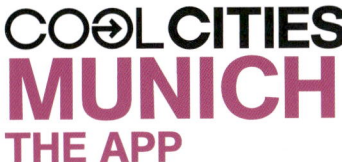

MUNICH
THE APP

W0049656

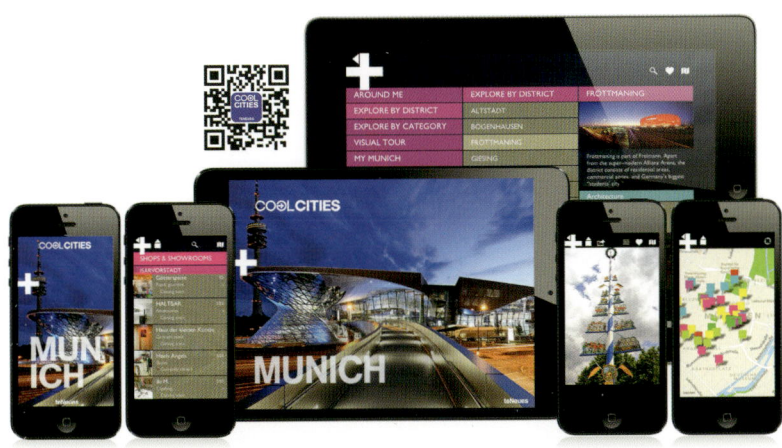

DOWNLOAD FOR FREE
FROM 15TH UNTIL 19TH OF JULY

COOL CITIES

MUN ICH

teNeues

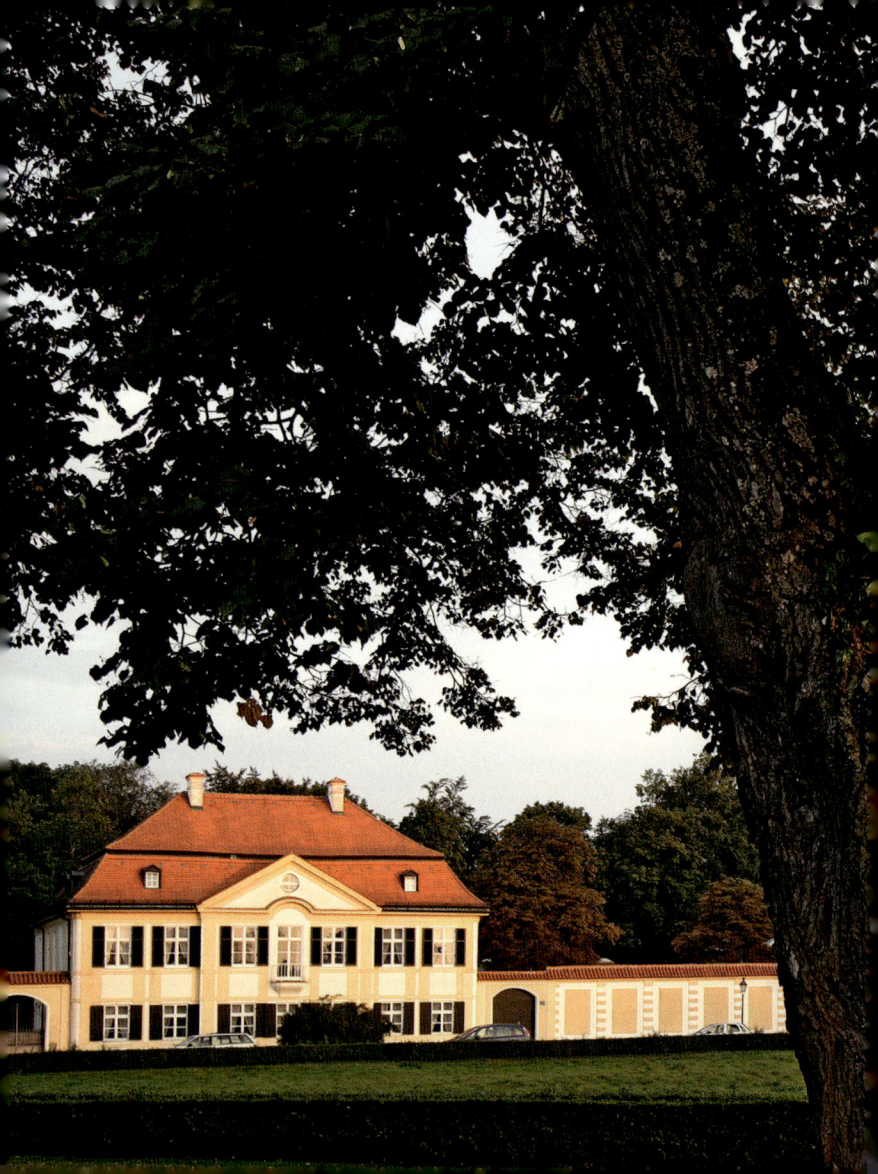

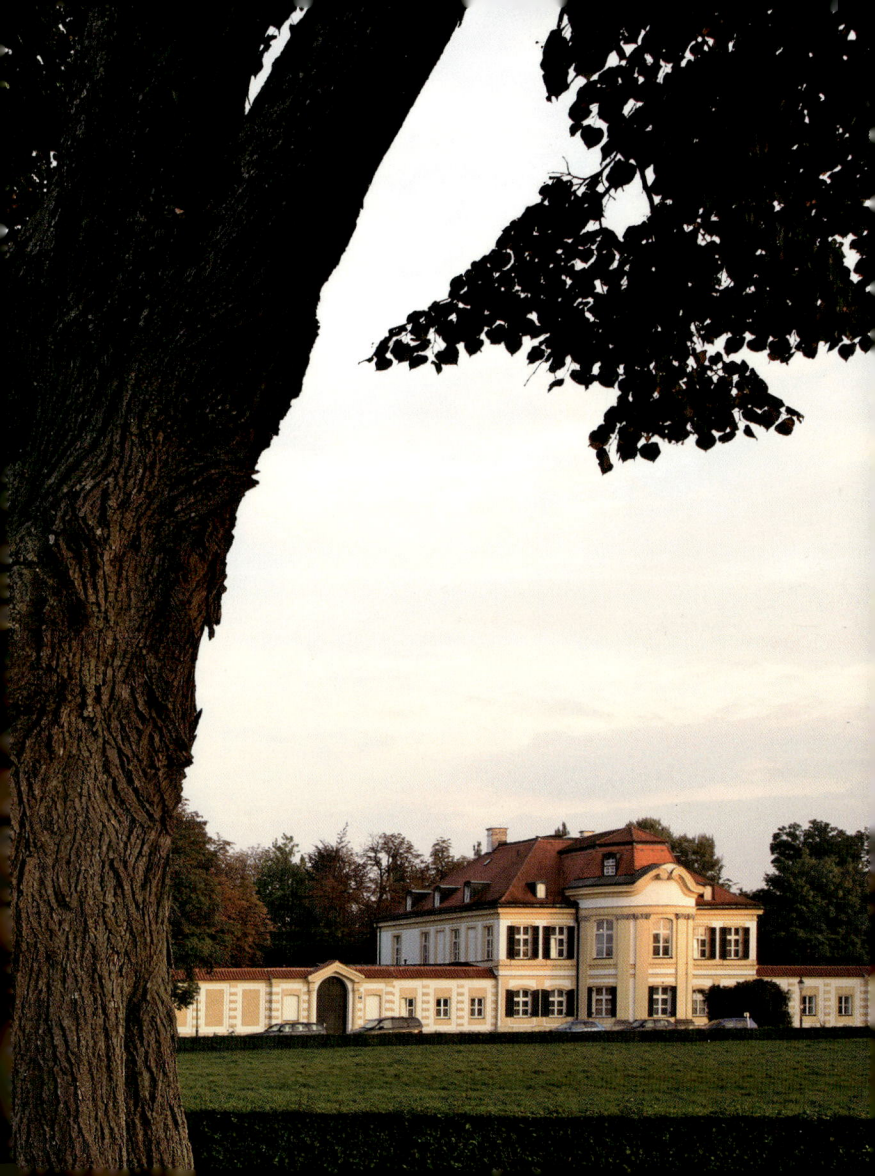

PRICE CATEGORY

$ = BUDGET $$ = AFFORDABLE $$$ = MODERATE $$$$ = LUXURY

COOL CONTENT

INTRO

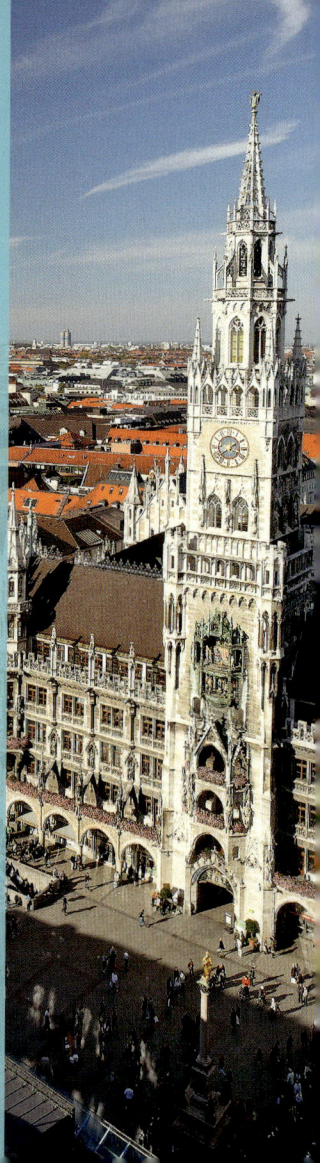

"YOU NEEDN'T BOTHER GOING ANYWHERE ELSE. I CAN TELL YOU: YOU CAN'T BEAT MUNICH, EVERYTHING ELSE IN GERMANY IS A WASTE OF TIME." THOUGH WE MIGHT NOT NECESSARILY PUT IT AS RADICALLY AS ERNEST HEMINGWAY DID, IT'S SOMETHING TO KEEP IN MIND. FEW CITIES ARE THE SUBJECT OF SO MANY PREPACKAGED IMAGES, MYTHS, AND MISUNDERSTANDINGS. MUNICH'S SELF-CONFIDENT RESIDENTS TAKE A RELAXED ATTITUDE, WITH A MIXTURE OF CHARMING BRAGGADOCIO AND HOMETOWN PRIDE. OF COURSE SOME PRECONCEPTIONS ABOUT MUNICH ARE TRUE: THE TAP WATER, FOR INSTANCE, REALLY IS THE BEST IN GERMANY, IF NOT EUROPE AND THE WORLD. IT MAY BE HARD TO SWALLOW THAT THE CITY NOT ONLY HAS AN INTERESTING HISTORY, CULTURAL LIFE, AND FOLKLORE BUT IS ALSO DAMN COOL. ALONGSIDE FRESH NEWCOMERS LIKE THE BOB BEAMAN CLUB, CHARLIE, AND HARVEST, SUCH CLASSIC INSTITUTIONS AS SCHUMANN'S, KÄFER, AND LODENFREY CHARACTERIZE A VEXINGLY DIVERSE, EMINENTLY LOVABLE CITY.

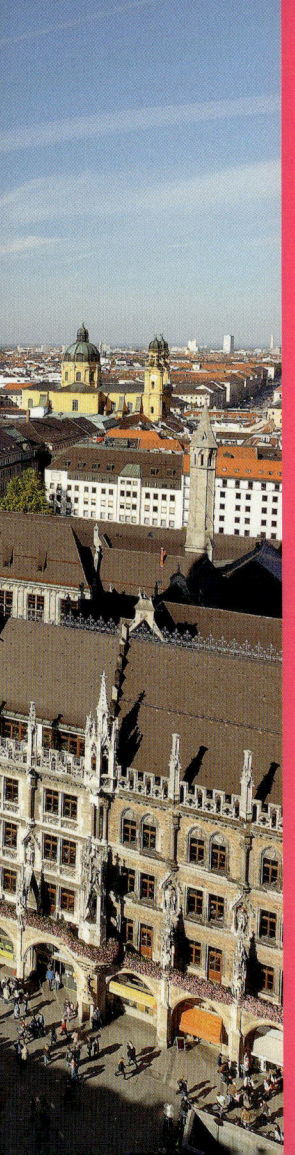

„FAHREN SIE GAR NICHT ERST WOANDERS HIN, ICH SAGE IHNEN, ES GEHT NICHTS ÜBER MÜNCHEN. ALLES ANDERE IN DEUTSCHLAND IST ZEITVERSCHWENDUNG." SO DRASTISCH WIE ERNEST HEMINGWAY MUSS MAN ES NICHT UNBEDINGT FORMULIEREN. ABER MAN SOLLTE ES IM KOPF BEHALTEN. ÜBER WENIGE STÄDTE KURSIEREN SO VIELE VORGEFERTIGTE BILDER, MYTHEN UND MISSVERSTÄNDNISSE. DIE SELBSTBEWUSSTEN MÜNCHNER GEHEN ENTSPANNT DAMIT UM, MIT EINER MISCHUNG AUS CHARMANTER GROSSMÄULIGKEIT UND HEIMATVERBUNDENHEIT. NATÜRLICH ENTSPRECHEN EINIGE VORURTEILE ÜBER MÜNCHEN DER REALITÄT; SO IST DAS DORTIGE LEITUNGSWASSER TATSÄCHLICH DAS BESTE DEUTSCHLANDS, WENN NICHT EUROPAS UND DER WELT. DASS DIE STADT NICHT NUR HISTORISCH, KULTURELL UND FOLKLORISTISCH INTERESSANT, SONDERN AUCH VERDAMMT COOL IST, KANN SCHWER ZU VERKRAFTEN SEIN. KLASSISCHE INSTITUTIONEN WIE DAS SCHUMANN'S, KÄFER ODER LODENFREY PRÄGEN NEBEN FRISCHEN NEUERSCHEINUNGEN WIE DEM BOB BEAMAN CLUB, CHARLIE ODER HARVEST DAS BILD EINER IRRITIEREND ABWECHSLUNGSREICHEN, UNBEDINGT LIEBENSWERTEN STADT.

HOTELS

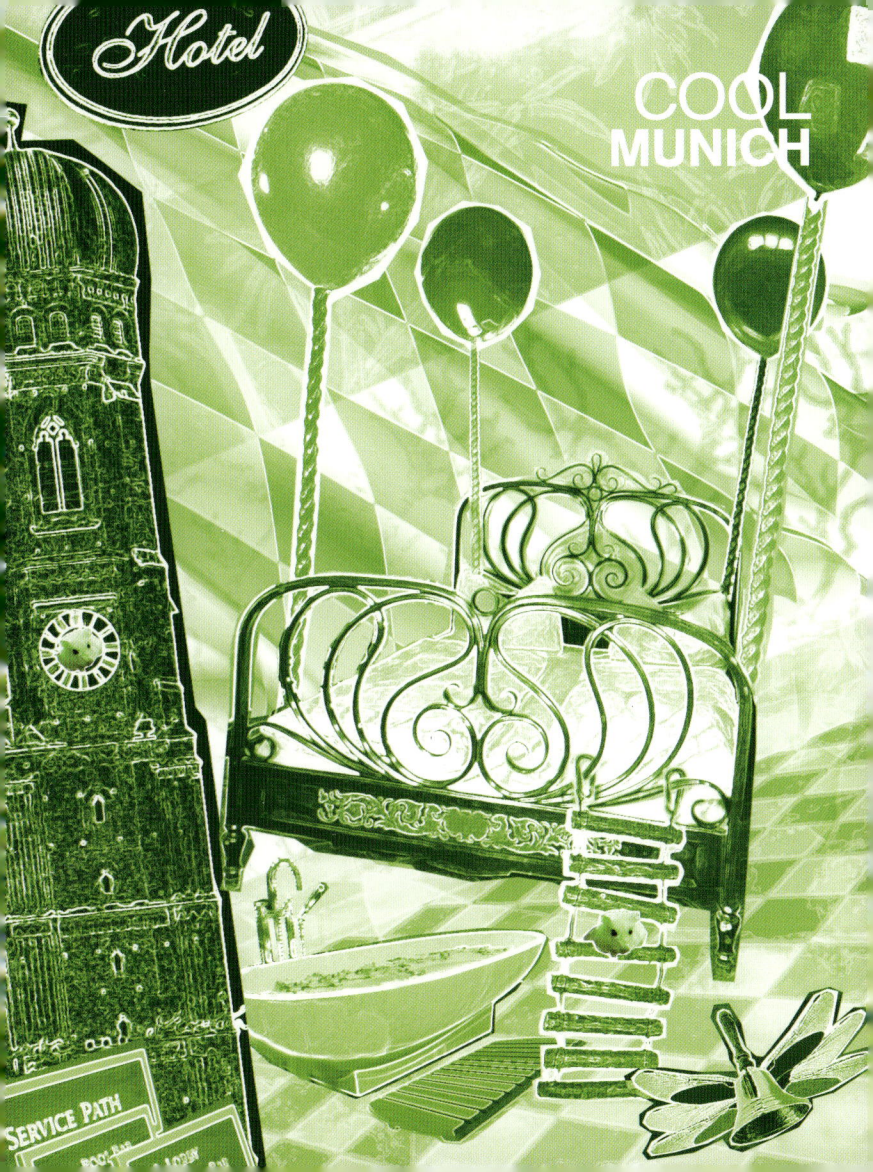

BAYERISCHER HOF

Promenadeplatz 2–6 // Altstadt
Tel.: +49 (0)89 2 12 00
www.bayerischerhof.de

S1–8, U3, U6 Marienplatz
Tram 19 Theatinerstraße

Prices: $$$$

KAREN WEBB'S SPECIAL TIP
Still—traditionally the leading
hotel of Munich!

MAP N°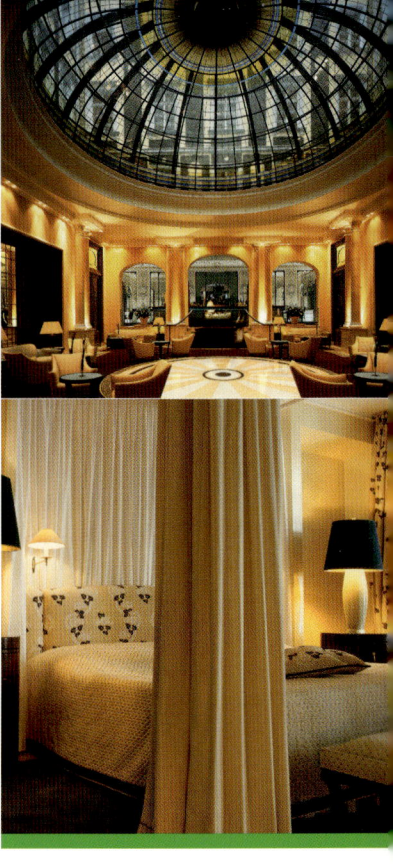

Commissioned by King Ludwig I, the Bayerischer Hof opened in 1841 to provide suitable accommodations for guests of state. Even if you're not a guest, the hotel is well worth a visit, not least because of the excellent falk's bar in the ballroom. Another highlight is the Restaurant Atelier, redesigned by Axel Vervoordt, whose use of elegant natural tones has turned the interior into a fitting backdrop for the star-awarded cuisine. The hotel's crown jewel, however, is the three-story Blue Spa with bar and roof terrace. A luxurious Cinema Lounge has just recently been opened.

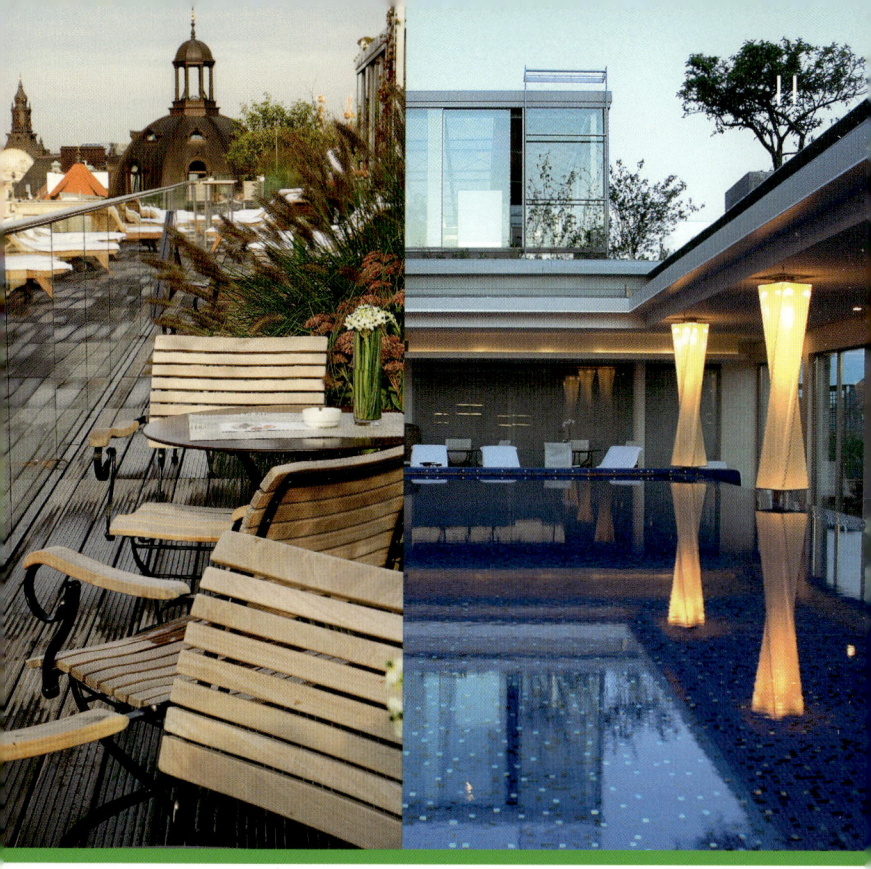

Der Bayerische Hof wurde 1841 auf Wunsch von König Ludwig I.
eröffnet und diente der standesgemäßen Unterbringung wichtiger
Staatsgäste. Auch Nicht-Hotelgästen sei ein Besuch empfohlen, z. B. in
der großartigen falk's Bar im Spiegelsaal. Oder im von Axel Vervoordt
eingerichteten Restaurant Atelier, dessen Interieur in eleganten Natur-
tönen die Sterneküche würdig umrahmt. Die Krönung ist das dreistö-
ckige Blue Spa mit Bar und Dachterrasse. Neu ist das kleine Luxuskino
Cinema Lounge.

CORTIINA

Ledererstraße 8 // Altstadt
Tel.: +49 (0)89 2 42 24 90
www.cortiina.com

S1–8, U3, U6 Marienplatz

Prices: $$$

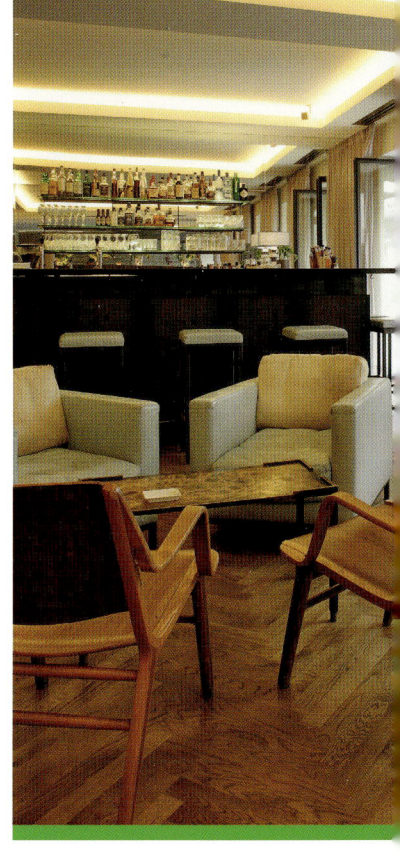

MAP N° 2

Natural colors and materials are dominant in this friendly hotel in Munich's city center. After visiting the outstanding Cortiina Bar with fireplace, you'll sleep like a log in the handsewn bedsheets of untreated cotton on the high-quality mattress made with natural rubber. Good thing they serve breakfast till noon on Sundays. A further intriguing detail—if needed—is the clear line of sight between bathtub and bed.

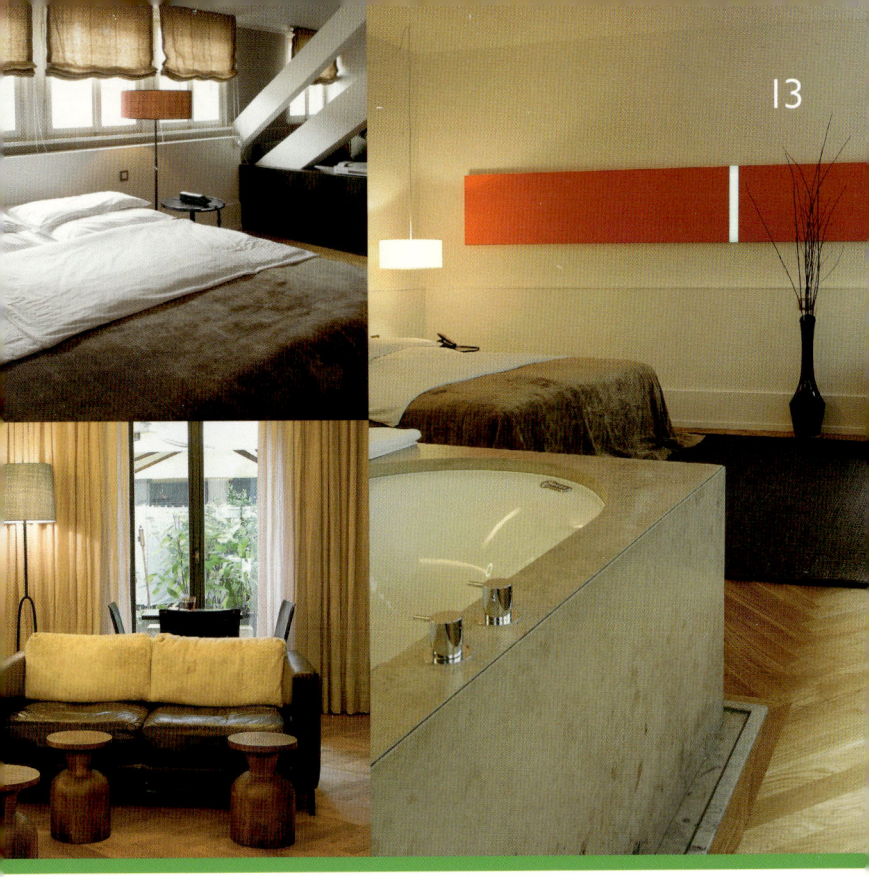

Naturfarben und -materialien dominieren dieses sympathische Hotel in der Innenstadt. Nach dem Besuch der ausgezeichneten Cortiina Bar mit Kamin schläft man hinterher in der handgenähten Bettwäsche aus unbehandelter Baumwolle und auf den hochwertigen Naturkautschukmatratzen wie ein Stein. Gut, dass es sonntags bis 12 Uhr Frühstück gibt. Ein weiteres spannendes Detail ist – bei Bedarf – die freie Sicht von der Badewanne aufs Bett und umgekehrt.

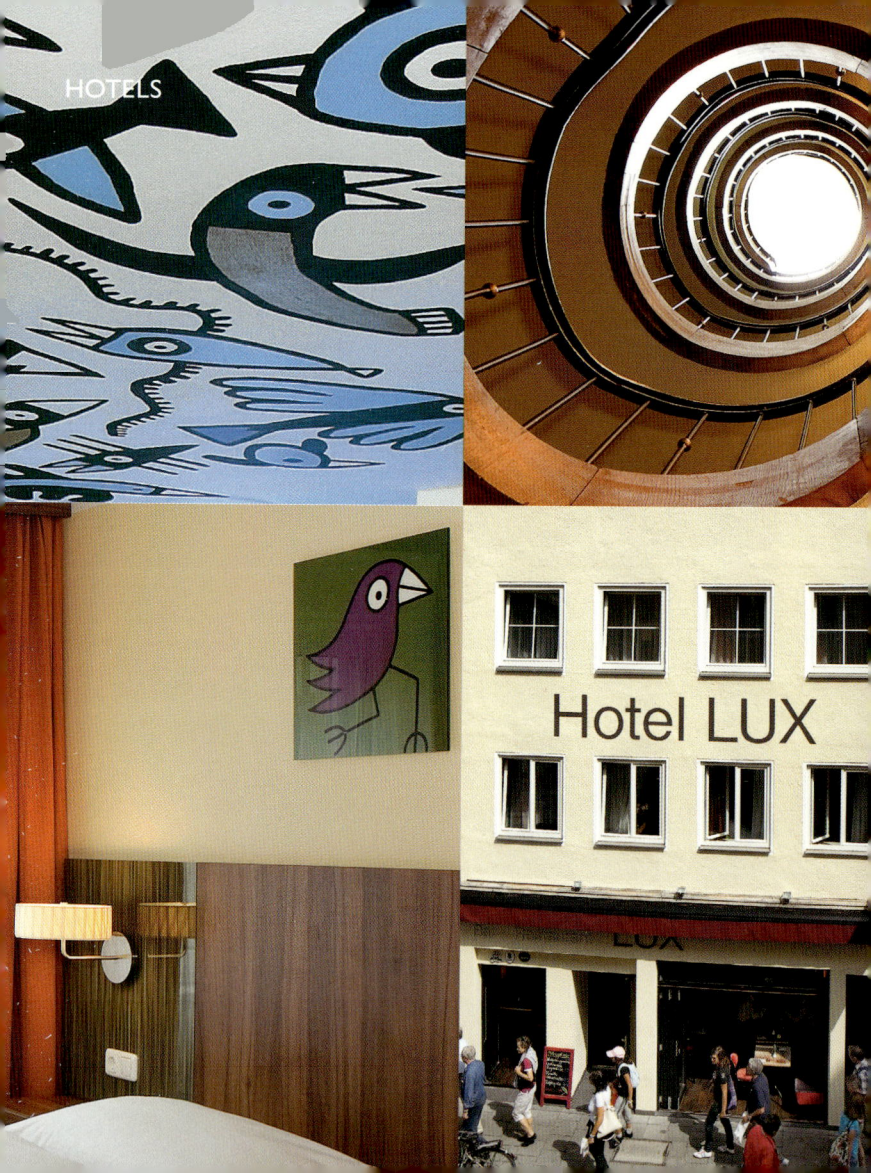

HOTEL LUX

Ledererstraße 13 // Altstadt
Tel.: +49 (0)89 45 20 73 00
www.hotel-lux-muenchen.de

S1—8, U3, U6 Marienplatz

Prices: $$

It begins with the fact that you check in at the bar—one of the best bars in the city, by the way, where you can also enjoy an outstanding meal. So really there's no reason ever to leave the Lux again—only it's so centrally located there's no other choice. The hotel owned by Aleks Vulic and Chris Dengler features rooms with a '70s orientation and straight lines (disregarding for a moment the psychedelic "Pony Farm" room), and moderate prices.

Es fängt damit an, dass man an der Bar eincheckt. An einer der besten Bars der Stadt übrigens, in der auch hervorragendes Essen serviert wird. Es gäbe also überhaupt keinen Grund, das Lux jemals wieder zu verlassen – wenn seine Lage nicht so zentral wäre, dass man keine andere Wahl hat. Die Zimmer des Hotels von Aleks Vulic und Chris Dengler sind an den 70ern orientiert und geradlinig (von dem psychedelischen „Ponyhof" mal abgesehen), die Preise moderat.

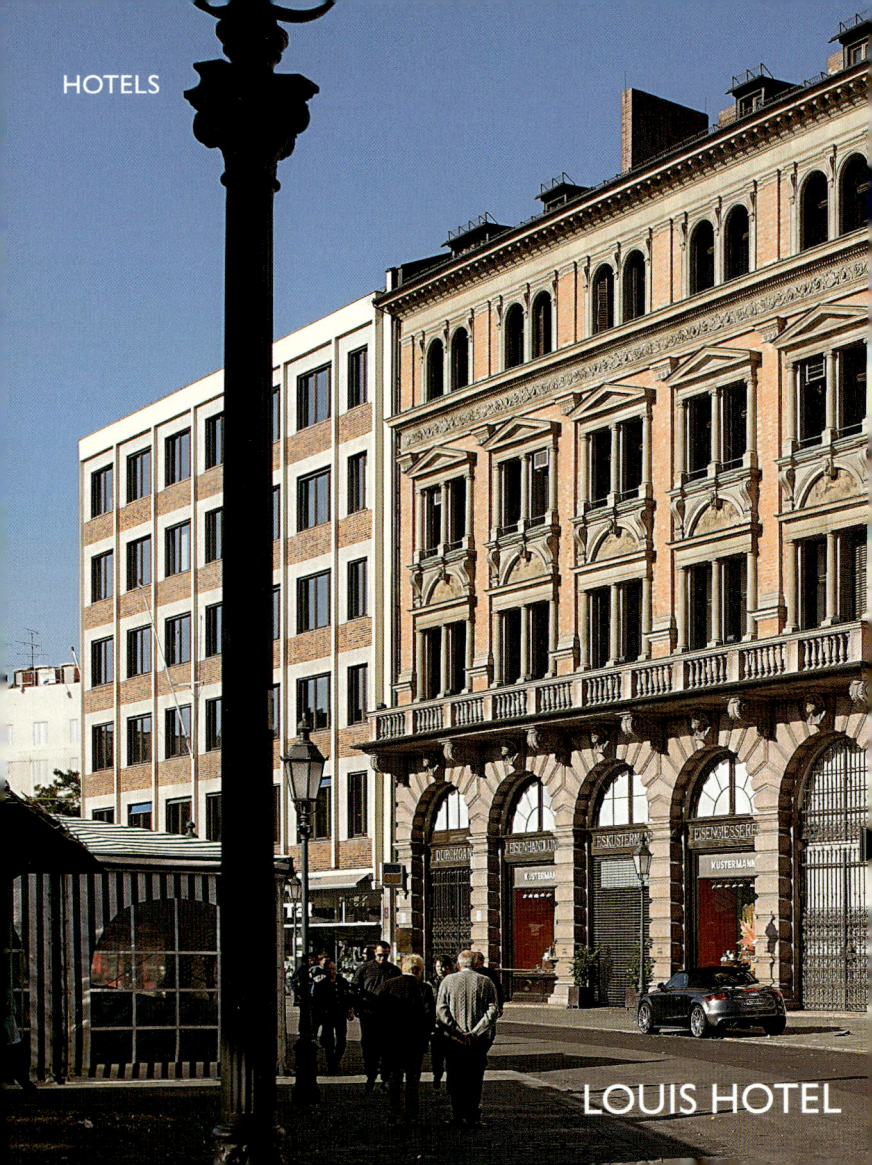

LOUIS HOTEL

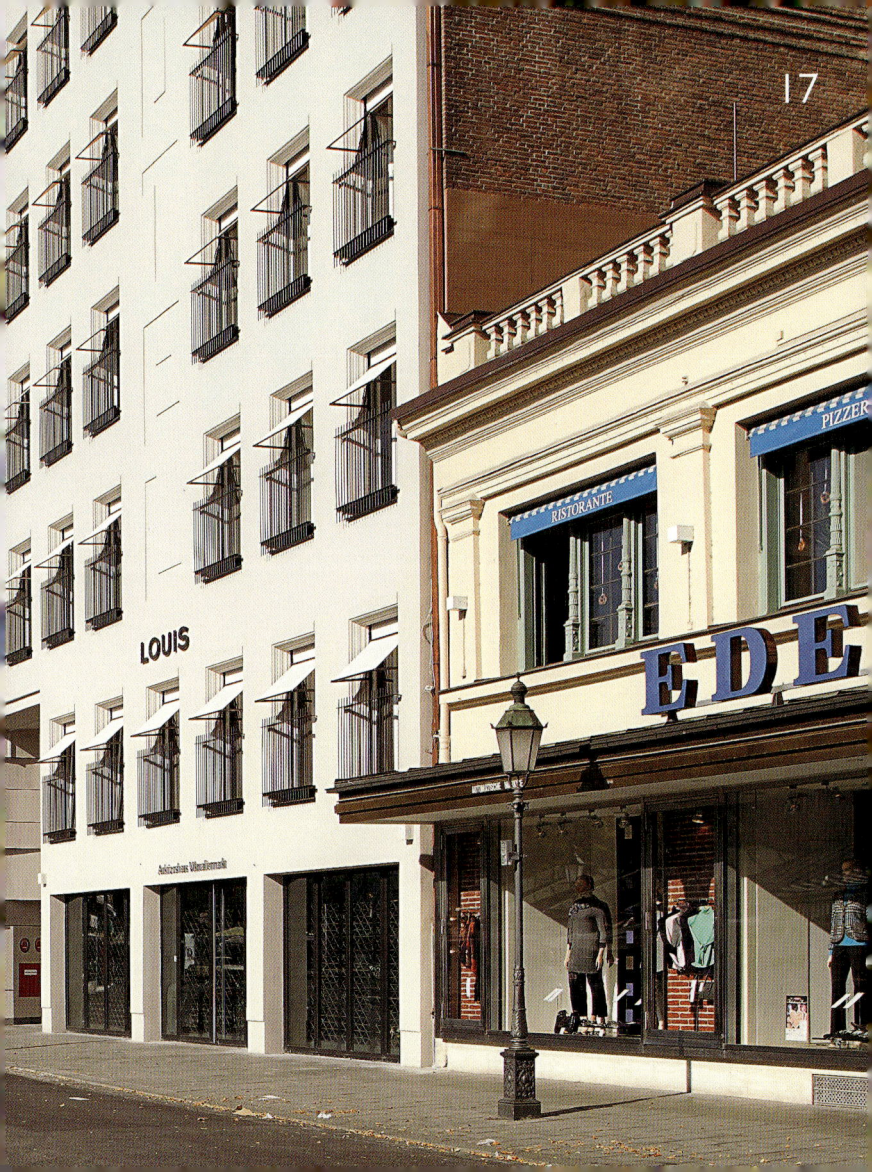

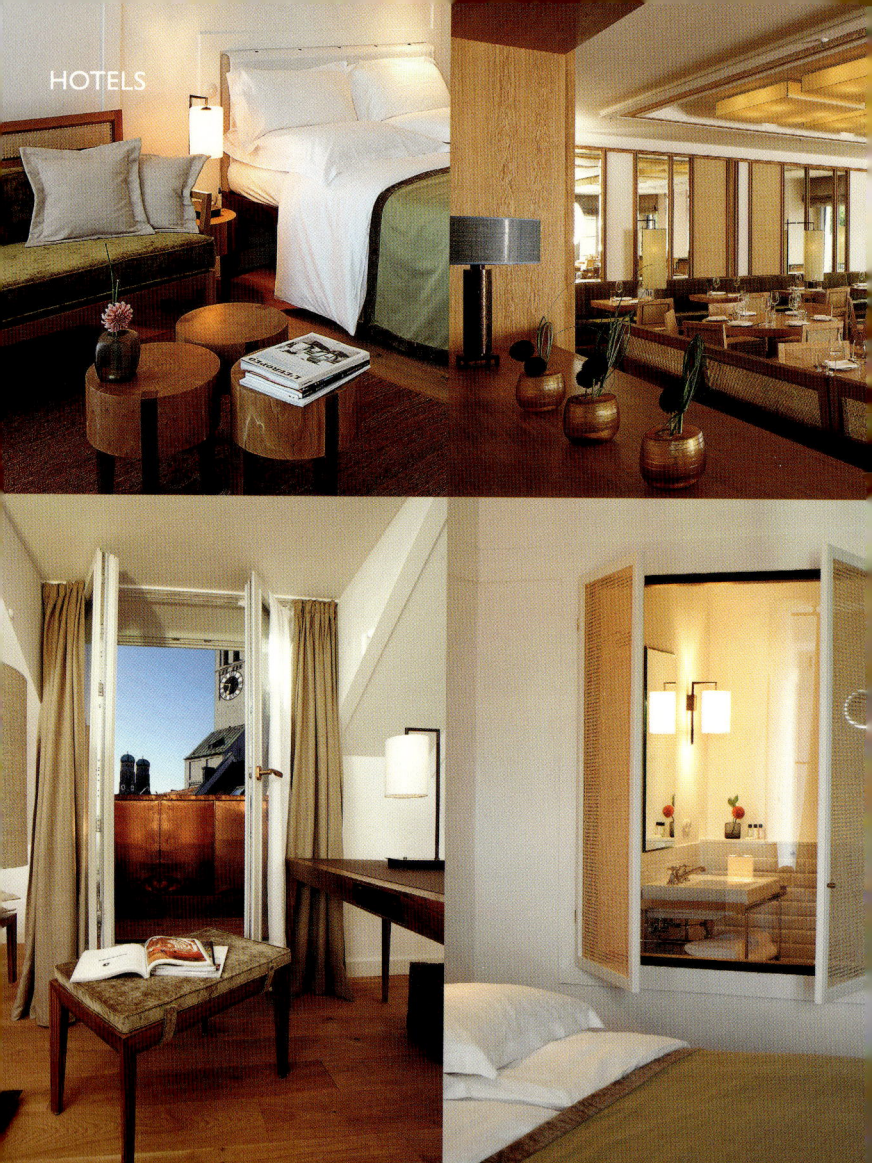

LOUIS HOTEL

Viktualienmarkt 6 // Altstadt
(access via Rindermarkt 2)
Tel.: +49 (0)89 41 11 90 80
www.louis-hotel.com

S1–8, U3, U6 Marienplatz

Prices: $$$

Tasteful through and through, this hotel is located directly on the Viktualienmarkt. The simple beauty of its façade is inescapable. And for the interior, Hild and K Architects used furnishings specially designed for the hotel. The 72 allergy-friendly rooms feature such loving details as "suitcase" wardrobes and the finest natural materials. The sunny terrace is another reason to make a reservation right away.

Direkt am Viktualienmarkt liegt dieses konsequent geschmackvolle Hotel. Seine Fassade ist in ihrer schlichten Schönheit nicht zu übersehen. Mit eigens für das Hotel entworfenem Mobiliar hat das Architekturbüro Hild und K das Design auch im Inneren maßgeblich geprägt. Die 72 allergikerfreundlichen Zimmer sind mit liebevollen Details wie „Reisekoffer"-Schränken und feinsten Naturmaterialien ausgestattet. Die Sonnenterrasse ist ein weiterer Grund sofort zu buchen.

MANDARIN ORIENTAL MUNICH

Neuturmstraße 1 // Altstadt
Tel.: +49 (0)89 29 09 80
www.mandarinoriental.com/munich

S1–8, U3, U6 Marienplatz
Tram 16, 18 Isartor
Tram 19 Kammerspiele

Prices: $$$$

MAP N° 5

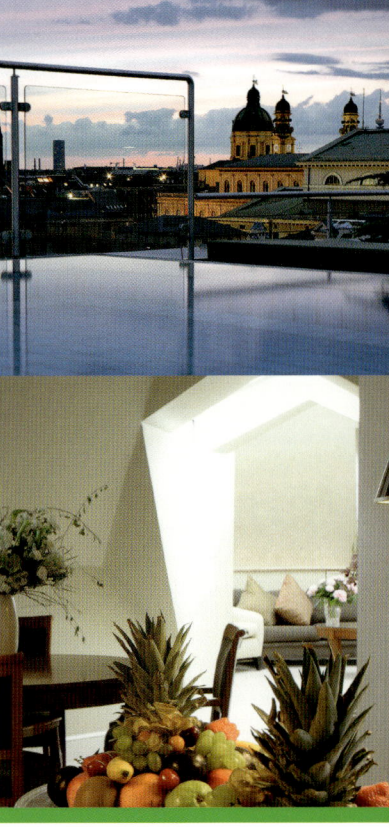

Built between 1875 and 1880, this handsome neo-Renaissance building is where Munich's upper crust once held their society balls. The classic hotel has been here since 1990, offering its clientele (still well-to-do) such amenities as the award-winning restaurant Mark's and a rooftop terrace with swimming pool, but most of all—as one guest put it—"the natural way you are treated like a king here and at the same time like a friend."

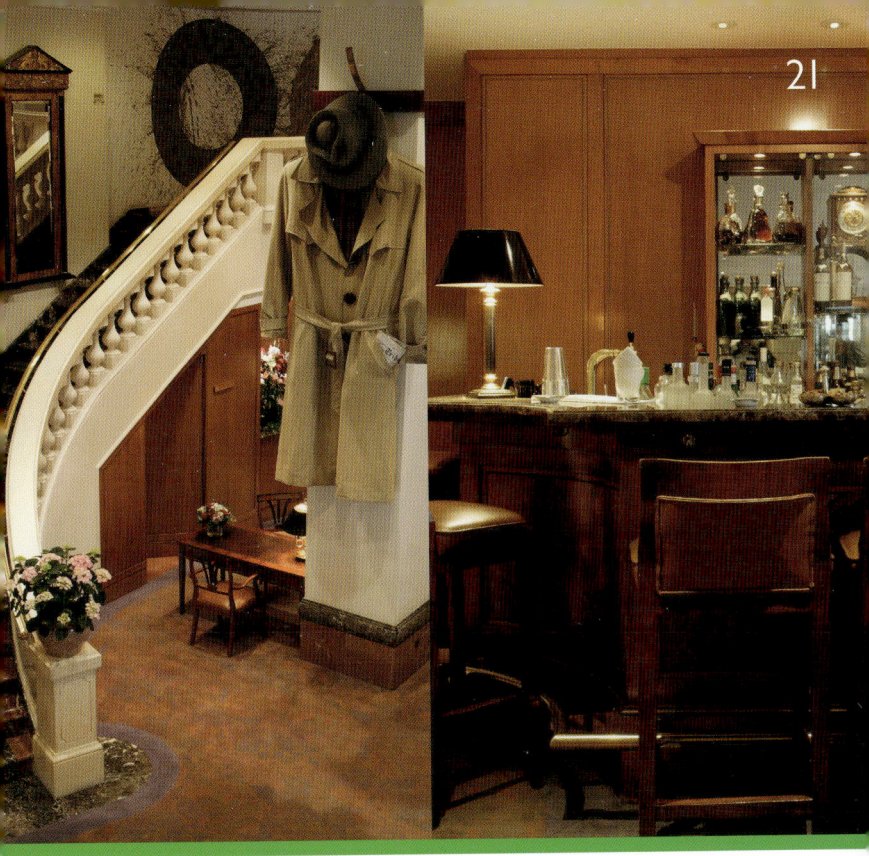

Das stattliche, zwischen 1875 und 1880 erbaute Neorenaissance-Gebäude diente einst der gehobenen Münchner Gesellschaft als Ballhaus. Seit 1990 befindet sich nun das klassische Hotel darin, das seiner nach wie vor gehobenen Klientel einiges zu bieten hat: das Sternerestaurant Mark's und die Dachterrasse mit Pool, vor allem aber – wie es ein Gast ausdrückte – „die Normalität, mit der man hier wie ein König und gleichzeitig wie ein Freund behandelt wird."

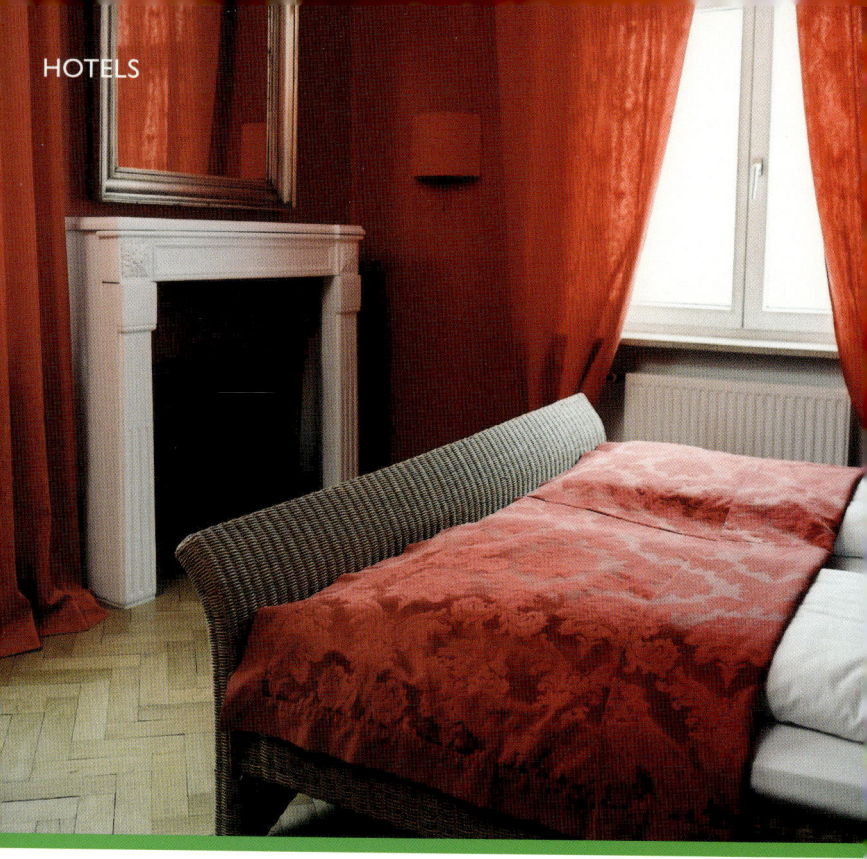

Each of this privately run hotel's 25 rooms is individually designed. It's worth inquiring when making a reservation—lest an Africa lover ends up in the Asia Room or a newly separated couple land in the romantic Red Room. The cozy building has a lovely location overlooking the river, not as central as other hotels but green and quiet and still with good traffic and transit connections. Villa Stuck and Haus der Kunst are within easy walking distance.

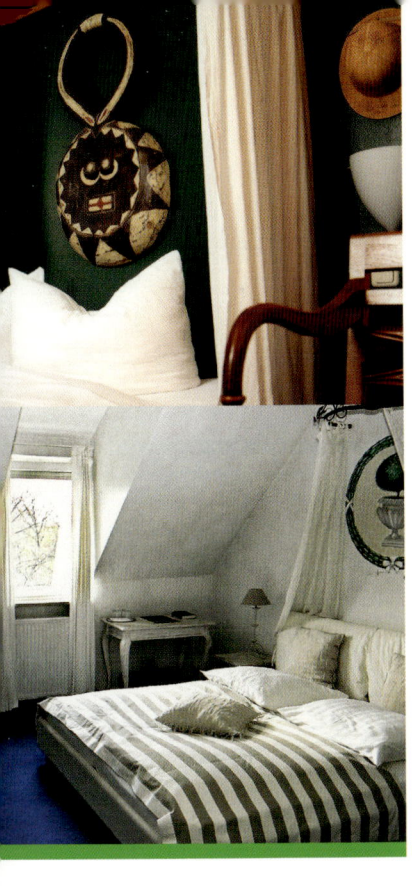

HOTEL RITZI

Maria-Theresia-Straße 2a
Haidhausen
Tel.: +49 (0)89 4 14 24 08 90
www.hotel-ritzi.de

U4, U5 Max-Weber-Platz
Tram 19 Maximilianeum

Prices: $$

MAP N° 6

Jedes der 25 Zimmer des privat geführten Hotels ist individuell gestaltet. Da lohnt sich beim Buchen das Nachfragen – nicht, dass man als Afrika-Freund im Asienzimmer oder frisch getrennt im romantischen Roten Zimmer landet. Das behagliche Haus liegt wunderschön am Isarhochufer, nicht ganz so zentral wie andere Hotels, aber dafür grün und ruhig und trotzdem gut angebunden. Die Villa Stuck und das Haus der Kunst sind zu Fuß perfekt erreichbar.

HOTEL OPÉRA

St.-Anna-Straße 10 // Lehel
Tel.: +49 (0)89 2 10 49 40
www.hotel-opera.de

U4, U5 Lehel

Prices: $$$

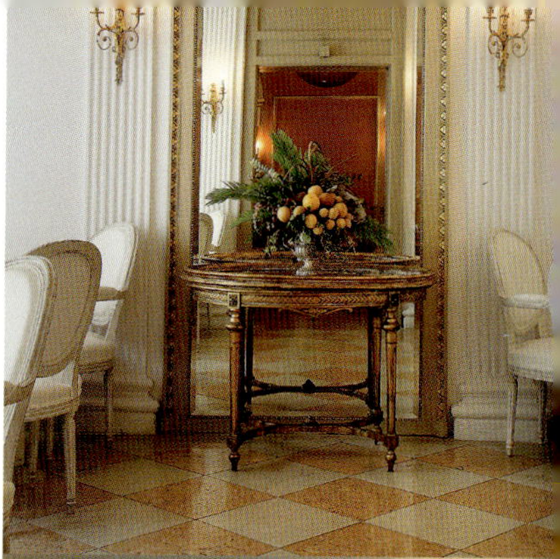

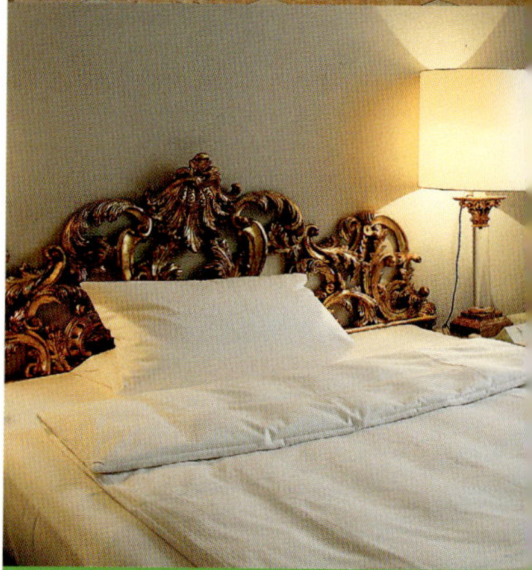

KAREN WEBB'S SPECIAL TIP
Breakfast is still served by
staff on the marvelous green
sunny yard—it's royal!

MAP N° 7

You'd be hard pressed to find more beautiful lodgings than this reno-
vated mansion from 1898. With its tranquil landscaped Renaissance
courtyard the Hotel Opéra is like an oasis. Sit beneath the shady col-
onnade and listen to the babbling brookwater of the Eisbach flowing
beneath the four-star establishment on St.-Anna-Platz. At one time a
purveyor to the royal court used this location for his gourmet foods
shop; fish and lobsters were kept fresh in the stream.

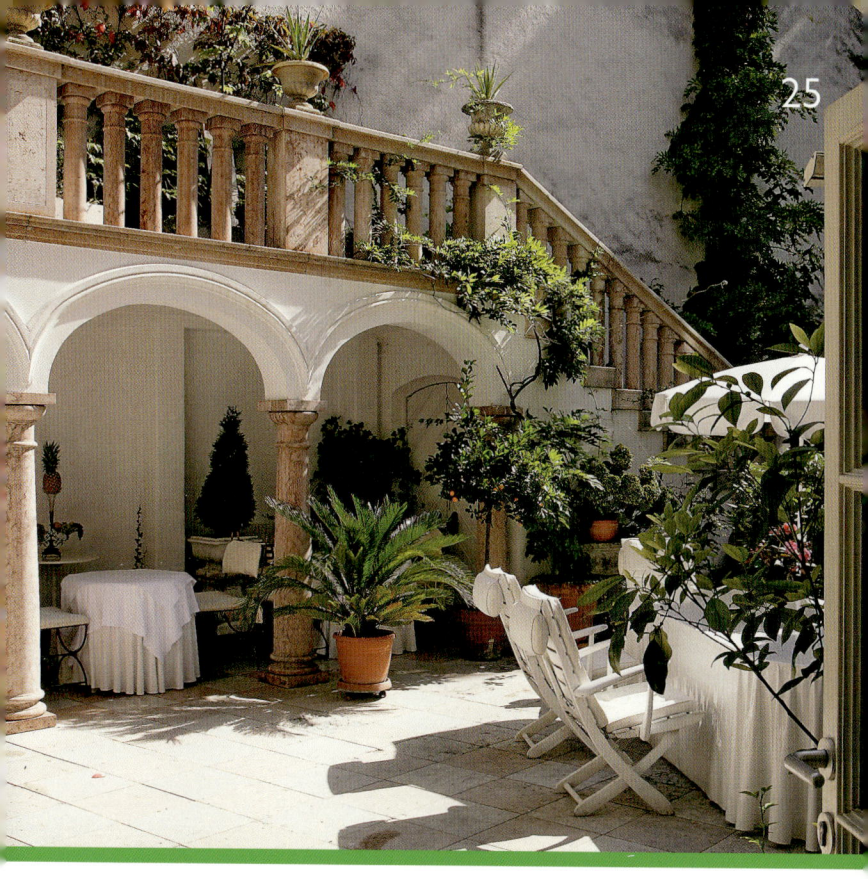

Schöner als in dem renovierten Stadtpalais von 1898 kann man fast nicht residieren: Mit seinem lauschigen, begrünten Renaissance-Innenhof gleicht das Hotel Opéra einer Oase. Unter den schattigen Arkaden sitzend hört man dem Plätschern des Eisbachs zu, der unter dem Vier-Sterne-Haus am St.-Anna-Platz durchfließt. Einst hatte ein königlicher Hoflieferant diesen Ort für sein feines Delikatessengeschäft gewählt – im Bach wurden Fische und Hummer frisch gehalten.

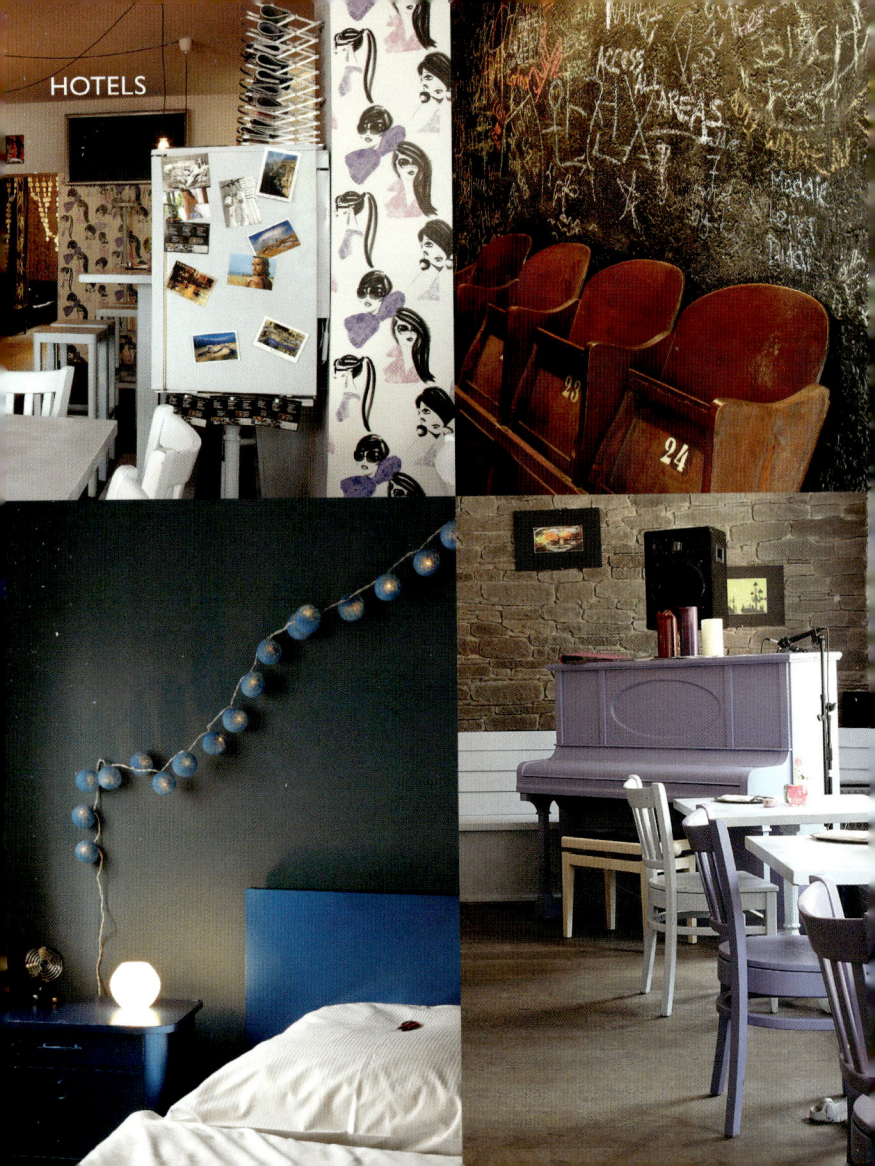

HOTEL ACHTERBAHN

Schwanthalerstraße 88 // Ludwigsvorstadt
Tel.: +49 (0)89 53 64 82
www.hotelachterbahn.de

U4, U5 Theresienwiese

Prices: $

The eight simple rooms make up an "emotional roller-coaster" (a play on Achterbahn, literally a "figure-8 track"): Pride, Melancholy, Fear, Euphoria, Ecstasy, Enlightenment, Happiness, and Relief. The Porodan siblings Ramona and Adrian have a heart for emotional people with small wallets. They offer good and affordable accommodation and meals very close to the train station. With the adorable Café Camera, this place is almost too good to be true.

Die Achterbahn der Gefühle: Übermut, Melancholie, Angst, Rausch, Ekstase, Erleuchtung, Glück und Erleichterung – so heißen die acht einfachen, aber liebevoll gestalteten Zimmer. Die Geschwister Ramona und Adrian Porodan haben ein Herz für emotionale Menschen mit kleinem Geldbeutel. Bei ihnen übernachtet und isst man günstig und gut, ganz in der Nähe des Hauptbahnhofs. Zusammen mit dem hübschen Café Camera ist dieser Ort fast zu schön um wahr zu sein.

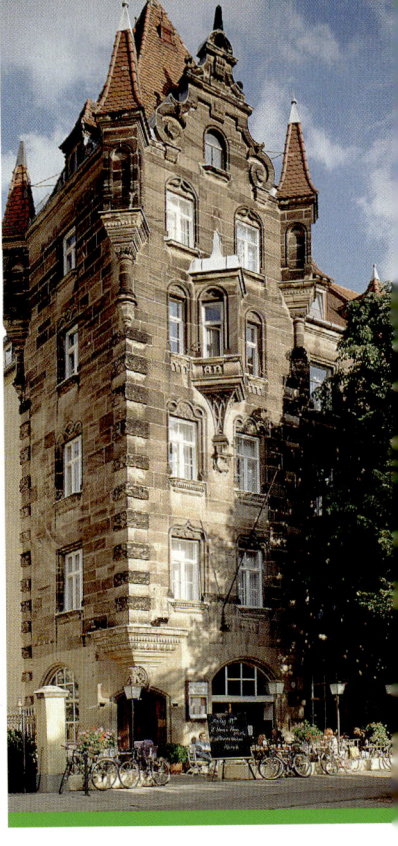

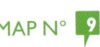

HOTEL MARIANDL

Goethestraße 51 // Ludwigsvorstadt
Tel.: +49 (0)89 5 52 91 00
www.mariandl.com

U3, U6 Goetheplatz

Prices: $$

MAP N° 9

Truly a one-of-a-kind Munich phenomenon, this Mariandl. The stately neo-Gothic building on Beethovenplatz houses the city's oldest concert café in addition to the hotel rooms with their true-to-style decor. The café features music almost every day—from jazz to classical—in a very Viennese atmosphere. If you value patina and character above spa and gourmet cuisine, the artistic charms of Mariandl are just the thing for you. We recommend the rooms with freestanding bathtubs!

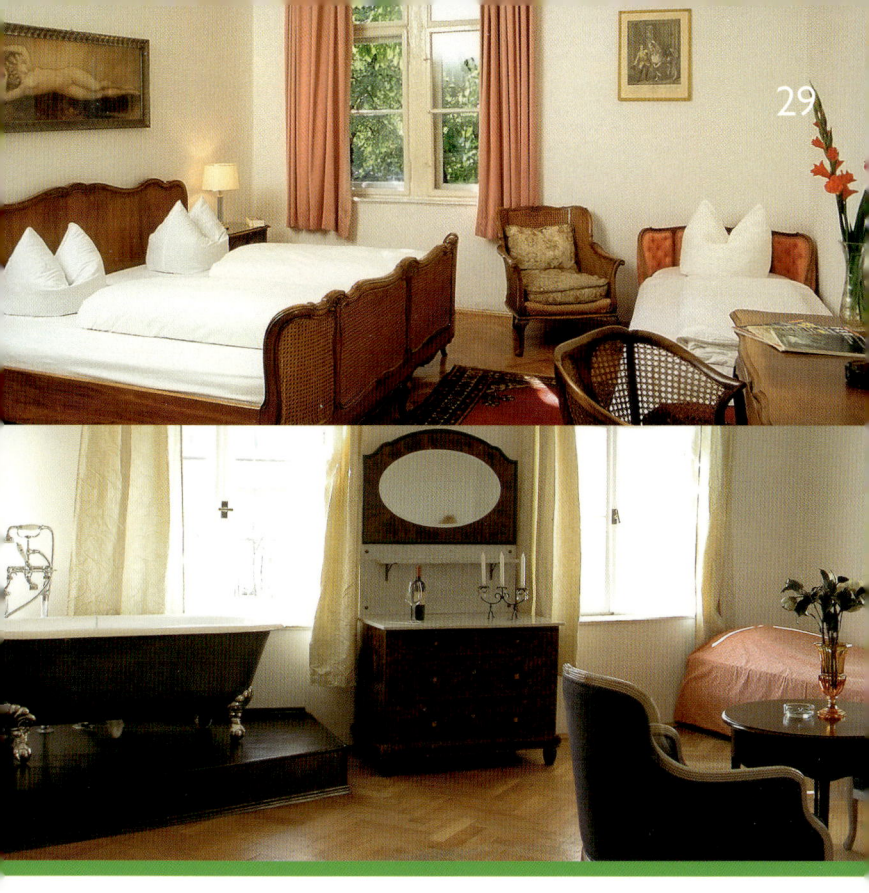

Ein echtes Münchner Unikat, das Mariandl. Der imposante neogotische Bau am Beethovenplatz beherbergt sowohl die stilecht eingerichteten Hotelzimmer als auch das älteste Konzertcafé der Stadt. Fast jeden Tag wird dort von Jazz bis Klassik musiziert, in sehr Wienerischer Atmosphäre. Wem Patina und Charakter wichtiger sind als Spa und Sterneküche, der ist im künstlerischen Mariandl genau richtig. Empfehlung: Die Zimmer mit der freistehenden Badewanne!

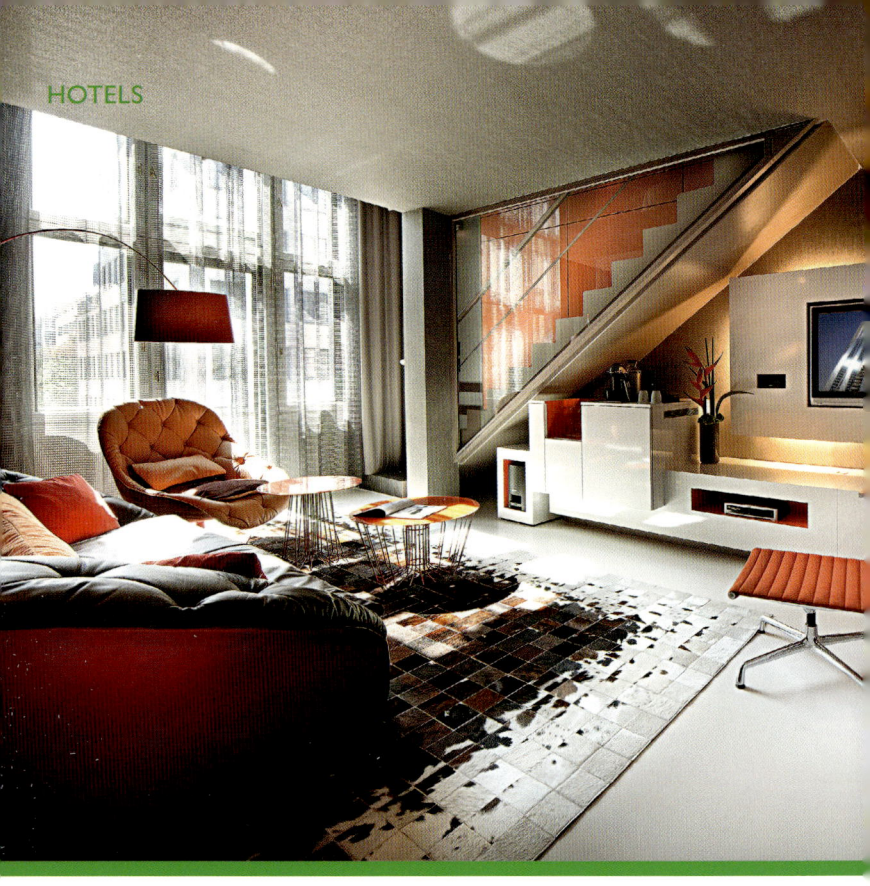

If the Main Station is your primary reference point, you won't find more centrally located accommodations in Munich than Sofitel Bayerpost. And you don't even have to make concessions when it comes to quality: this five-star establishment is especially favored by discerning business travelers. The Wilhelminian architecture blends harmoniously with the rooms' modern design and high-tech details. The maisonette suite on the 8th floor affords a fantastic view of the city.

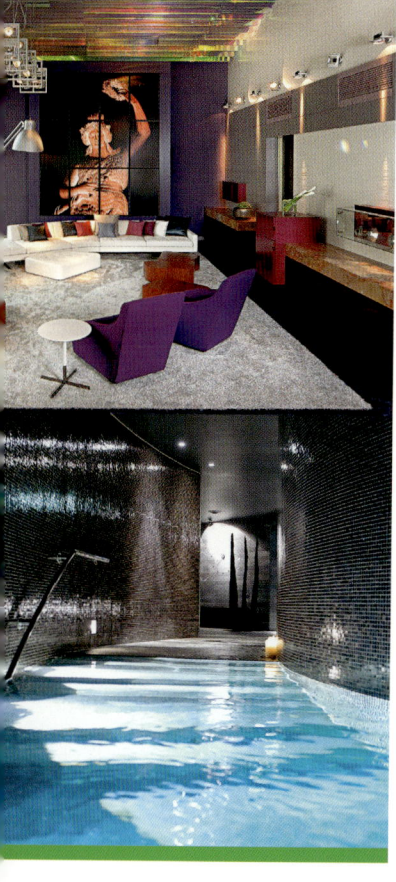

SOFITEL MUNICH BAYERPOST

Bayerstraße 12 // Ludwigsvorstadt
Tel.: +49 (0)89 59 94 80
www.sofitel.com

S1–8, U1, U2, U4, U5, U7
Tram 16, 17, 19, 20, 21 Hauptbahnhof

Prices: $$$$

MAP N°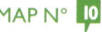

Wenn man den Hauptbahnhof als Maßstab nimmt, kann man in München nicht zentraler wohnen als im Sofitel Bayerpost. Und dabei muss man nicht mal Abstriche bei der Qualität machen: Das Fünf-Sterne-Haus ist besonders bei anspruchsvollen Geschäftsleuten beliebt. Die wilhelmini-sche Architektur verbindet sich harmonisch mit dem modernen Design und den High-Tech-Details der Zimmer. Von der Maisonette-Suite im 8. Stock genießt man einen prächtigen Blick über die Stadt.

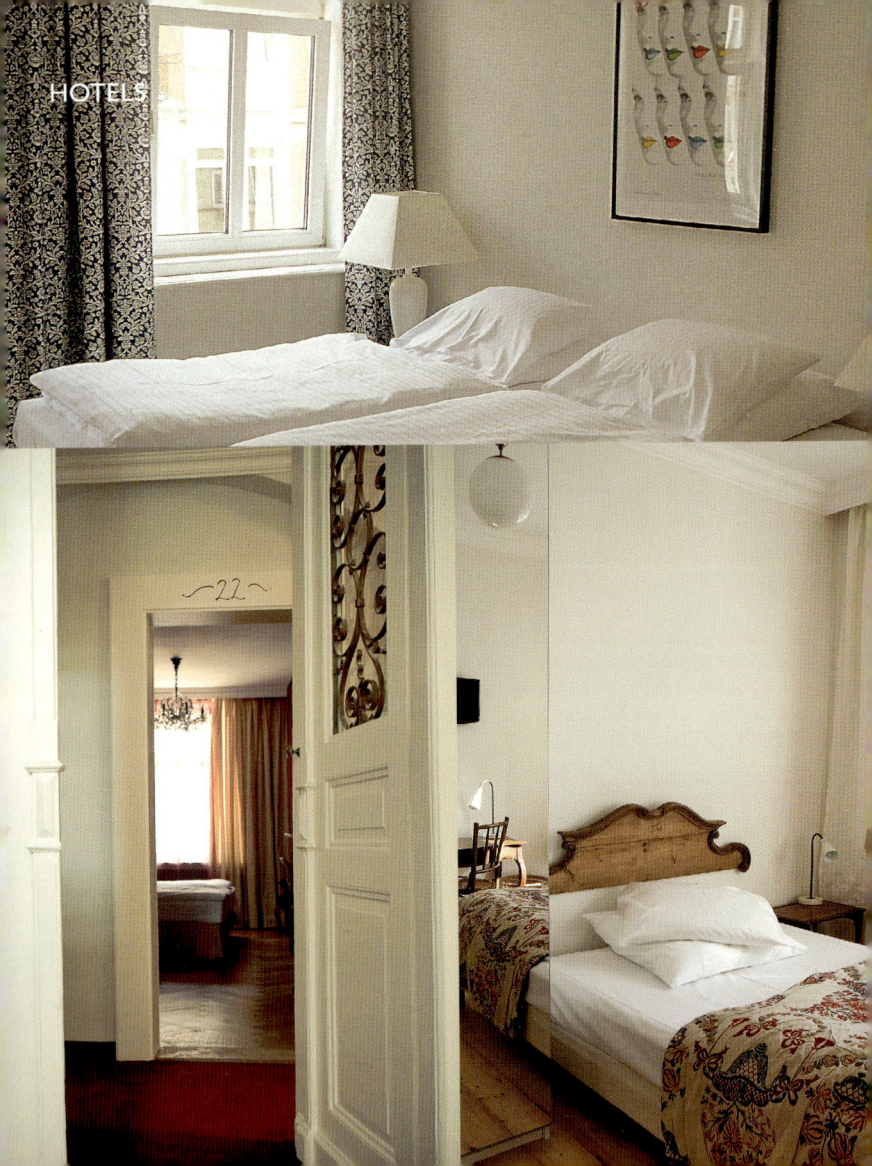

DAS HOTEL
IN MÜNCHEN

Türkenstraße 35 // Maxvorstadt
Tel.: +49 (0)89 2 88 14 00
www.das-hotel-in-muenchen.de

U3, U6 Universität

Prices: $$

Reopened in 2009, the establishment called simply Das Hotel stands on lively Türkenstraße in the middle of the university district. The Pinakothek museums are just a stone's throw away and you will also find some of the best galleries and countless cafés in the immediate vicinity. The rooms are all decorated differently, but with the same loving attention. A vacation suite with space for up to four guests is located on the 5th floor.

Das 2009 wiedereröffnete Haus mit dem simplen Namen Das Hotel befindet sich in der lebendigen Türkenstraße mitten im Universitätsviertel. Von hier aus ist das Pinakotheken-Areal nur einen Steinwurf entfernt, außerdem gibt es einige der besten Galerien und unendlich viele Cafés in der direkten Nachbarschaft. Die Zimmer sind alle unterschiedlich, aber gleichsam liebevoll eingerichtet. Im 5. Stock wartet ein Appartement, das bis zu vier Personen Platz bietet.

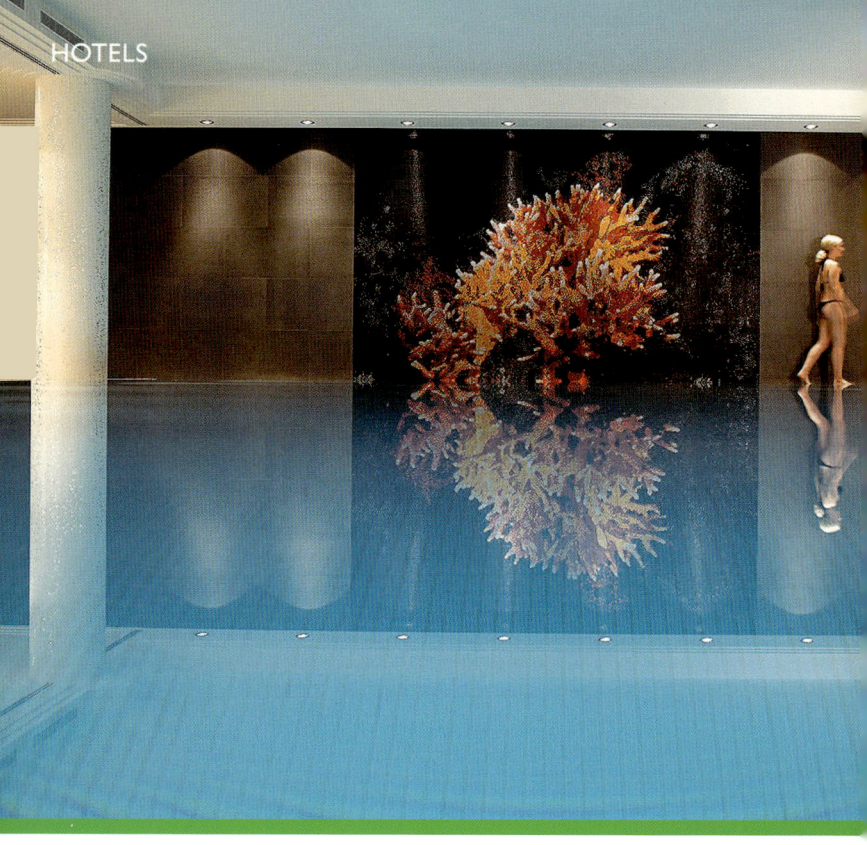

The Charles is the twelfth hotel in Sir Rocco Forte's exclusive portfolio. It's not named for the city's most famous bartender and host, but Sir Rocco's father. The curving building at the Old Botanical Garden conveys understatement both inside and out, but when it comes to furnishings and service, it is among Munich's most luxurious establishments. Along with the 160 rooms there are 27 suites and the 2,150 sq. ft. Presidential Suite.

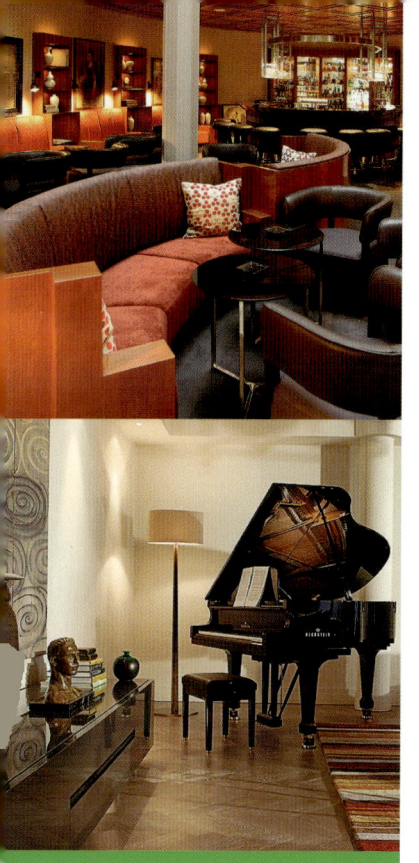

THE
CHARLES HOTEL

Sophienstraße 28 // Maxvorstadt
Tel.: +49 (0)89 5 44 55 50
www.charleshotel.de

S1–8, U4, U5 Karlsplatz (Stachus)
U1, U2, U7 Hauptbahnhof
Tram 16, 17, 20, 21 Hauptbahnhof Nord

Prices: $$$$

MAP N° 12

The Charles ist das zwölfte Hotel im exklusiven Portfolio von Sir Rocco
Forte. Benannt ist es nicht etwa nach dem berühmtesten Bartender
und Gastgeber der Stadt, sondern nach Sir Roccos Vater. Der ge-
schwungene Bau am Alten Botanischen Garten vermittelt außen und
innen Understatement, gehört aber in Sachen Ausstattung und Service
zum Luxuriösesten, was München zu bieten hat. Zu den 160 Zimmern
zählen 27 Suiten sowie die 200 m² große Präsidentensuite.

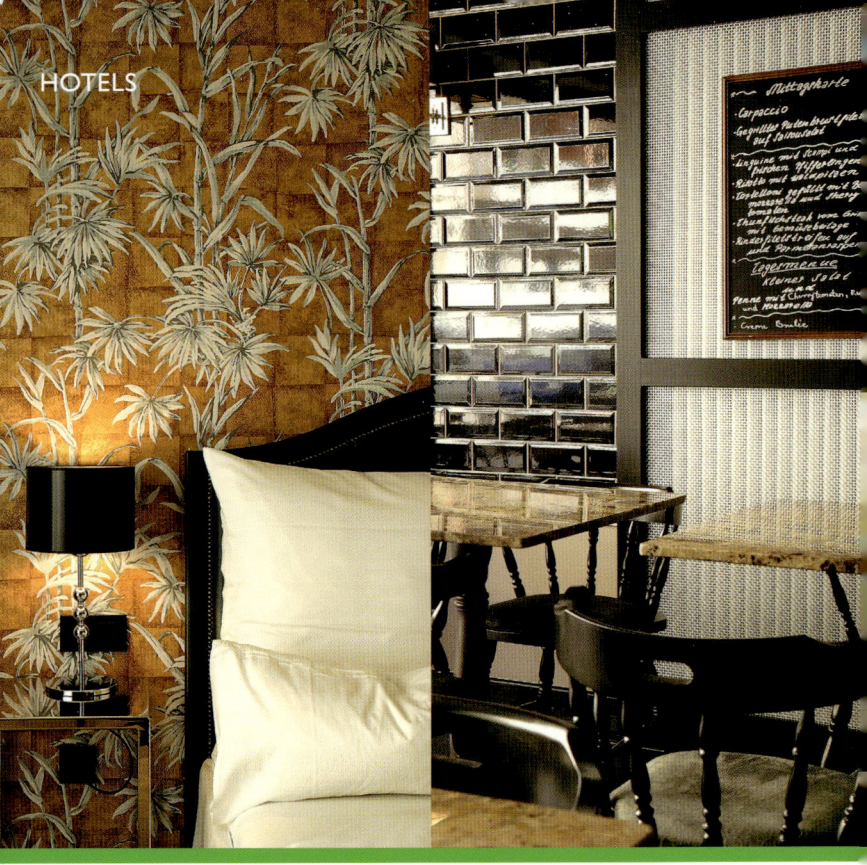

At just 31 rooms, La Maison is small and personal. Its quiet location between Leopoldstraße and the English Garden makes the boutique hotel run by Philipp Kretschmer the ideal starting point for a relaxing and varied sojourn. Lovers of extravagant and elaborate design will find their heart's content here. The complete interior decor comes from interior designers Koubek & Hartinger.

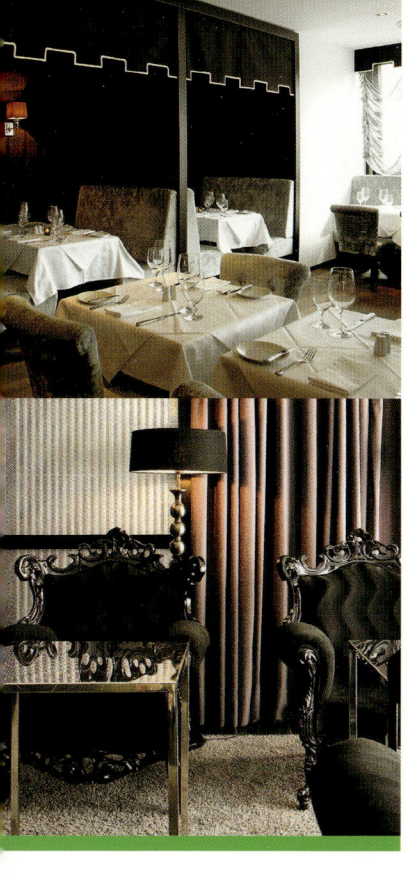

HOTEL
LA MAISON

Occamstraße 24 // Schwabing
Tel.: +49 (0)89 33 03 55 50
www.hotel-la-maison.com

U3, U6, Tram 23 Münchner Freiheit

Prices: $$

MAP N° 13

Mit nur 31 Zimmern ist das von Philipp Kretschmer geführte La Maison ein kleines, persönliches Haus. Seine ruhige Lage zwischen Leopold-straße und dem Englischen Garten macht das Boutique-Hotel zum perfekten Ausgangspunkt für einen entspannten und abwechslungs-reichen Aufenthalt. Liebhaber von extravagantem, verschnörkeltem Design kommen hier voll auf ihre Kosten. Die gesamte Inneneinrichtung stammt von den Innenarchitekten Koubek & Hartinger.

RESTAURANTS
+CAFÉS

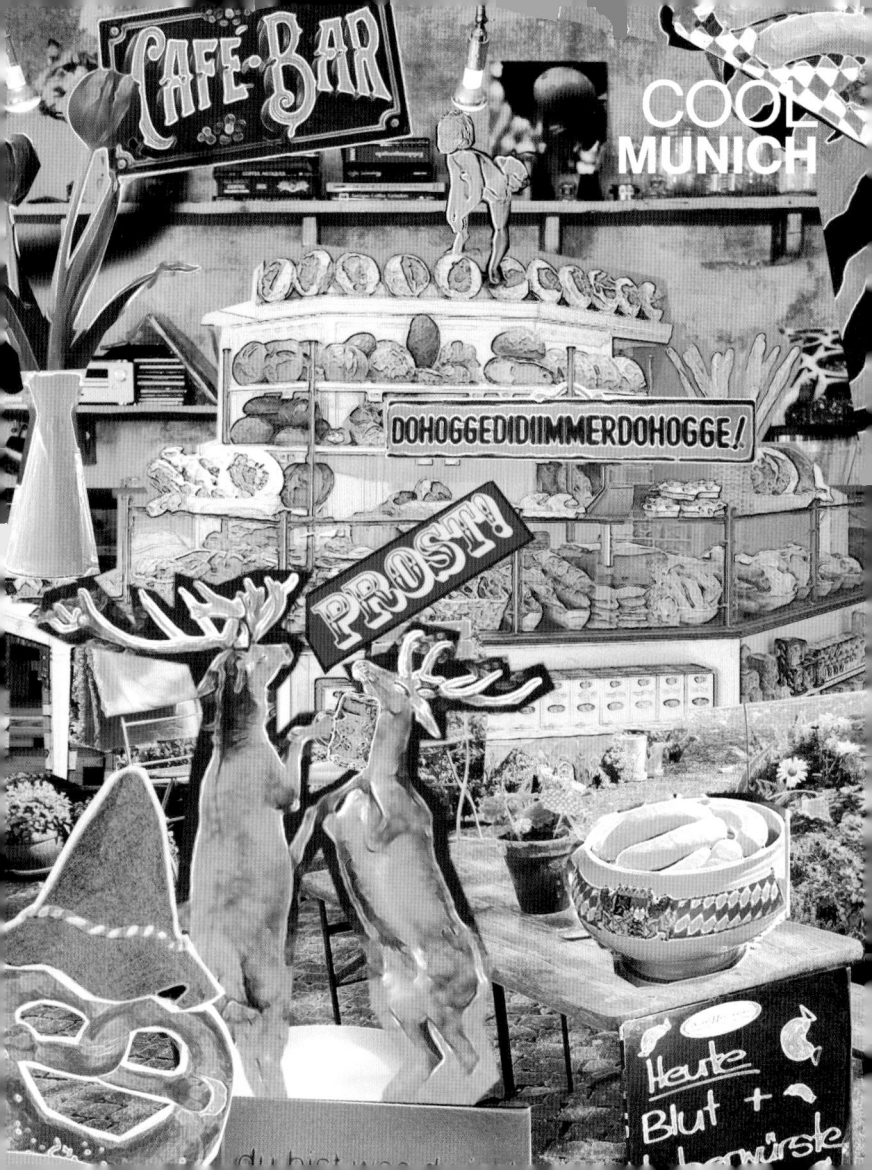

BON VALEUR

Sonnenstraße 17 // Altstadt
Tel.: +49 (0)89 54 88 39 94
www.bonvaleur.de

Mon–Thu 10 am to midnight
Fri–Sat 10 am to 1 am

S1–8, U4, U5
Tram 16–21, 27 Karlsplatz (Stachus)

Prices: $$
Cuisine: International

MAP N° 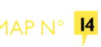 14

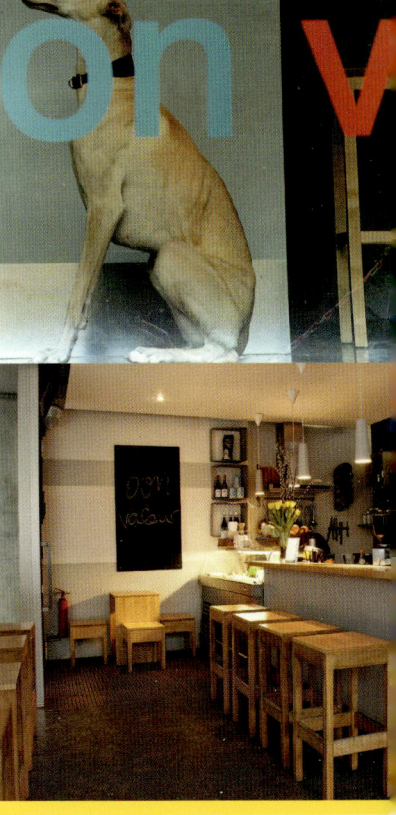

Although from the outside Bon Valeur is simply a minimalist glass cube—not particularly inviting as it sits between Sonnenstraße and hulking office buildings—it's a real insider secret. Max Grauer's relaxed eatery serves up delicious food for the soul, not necessarily vegetarian but always healthy. The small favorite is bustling until late, when the gas station across the street also awakens its beauty to become an urban backdrop.

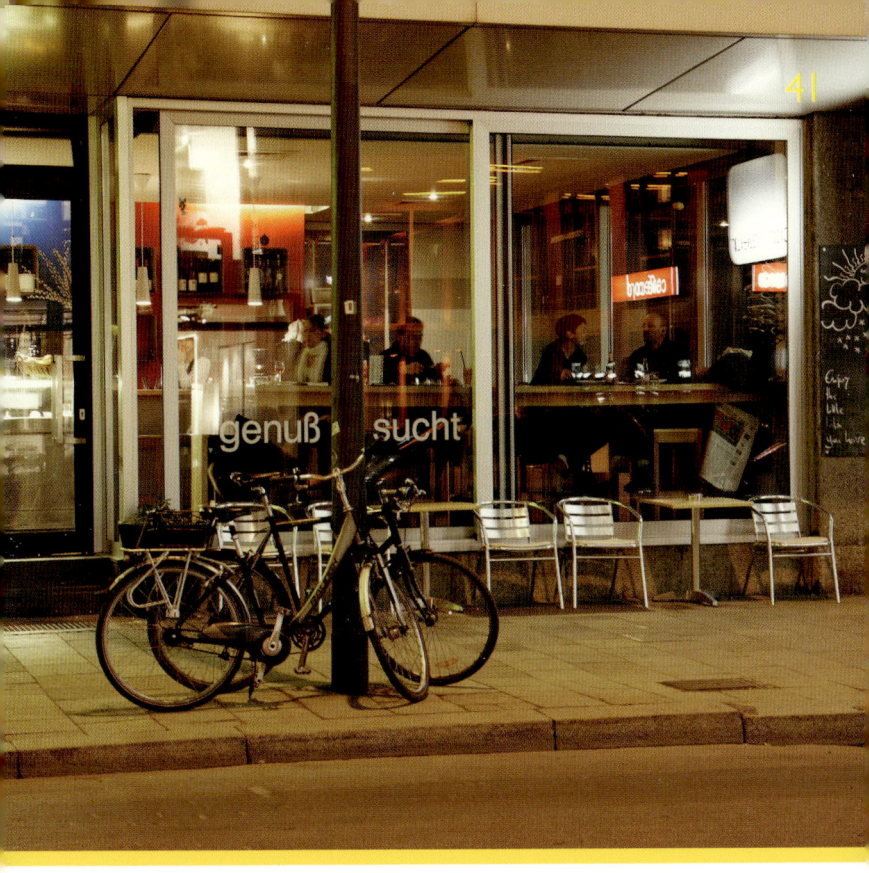

Obwohl das Bon Valeur – rein äußerlich – nur ein minimalistischer Glaskubus ist und wenig einladend zwischen der Sonnenstraße und Büroklötzen liegt, ist es ein echter Geheimtipp. In dem unverkrampften Lokal von Max Grauer gibt es lecker Soul Food, nicht zwingend vegetarisch, aber immer gesund. Bis zu vorgerückter Stunde geht es herzlich zu im kleinen Lieblingsladen. Dann entfaltet die Tankstelle gegenüber auch ihre Schönheit und wird zur urbanen Kulisse.

BRENNER

Maximilianstraße 15 // Altstadt
Tel.: +49 (0)89 4 52 28 80
www.brennergrill.de

Mon–Thu 8.30 am to 1 am
Fri–Sat 8.30 am to 2 am
Sun 9.30 am to 1 am

S1–8, U3, U6 Marienplatz
U4, U5 Lehel

Prices: $$

KAREN WEBB'S SPECIAL TIP
Sunday is Family Day! The playground
in the back includes childcare and the
waiters gently manage the buggies and
heat up your baby food.

MAP N°

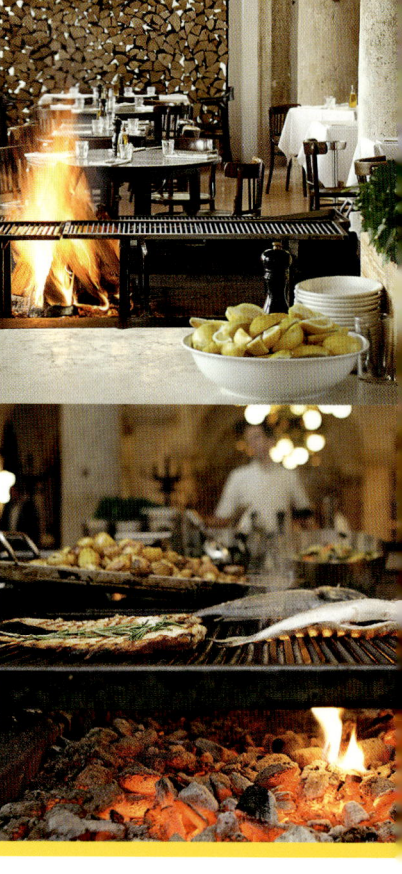

There is a growing habit among locals and tourists alike to visit Brenner
on a regular basis. This might be due to it being located on the presti-
gious Maximilianstraße, or simply because everything is just right here.
For friends of upscale cuisine and a relaxed ambience, this is the place
to be—a place to see and be seen, to have a Kir Royal, and to feel that
you have finally arrived in Munich. Reservation recommended!

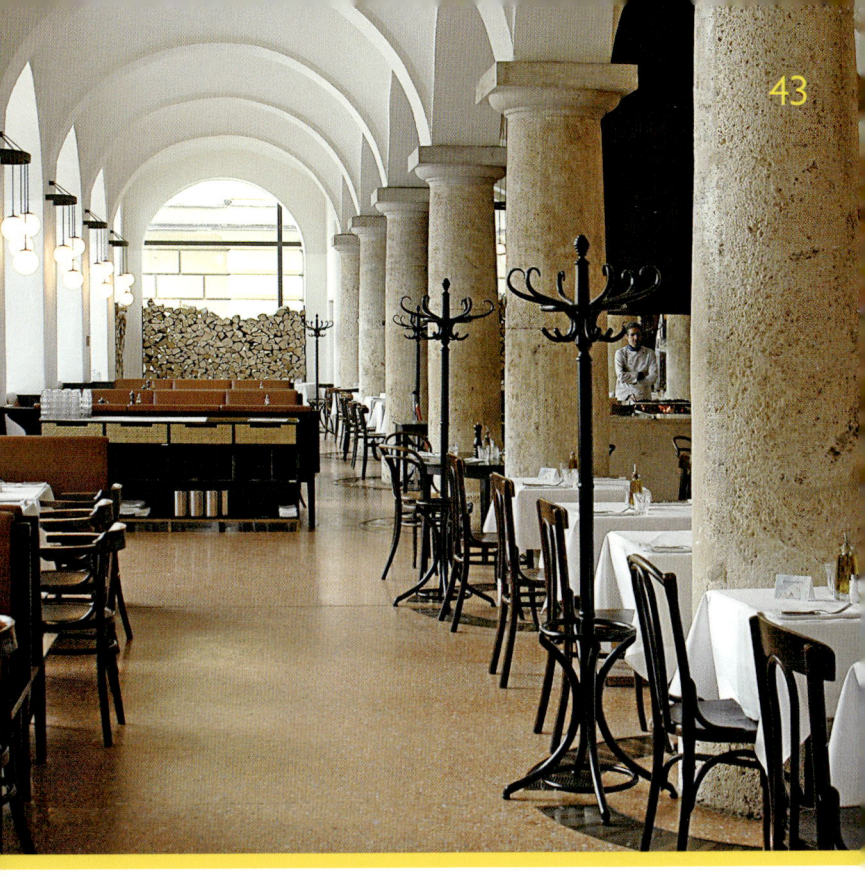

Münchner und Gäste der Stadt schauen gewohnheitsmäßig gern im Brenner vorbei. Was an der prestigeträchtigen Lage direkt auf der Maximilianstraße liegen kann, oder vielleicht auch der Tatsache geschuldet ist, dass hier einfach alles stimmt. Wer auf gehobene frische Küche und entspanntes Ambiente Wert legt, ist hier richtig. Hier sieht man, wird gesehen und mit einem Kir Royal in der Hand ist man in München angekommen. Reservierung empfehlenswert!

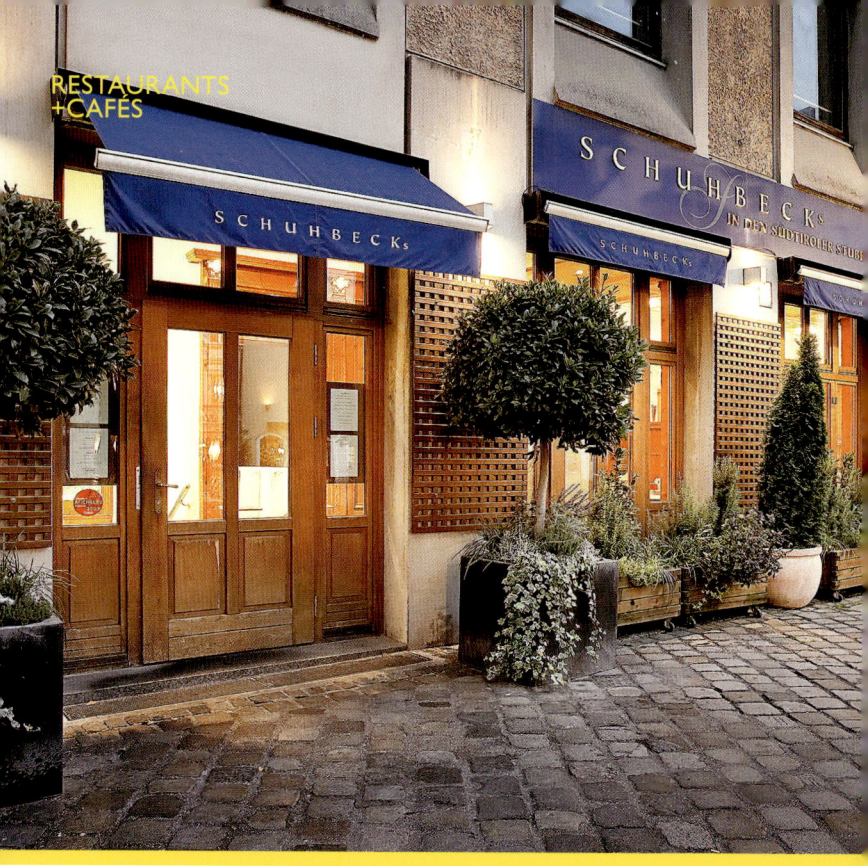

Star cook Alfons Schuhbeck is everywhere: In books, on TV, on the radio, in gourmet shows—you name it. Cooking is always the topic of choice, and even more so in his spice store near the Hofbräuhaus at the central Platzl. This is also where the Munich grandee has his flagship venue, Südtiroler Stuben. The somewhat conservatively furnished luxury brasserie offers cuisine of the highest standards with a focus on local specialties. With a little bit of luck the chef might stroll by your table in person—provided that he is not out of town.

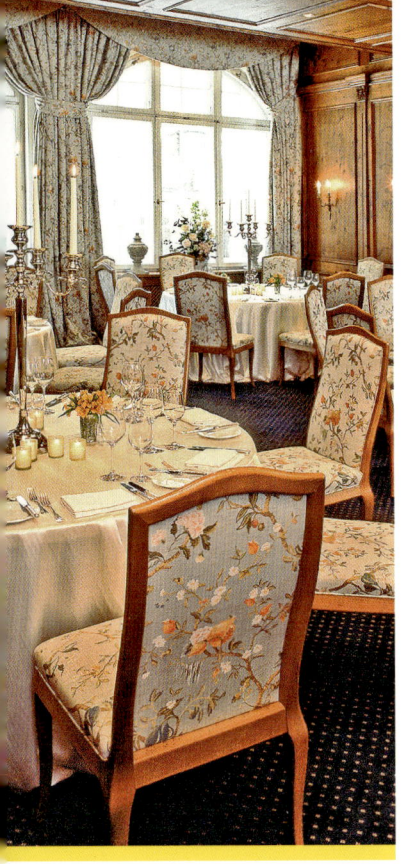

SCHUHBECKS IN DEN SÜDTIROLER STUBEN

Platzl 6–8 // Altstadt
Tel.: +49 (0)89 2 16 69 00
www.schuhbeck.de

Mon from 6 pm
Tue–Sat noon to 3 pm
and from 6 pm

S1–8, U3, U6, Tram 19 Marienplatz

Prices: $$$$
Cuisine: Bavarian

MAP N° 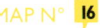 16

Der Meisterkoch Alfons Schuhbeck ist auf allen Kanälen: Bücher, Fernsehen, Radio, Gourmet-Shows. Immer geht es ums Kochen. Erst recht in seinem Gewürzladen am zentralen Platzl, unweit vom Hofbräuhaus. Dort betreibt das Münchner Urgestein auch sein Flaggschiff, die Südtiroler Stuben. Die etwas bieder eingerichtete Luxusbrasserie bietet Küche auf höchstem Niveau – mit dem Fokus auf regionalen Spezialitäten. Mit ein wenig Glück schaut der Chef auch einmal persönlich am Tisch vorbei. Vorausgesetzt, er weilt überhaupt im Haus.

PRINZ MYSHKIN

Hackenstraße 2 // Altstadt
Tel.: +49 (0)89 26 55 96
www.prinzmyshkin.com

Mon–Sun 11 am to 12.30 am

S1–8, U3, U6 Marienplatz

Prices: $$$
Cuisine: Vegetarian

MAP N° 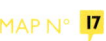 17

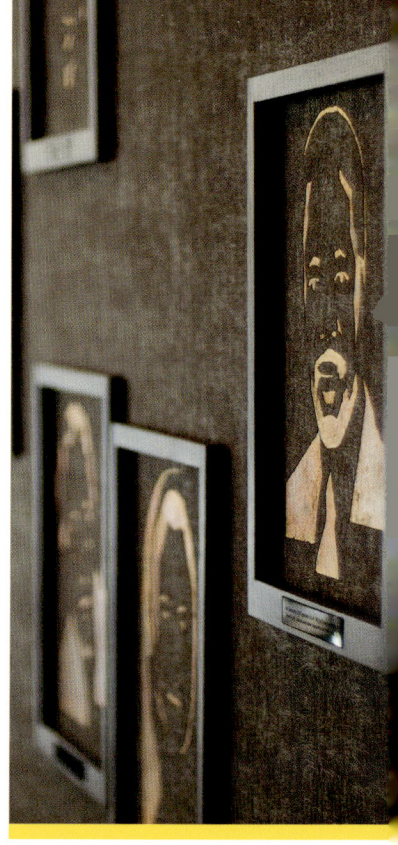

The restaurant between Marienplatz and Sendlinger Tor has been
here since 1984, making it a pioneer in Munich's vegetarian subculture.
But you won't find many hippies in Birkenstocks here, as the clientele
drawn to Prinz Myshkin, while health-conscious, tend more toward
the chic and stylish. Vegan and vegetarian dishes from all over the
world, such as Tofu Stroganoff or Indian lentils, are served in the high-
vaulted space or somewhat quieter side room.

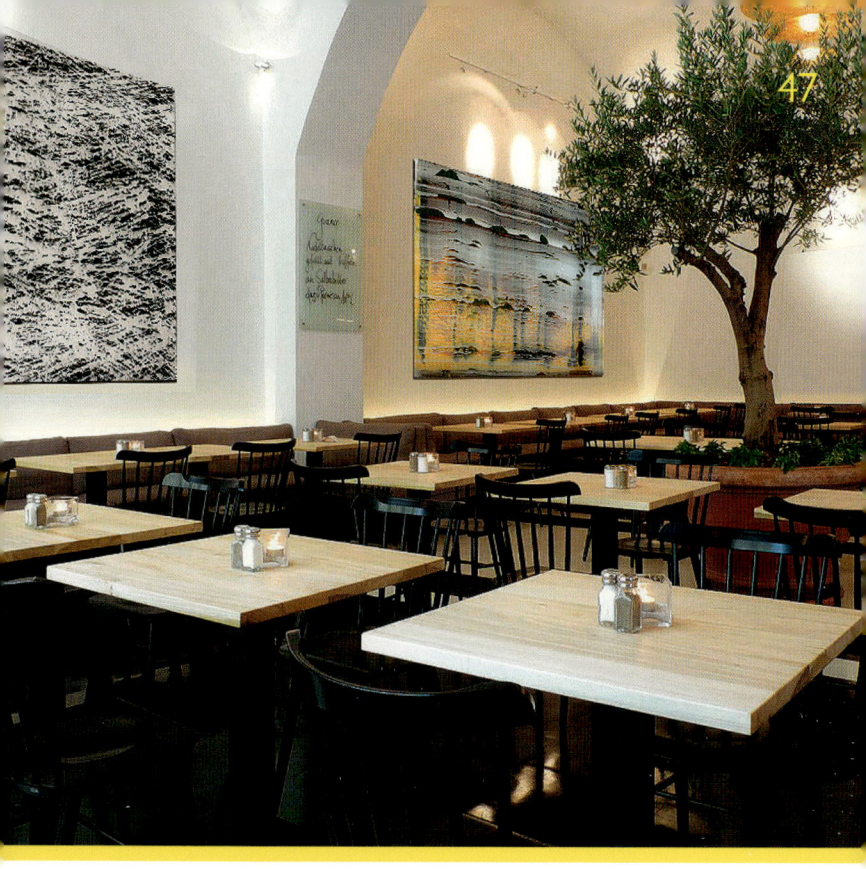

Das Restaurant zwischen Marienplatz und Sendlinger Tor gibt es bereits seit 1984 – damit hat es in München vegetarische Pionierarbeit geleistet. Alternative Sandalenträger wird man dort jedoch kaum antreffen, da das Prinz Myshkin zwar eine gesundheitsbewusste, aber eher schicke Klientel anzieht. In dem hohen Gewölberaum und einem etwas ruhigeren Seitenraum genießt man Veganes und Vegetarisches aus aller Welt, zum Beispiel Tofu Stroganoff oder indische Linsen.

SCHIFFMACHER
EIS CAFÉ BAR

Prälat-Zistl-Straße 4 // Altstadt
Tel.: +49 (0)89 2 38 89 99 81

Mon–Fri from 8 am
Sat from 9 am

S1–8, U3, U6 Marienplatz

Prices: $$$
Cuisine: Ice cream

MAP N° 18

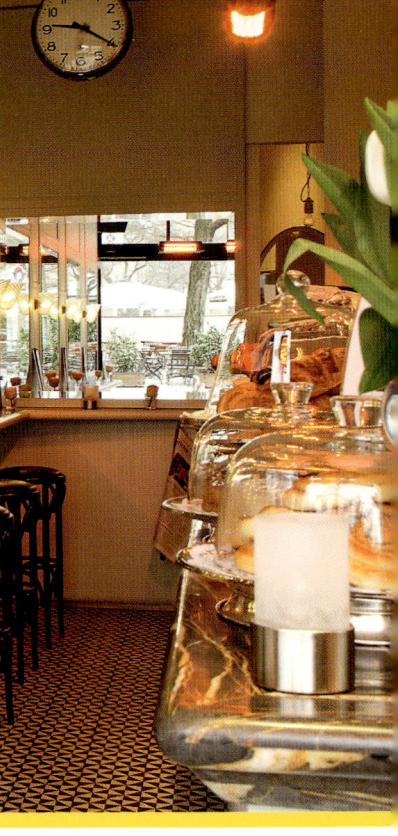

Amid the greatest hustle and bustle Uwe Häussler and Bekim Avdiji still always recount the origin of the bean, who roasts it (Johannes Bayer in this case), and explain that perfectly foamed milk should glide from the spoon. "Good enough" isn't sufficient here—the owners' love of perfection reigns at Schiffmacher, alongside La Marzocco of Florence, queen of espresso machines. In the winter delightful waffles are served, and in summer, ice cream from the Italian gelatiere.

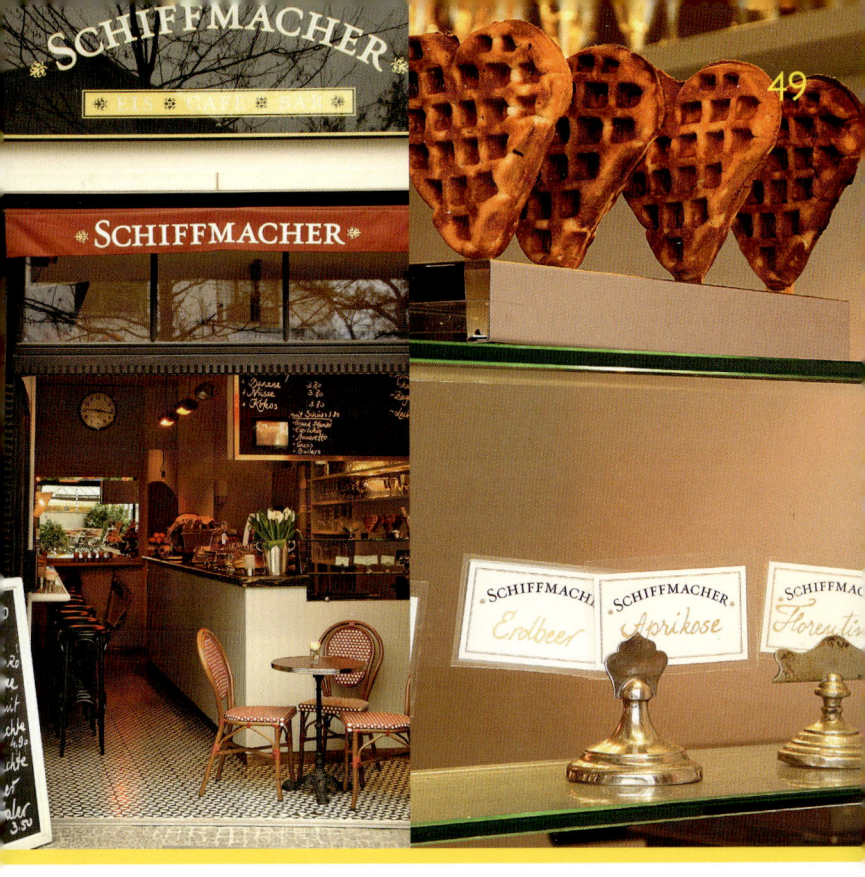

Selbst im größten Trubel erklären Uwe Häussler und Bekim Avdiji, woher die Bohne kommt, wer sie röstet (Johannes Bayer nämlich), und dass der perfekte Milchschaum vom Löffel gleiten muss. Ein „Passt schon" gibt es nicht – im Schiffmacher regieren der liebevolle Perfektionismus der Betreiber und die florentinische Marzocco, die Königin der Kaffeemaschinen. Im Winter nascht man dazu köstliche Waffeln, im Sommer Eis vom italienischen Gelatiere.

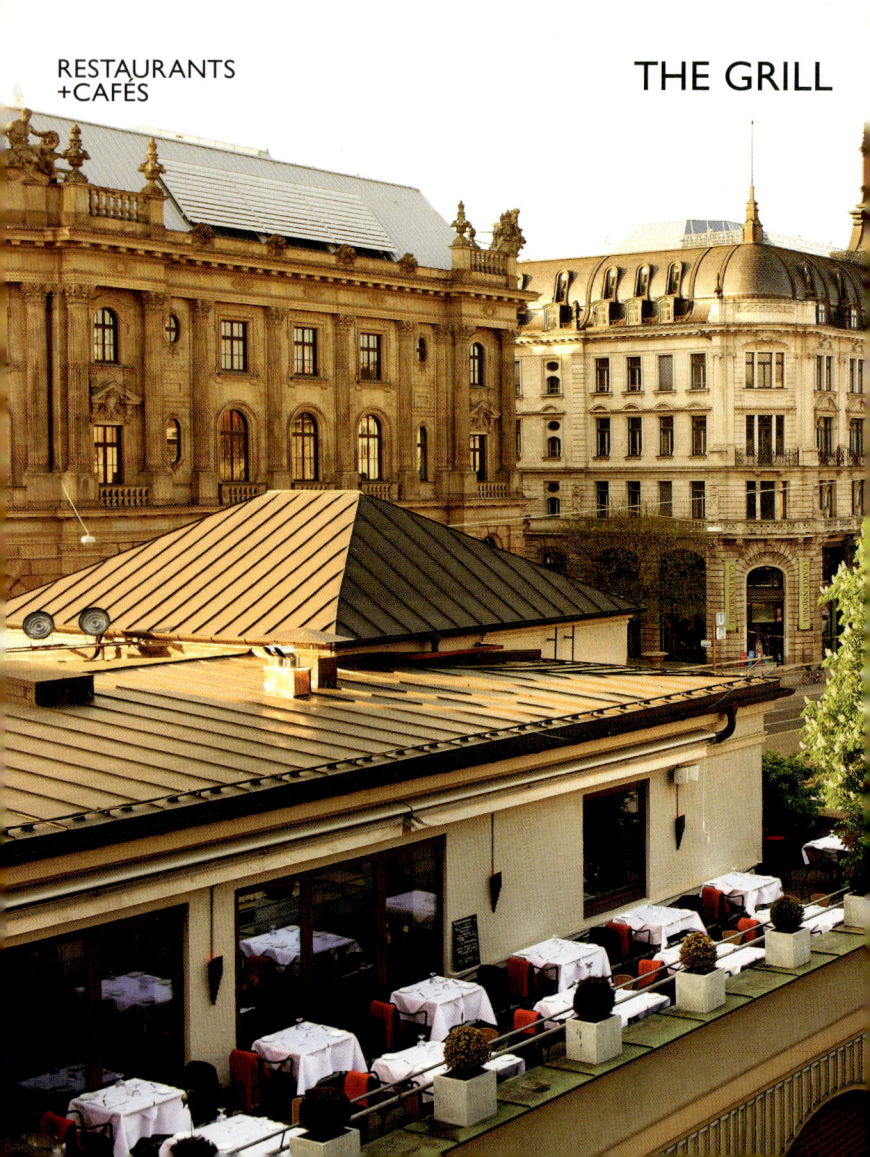

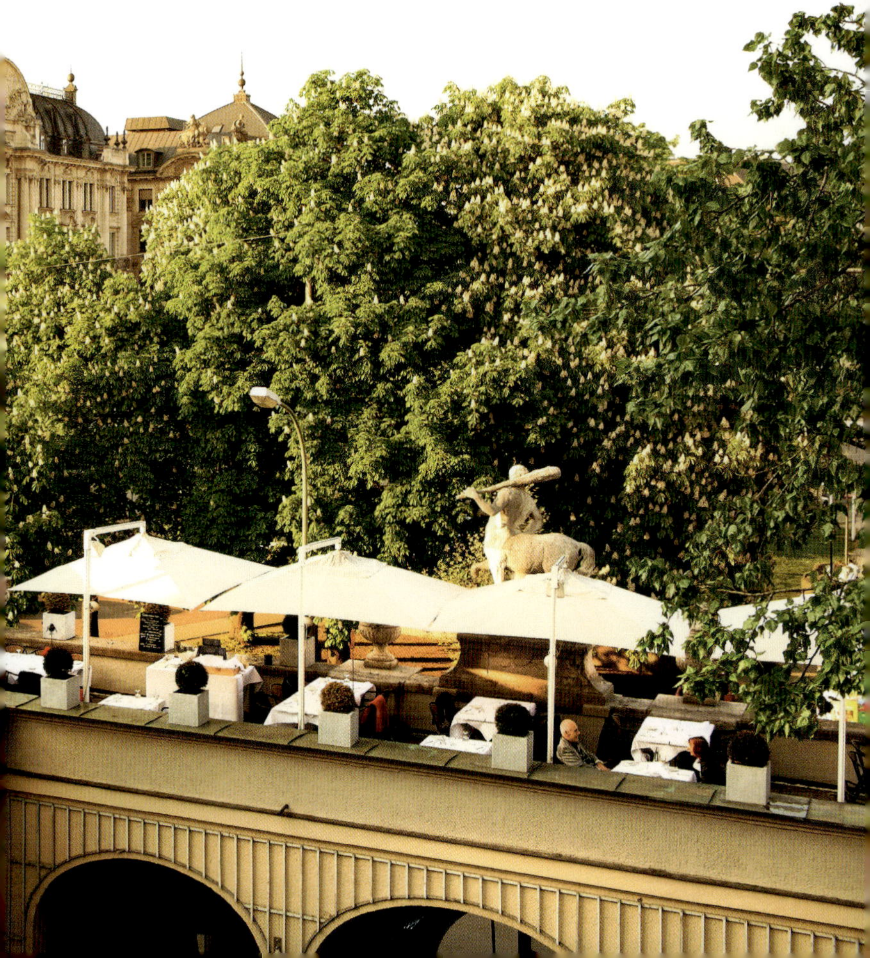

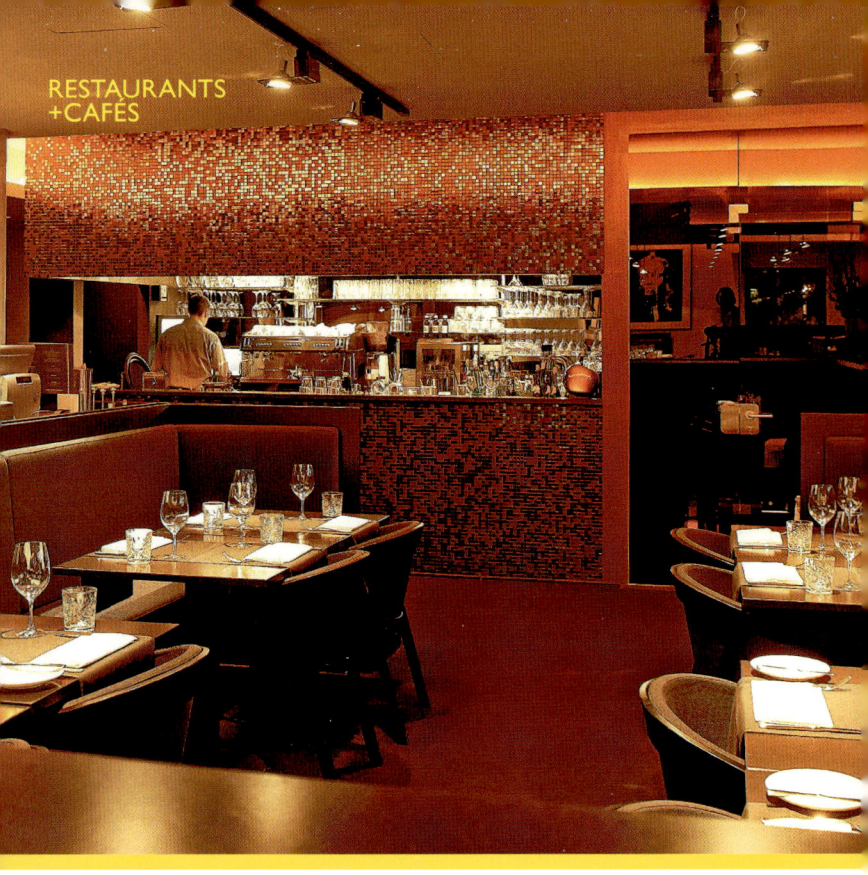

Built by Gabriel von Seidl and dedicated in 1900, the House of Artists originally served as a clubhouse to the artists surrounding "Artist Prince" Franz von Lenbach. Since the restaurant took over the upper floor in April 2010 and chef Max Lechner started serving meat, fish, and vegetables from the grill, it has turned into the perfect place for a drink at sunset. If it gets too chilly on the terrace you can go inside to feast your eyes on Nitzan Cohen's interior design.

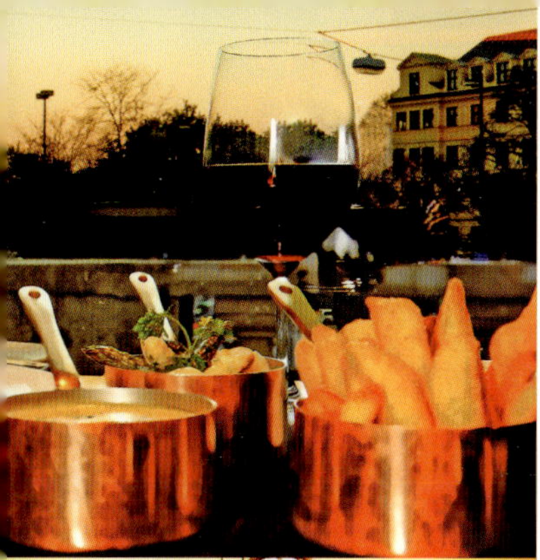

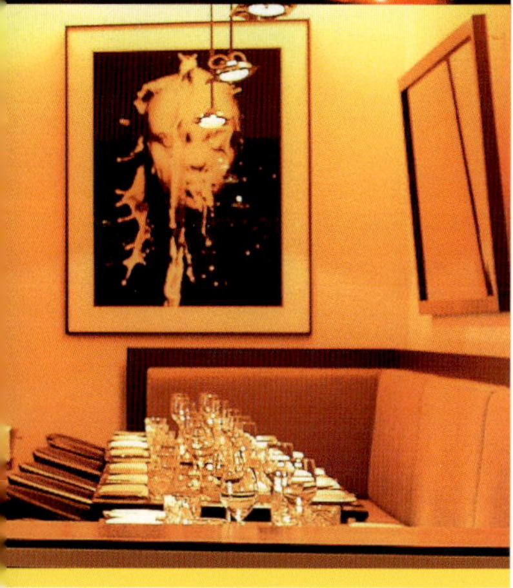

THE GRILL

Lenbachplatz 8 // Altstadt
Tel.: +49 (0)89 45 20 59 50
www.the-grill-munich.de

Mon–Thu 6 pm to midnight
Fri–Sat 6 pm to 1 am

S1–8, U4, U5
Tram 16–21, 27 Karlsplatz (Stachus)

Prices: $$$
Cuisine: International

MAP N° 19

Ursprünglich diente das von Gabriel von Seidl gebaute und 1900 ein-geweihte Künstlerhaus den Künstlern rund um den „Malerfürsten" Franz von Lenbach als Clubhaus. Seit das Restaurant im April 2010 das Obergeschoss bezogen hat und Küchenchef Max Lechner Fleisch, Fisch und Gemüse vom Grill kredenzt, ist es zu einem idealen Ort für einen Sundowner geworden. Wenn es auf der Terrasse zu kalt wird, kann sich das Auge drinnen an Nitzan Cohens Design weiden.

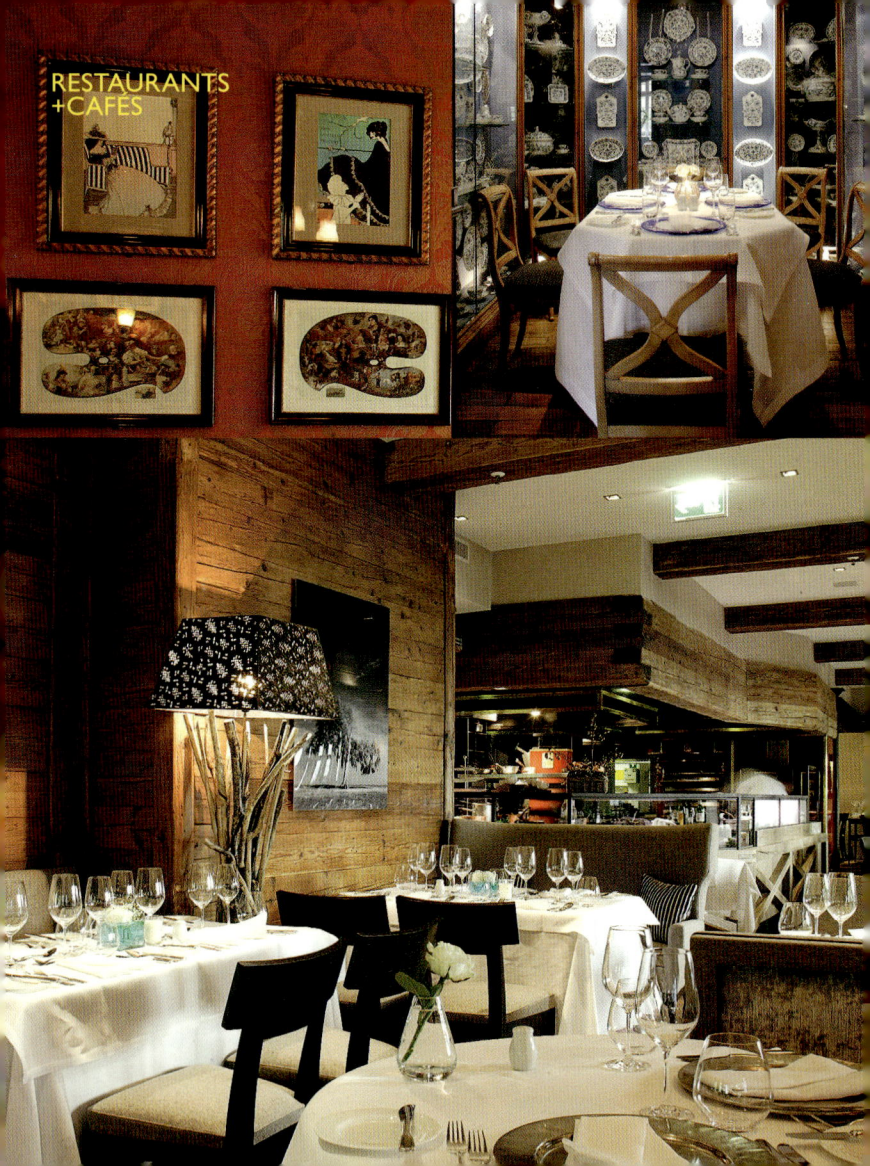

KÄFER-SCHÄNKE

Prinzregentenstraße 73 // Bogenhausen
Tel.: +49 (0)89 4 16 82 47
www.feinkost-kaefer.de

Mon–Sat 11 am to 11 pm

U4 Prinzregentenplatz
Tram 18 Friedensengel

Prices: $$$$
Cuisine: International

It all began in 1930 with Paul and Elsa Käfer's imported foods store on Amalienstraße. Today, Käfer is a Munich institution with worldwide connections. The flagship store on Prinzregentenstraße is a foodie's and connoisseur's dream. Head chef Volker Eisenmann demonstrates what kind of dishes you can conjure up with the exquisite products sold in the gourmet food store. This magic is also worshipped by the many Munich celebrities you'll meet here.

Mit dem Kolonialwarengeschäft von Paul und Elsa Käfer in der Amalienstraße fing 1930 alles an. Heute ist Käfer eine weltweit agierende Münchner Institution. Das Stammhaus in der Prinzregentenstraße ist ein Traum für Feinschmecker und Genießer. Was man aus den edlen Produkten, die im Feinkostladen verkauft werden, zaubern kann, führt Küchenchef Volker Eisenmann vor. Auf diese Magie steht auch die Münchner Prominenz, die man hier zahlreich antrifft.

CHARLIE

Schyrenstraße 8 // Giesing
Tel.: +49 (0)89 48 05 82 44
www.charl.ie

Tue–Sat 4 pm to 1 am
Sun 5 pm to 11 pm
Bar: Sat from 10 pm

U1, U2, U7 Kolumbusplatz
Bus 58 Claude-Lorrain-Straße

Prices: $$
Cuisine: Vietnamese

MAP N° 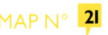 21

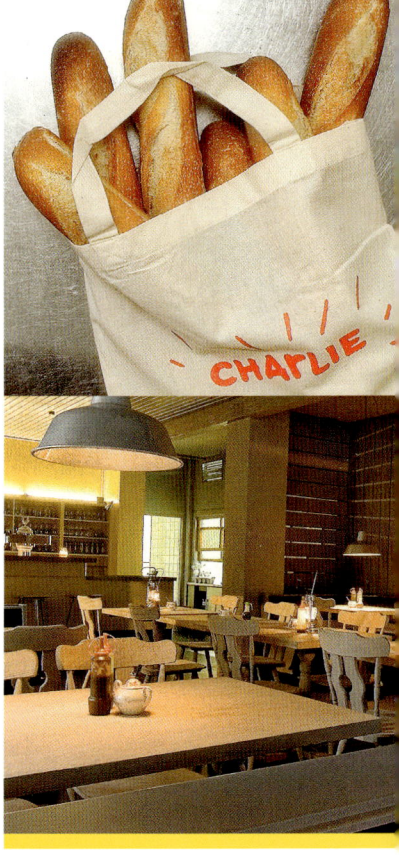

With designer Nitzan Cohen and a slender budget, Sandra Forster and Luc Nguyen took a dark, dusty tavern and transformed it into a friendly place—rescuing the outlying Untergiesing district from oblivion in the process. You can still see signs of the partly vegan Vietnamese restaurant's Bavarian past, which is pretty cool. Charlie's large, sunny outdoor area and the small downstairs bar make it absolutely irresistible.

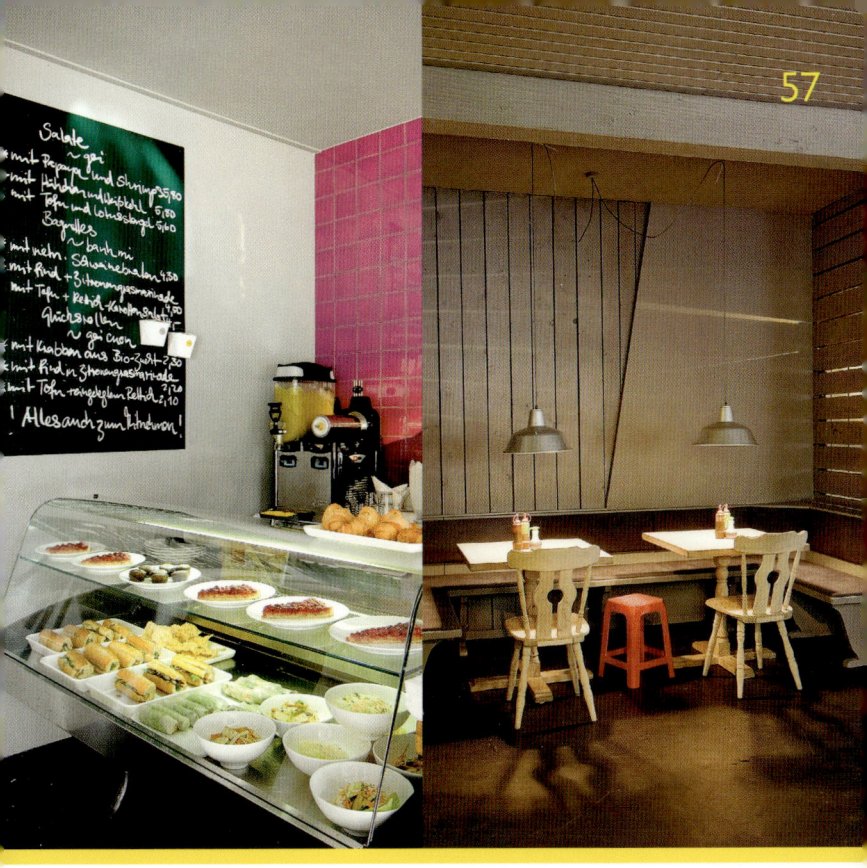

Mit dem Designer Nitzan Cohen und schmalem Budget haben Sandra Forster und Luc Nguyen ein angestaubtes, dunkles Wirtshaus in einen freundlichen Ort verwandelt – und damit auch das etwas abseits gelegene Untergiesing aus der Versenkung geholt. Dass man dem teils veganen vietnamesischen Restaurant seine bayerische Vergangenheit ansieht, ist ziemlich cool. Charlies großer, sonniger Außenbereich und seine kleine Kellerbar machen es endgültig unwiderstehlich.

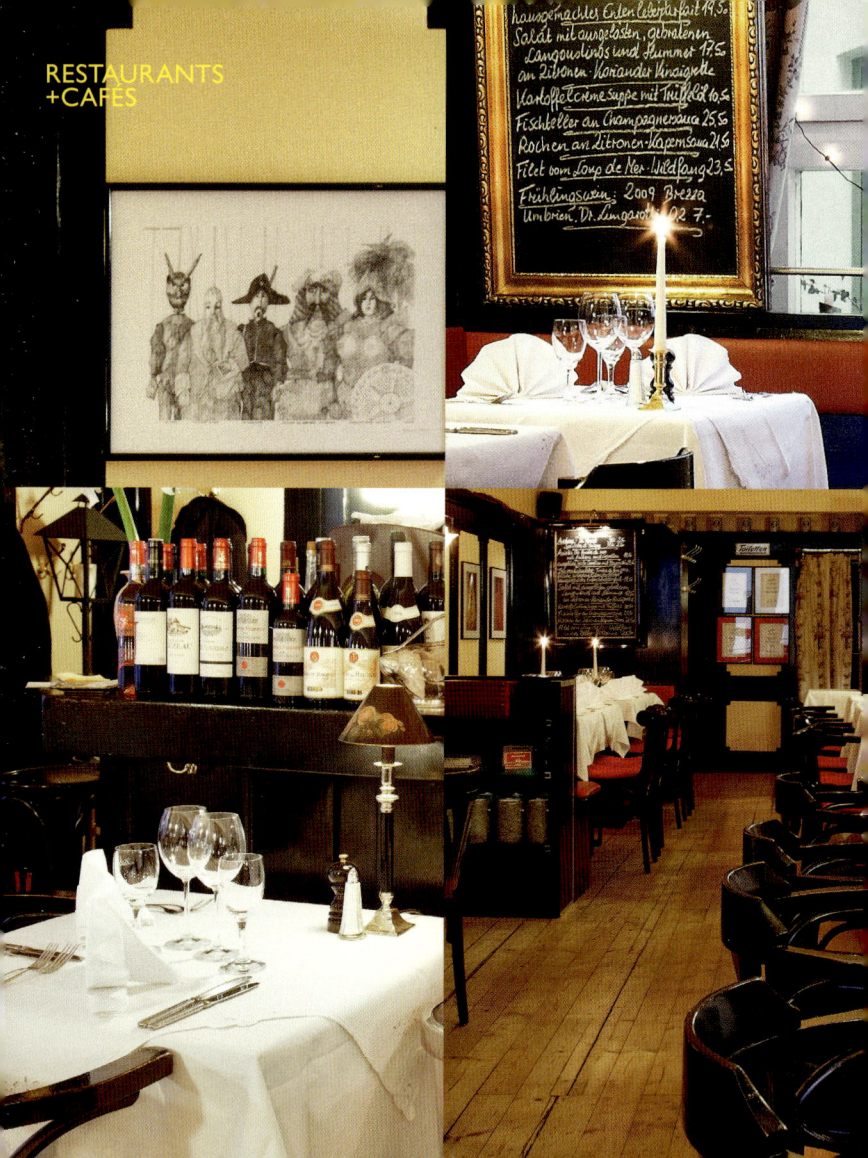

Steinstraße 63 // Haidhausen
Tel.: +49 (0)89 47 08 40 00
www.saint-laurent.eu

Tue–Sun 6 pm to 1 am

S1–8 Rosenheimer Platz
Tram 15, 19, 25 Wörthstraße

Prices: $$$
Cuisine: French

KAREN WEBB'S SPECIAL TIP
For fanciers of the haute cuisine—this is the place to rendez-vous!

The Pezerons' theme is a "liaison between countries," the fruits of which are enjoyed by the guests in their passionate, first-class restaurant. Originally from Brittany and a namesake of the patron saint of cooks, Laurent unites France and Germany in his creations. Meanwhile, his wife Claudia makes sure each guest feels more than at home. "What a mistake not to have been here in such a long time," writes Boris Becker in the guestbook.

Die „Liaison der Länder" ist bei den Pezerons Programm. Von den Früchten profitieren die Gäste ihres mit Herzblut geführten, erstklassigen Lokals. Der Bretone Laurent, namensverwandt mit dem Schutzpatron der Köche, vermählt in seinen Kreationen Frankreich und Deutschland. Seine Frau Claudia sorgt indessen dafür, dass sich jeder wohler als zu Hause fühlt. „Was für ein Fehler, so lange nicht hier gewesen zu sein", schreibt Boris Becker ins Gästebuch.

ZUM KLOSTER

Preysingstraße 77 // Haidhausen
Tel.: +49 (0)89 4 47 05 64

Mon–Sat 10 am to 1 am
Sun noon to 1 am

S1–8 Rosenheimer Platz
Tram 15, 19, 25 Wörthstraße

Prices: $$
Cuisine: German

MAP N° 23

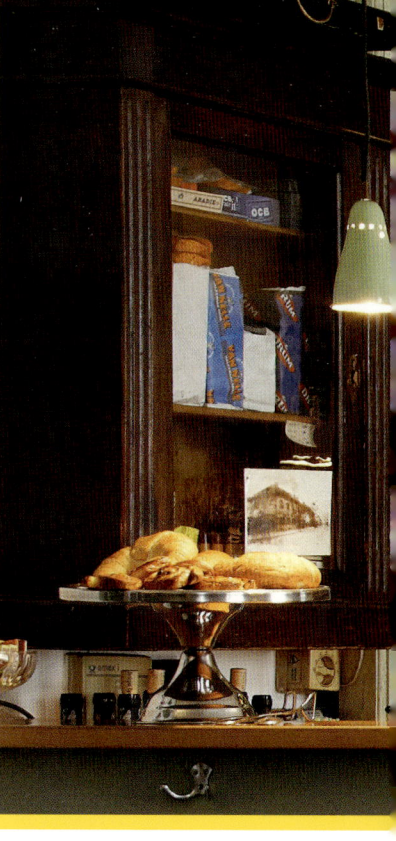

Amazing how beautiful it is up in Haidhausen, and so quiet! The rustic Zum Kloster inn strengthens the impression that you're in the countryside, only the pleasantly mixed crowd reminding you that you're still in the city. Breakfast in the shade of the trees is a wonderful summertime experience. The menu also features traditional Bavarian fare, with different cakes and pastries each day.

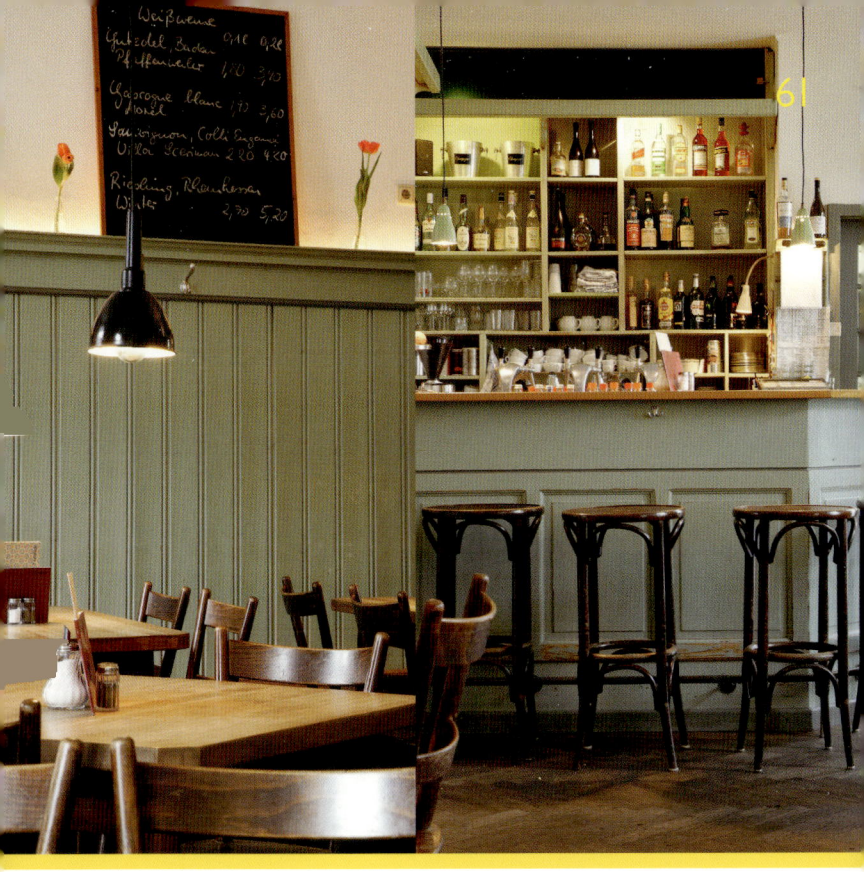

Man fasst es nicht, wie schön es da oben in Haidhausen ist. Und vor allem ruhig. Die rustikale Gaststätte Zum Kloster verstärkt den Eindruck, sich irgendwo auf dem Land zu befinden. Nur das angenehm durchmischte Publikum deutet darauf hin, dass man nach wie vor in der Stadt ist. Im Schatten der Bäume kann man hier im Sommer wunderbar frühstücken. Außerdem bietet die Karte traditionelle bayerische Gerichte und täglich wechselnde Kuchensorten.

BANYAN

Goethestraße 68 // Isarvorstadt
Tel.: +49 (0)89 5 30 93 21
www.banyan-restaurant.de

Mon–Sat 11.30 am to 2.30 pm
6 pm to midnight

U3, U6 Goetheplatz

Prices: $$$
Cuisine: Vietnamese

MAP N° 24

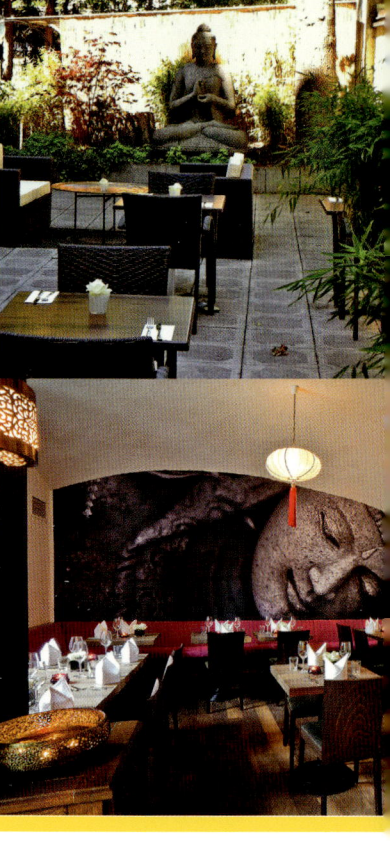

Banyan's kitchen chef and co-owner Anh Thu prepares tasty
Vietnamese meals by faithfully following her mother's recipes.
Apart from that, the stylish venue is also a treat for the eyes. Heavy
wooden furniture and traditional ornaments are combined with
color-intensive light installations. The right mixture of pleasure and
design is provided to make the place a popular and hip meeting spot.

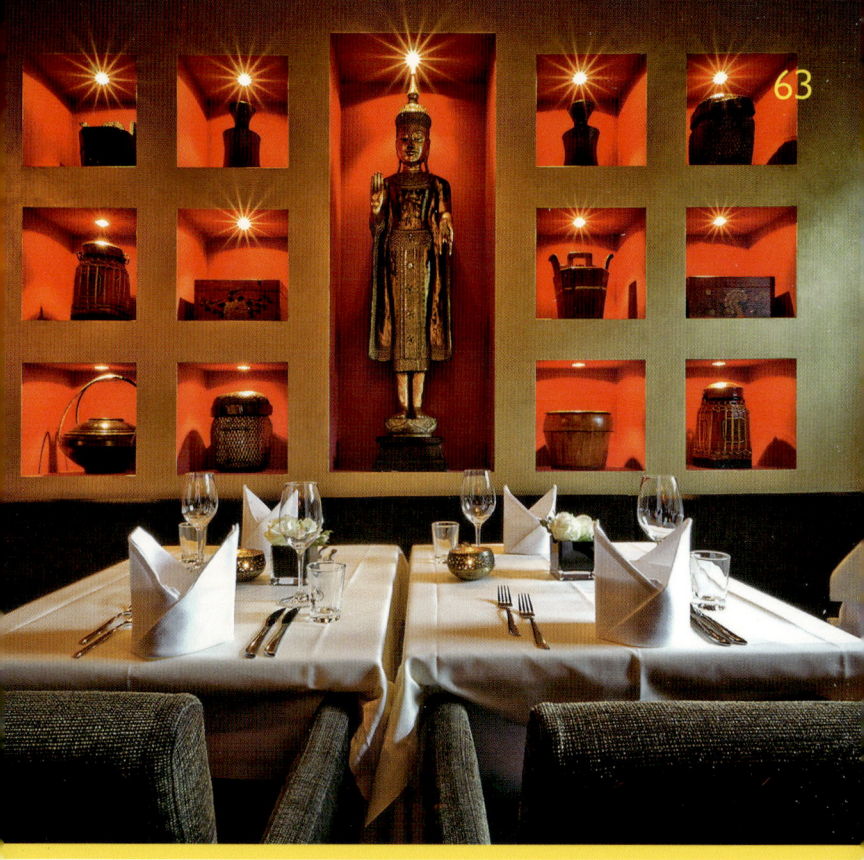

Die Küchenchefin und Mitbesitzerin Anh Thu bereitet im Banyan leckere vietnamesische Gerichte zu, ganz nach den Rezepten ihrer Mutter. Abgesehen davon ist das stylische Lokal auch ein Augenschmaus. Schwere Holzmöbel und traditionelle Ornamente sind mit farbintensiven Lichtinstallationen kombiniert. Die richtige Mischung aus Genuss und Design, um zum In-Treffpunkt zu werden.

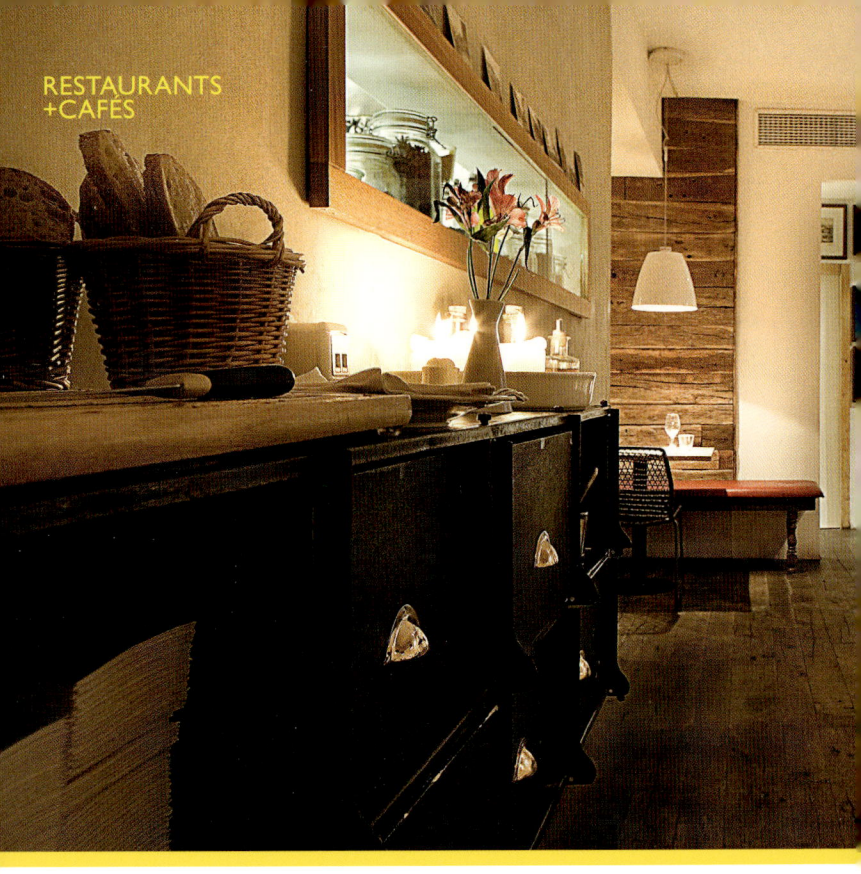

This smart all-day bar is located on bustling Müllerstraße at the entrance to the Glockenbach district. An ideal location for observing flaneurs and enjoying a beverage and light meal, at any time of day. Besides the organic products sourced from the nearby Bavarian countryside, the Corso is very north-Italian. This is clear from the decor: 300-year-old oak beams from a castle in Alto Adige meet unembellished designs.

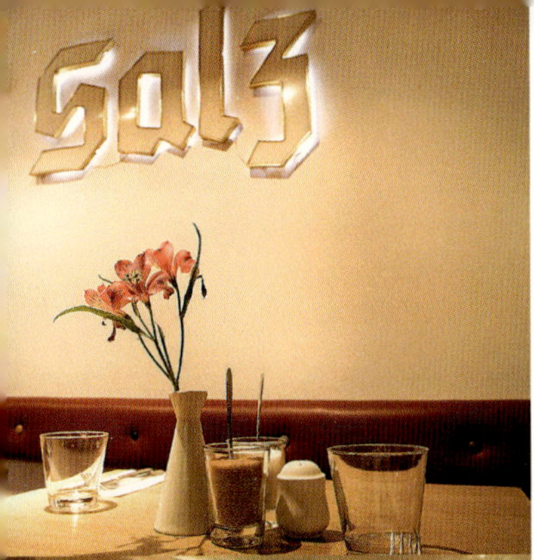

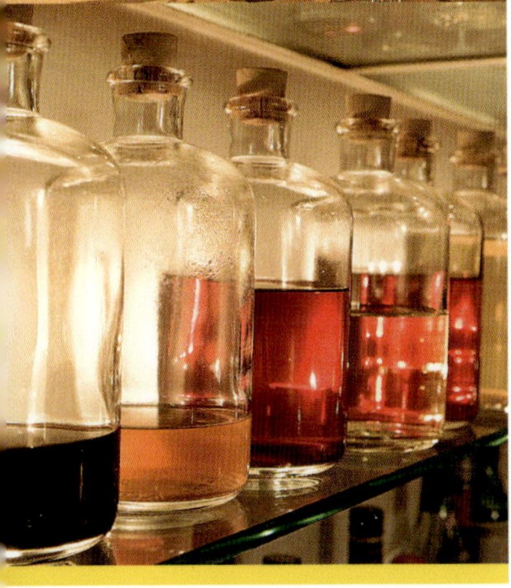

BAR CORSO

Müllerstraße 51 // Isarvorstadt
Tel.: +49 (0)89 24 21 61 15
www.barcorso.de

Daily 10 am to 1 am

U1, U2, U3, U6, U7
Tram 16, 17, 18, 27 Sendlinger Tor

Prices: $$
Cuisine: German-Austrian

MAP N° 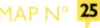 25

Diese schmucke Tagesbar liegt am Eingang des Glockenbachviertels in der belebten Müllerstraße. Der ideale Ort, um die Flaneure zu beobachten und dabei ganztägig Getränke und leichte Speisen zu sich zu nehmen. Die verwendeten Bio-Produkte stammen aus dem bayerischen Umland, aber sonst ist das Corso sehr norditalienisch, was sich auch in der Einrichtung zeigt: 300-jährige Eichenbalken aus einem Südtiroler Schloss treffen auf schnörkelloses Design.

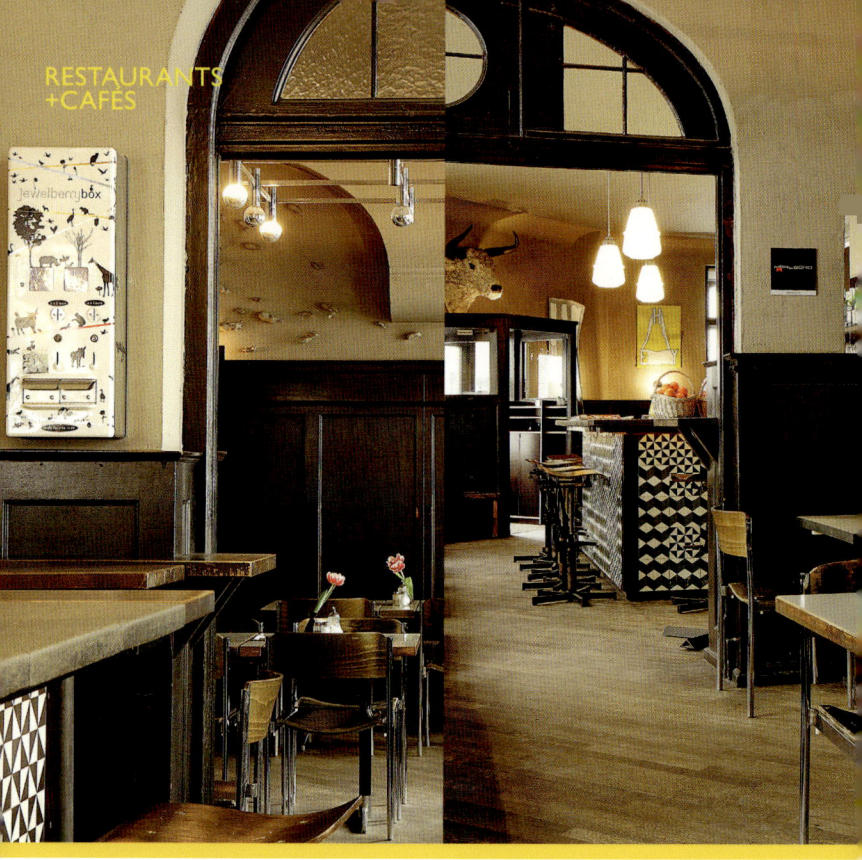

At Hey Luigi you can inadvertently get into the party spirit though all you wanted was to grab a bite to eat. Maybe something simple and satisfying, like "Leberkäs" (a type of meat loaf) with a fried egg. The former corner pub is a meeting point for the cool crowd that also frequents this eatery for good food, generous portions, and fair prices. The outdoor seating is great in the summer, ideally with sunglasses, in the middle of the colorful neighborhood.

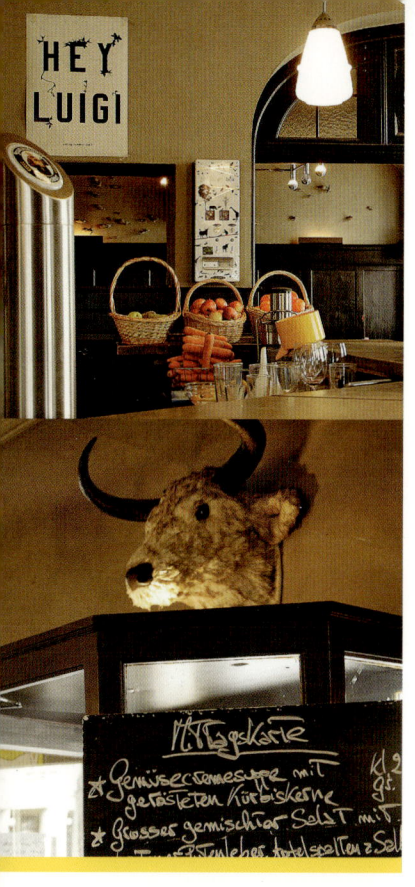

HEY LUIGI

Holzstraße 29 // Isarvorstadt
Tel.: +49 (0)89 46 13 47 41
www.heyluigi.de

Mon–Fri noon to 1 am
Sat 5 pm to 1 am
Sun and holidays 5 pm to midnight

Tram 16, 17, 18 Müllerstraße
U1, U2, U3, U6, U7 Sendlinger Tor

Prices: $
Cuisine: International

MAP N° **26**

Im Hey Luigi kann man unabsichtlich in Partystimmung geraten, obwohl man doch nur schnell etwas essen wollte. Zum Beispiel was einfaches, deftiges, wie Leberkäs mit Spiegelei. Die einstige Eckkneipe ist ein Treffpunkt für das Szenevolk, das sich hier auch gerne mittags einfindet, weil man gut isst, die Portionen üppig und die Preise fair sind. Im Sommer sitzt man draußen sehr gut, am besten mit großer Sonnenbrille – mitten im bunten Viertel.

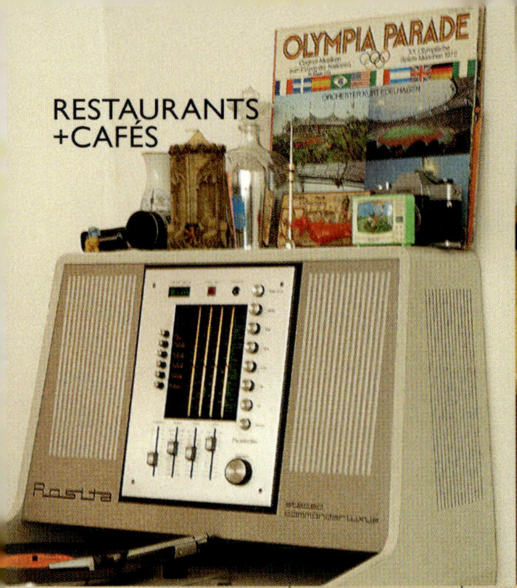

RESTAURANTS
+CAFÉS

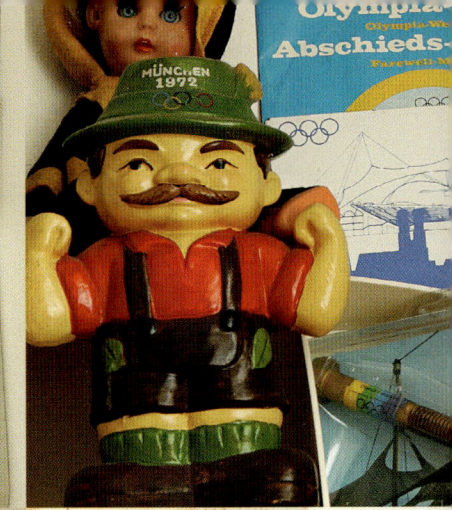

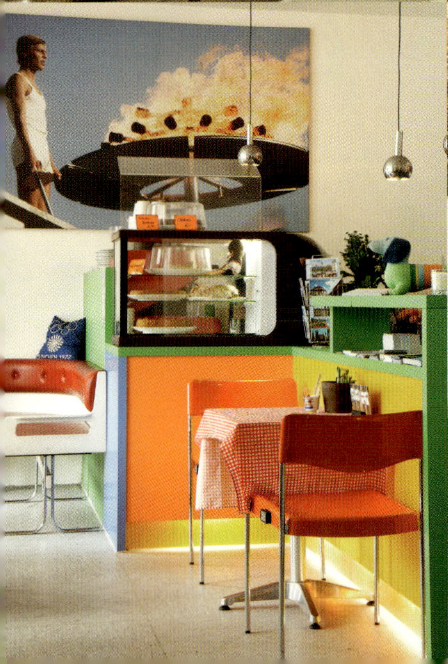

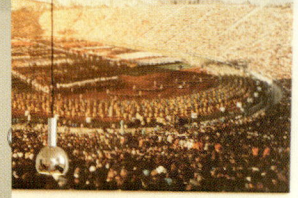

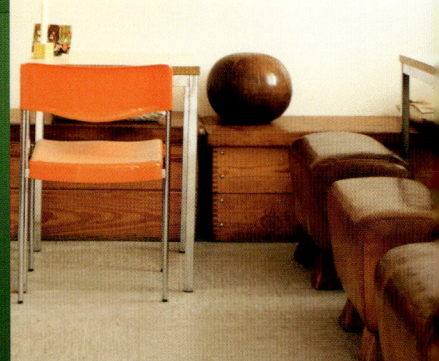

MÜNCHEN 72

Morassistraße 26 // Isarvorstadt
(access via Kohlstraße)
Tel.: +49 (0)89 97 34 37 85
www.muenchen72.de

Tue–Thu 10 am to midnight
Fri–Sat 10 am to 1.30 am
Sun 10 am to 10 pm

S1–8, Tram 16, 18 Isartor

Prices: $
Cuisine: German

This truly sporty locale is a loving tribute to the '70s and particularly to the 1972 Munich Summer Olympics. Although the café gets plenty of media attention for its retro interior made of old gymnastic equipment, Tom Zufall's place is still something of an insider secret. Hard to understand, considering the friendly service, all-day sun, and terrific hearty breakfast.

Das im wahrsten Sinne sportliche Lokal ist eine liebevolle Hommage an die 70er Jahre und insbesondere die – in München ausgetragenen – Olympischen Sommerspiele von 1972. Obwohl das Café wegen seines Retro-Interieurs aus alten Turngeräten viel mediale Aufmerksamkeit bekommt, hat Tom Zufalls Laden immer noch etwas von Geheimtipp. Eigentlich völlig unverständlich, bei dem freundlichen Service, ganztägig Sonne und dem herzhaft köstlichen Frühstück.

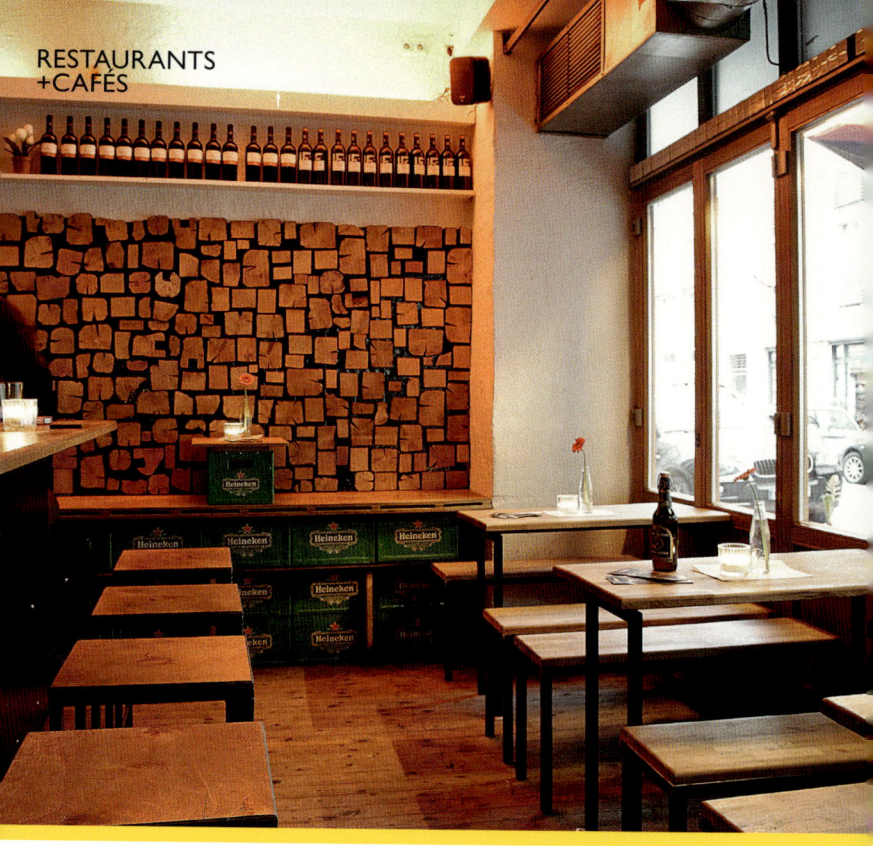

The love may be fast, as the name suggests, but it is ardent: shortly before opening time, the hungry mob is already waiting outside and the place fills up fast. This makes perfect sense, actually, given the sensational burgers and the fact that the attractive and friendly lady at the grill wears black latex gloves. The later the hour, the more fans of Schnelle Liebe pile up in the little room with the bar in the middle. A snack becomes a party.

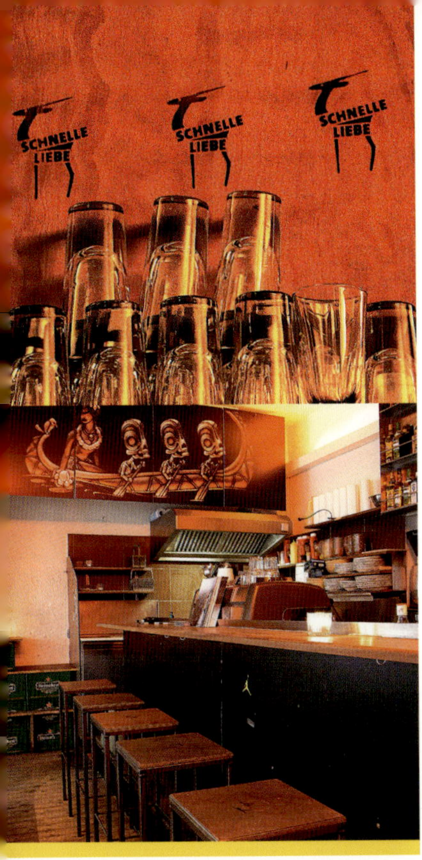

SCHNELLE LIEBE

Thalkirchnerstraße 12 // Isarvorstadt
Tel.: +49 (0)89 21 57 87 52
www.schnelleliebe.de

Daily from 5.30 pm
Sun closed during winter

U1, U2, U3, U6, U7
Tram 16, 17, 18, 27 Sendlinger Tor

Prices: $$
Cuisine: German Bistro

MAP N° 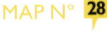 28

Die Liebe mag schnell sein, aber sie ist inbrünstig: kurz vor Öffnung wartet draußen bereits die hungrige Meute, das Lokal füllt sich schnell. Was vollkommen logisch ist, angesichts des sensationellen Burgers und der Tatsache, dass die attraktive, freundliche Dame vom Grill schwarze Latexhandschuhe trägt. Je später die Stunde, desto mehr Fans der Schnellen Liebe stapeln sich in dem kleinen Raum mit der Bar in der Mitte. Der Imbiss wird zur Party.

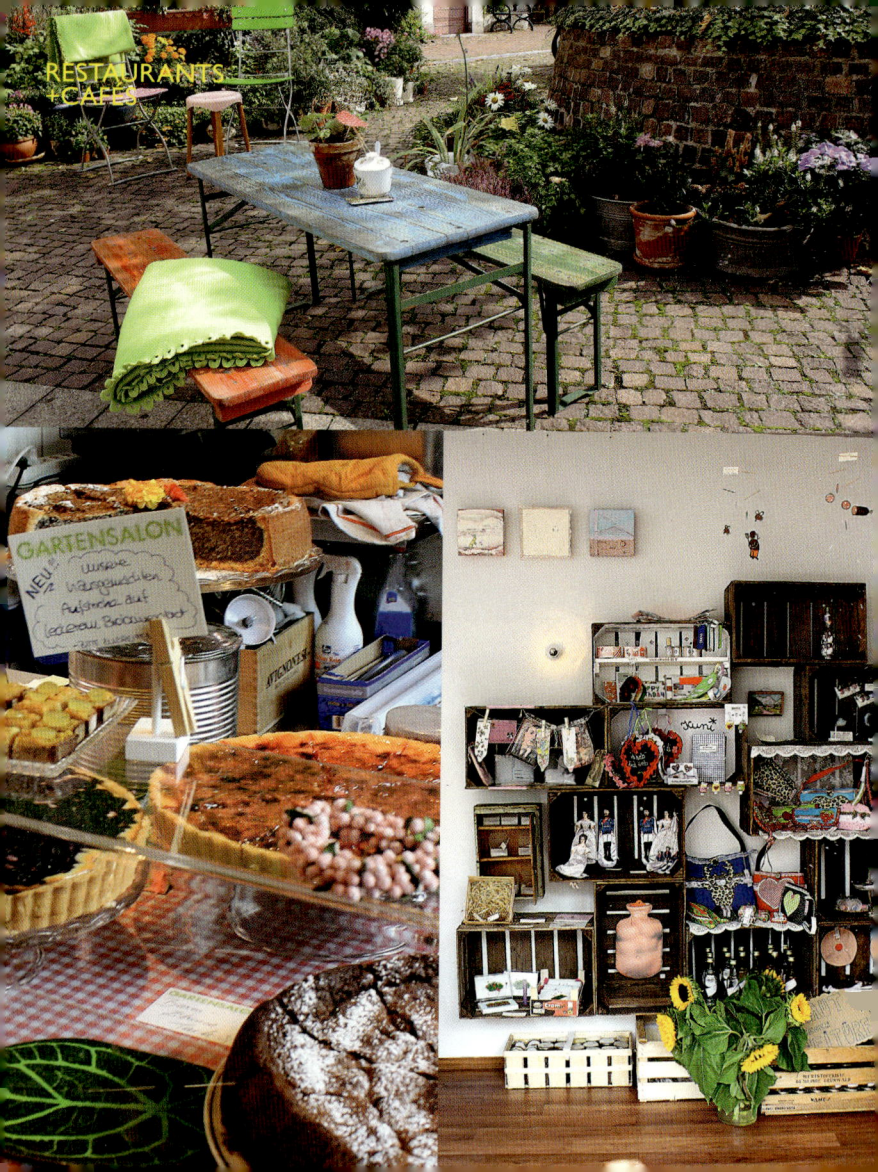

GARTENSALON

NEU!

GARTENSALON

Türkenstraße 90 / Amalienpassage
Maxvorstadt
Tel.: +49 (0)89 28 77 86 04
www.gartensalon.net

Tue–Sat 9 am to 7 pm
Sun 10 am to 7 pm

U3, U6 Universität

Prices: $$
Cuisine: Homemade

Gartensalon is in the middle of the lively Maxvorstadt area, in a passageway connecting Amalienstraße and Türkenstraße, yet it's extremely quiet. Breakfast or the "Lunch Box Deluxe" are especially delicious at this oasis. Anglophile Ines Stöhr prepares soft drinks, marmalade, and scones to original English recipes. The shop also holds small works of art and objects by various artists—affordable art-to-go.

Der Gartensalon liegt mitten in der quirligen Maxvorstadt, in einer Passage zwischen Amalien- und Türkenstraße, und dennoch ganz ruhig. In dieser Oase schmecken das Frühstück oder das „Pausenbrot Deluxe" besonders gut. Die anglophile Ines Stöhr bereitet Limonaden, Marmeladen und Scones nach original englischem Rezept zu. Im Ladenlokal finden sich des Weiteren kleine Kunstwerke und Objekte von verschiedenen Künstlern – erschwingliche „Art to go".

PAVESI PICNIC

Türkenstraße 61 // Maxvorstadt
Tel.: +49 (0)89 23 54 50 45
www.pavesipicnic.de

Mon–Fri 10 am to 8 pm
Sat 10 am to 6 pm

U3, U6 Universität

Prices: $$
Cuisine: Asian

MAP N° 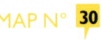 30

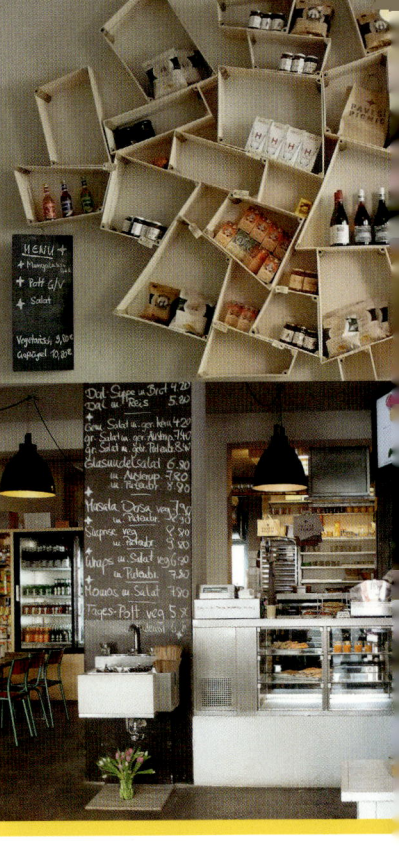

Pavesi Picnic sounds like Italian panini but actually features Indian-inspired cuisine that feels so good it should be prescribed by doctors. Take the momos: impressive proof that healthy and delicious are not mutually exclusive. Homemade masala spice blends complement the seasonal goods of the region, resulting in light delicacies. "Picnics make people happy," Markus Härle and Martin Küttner claim. How true.

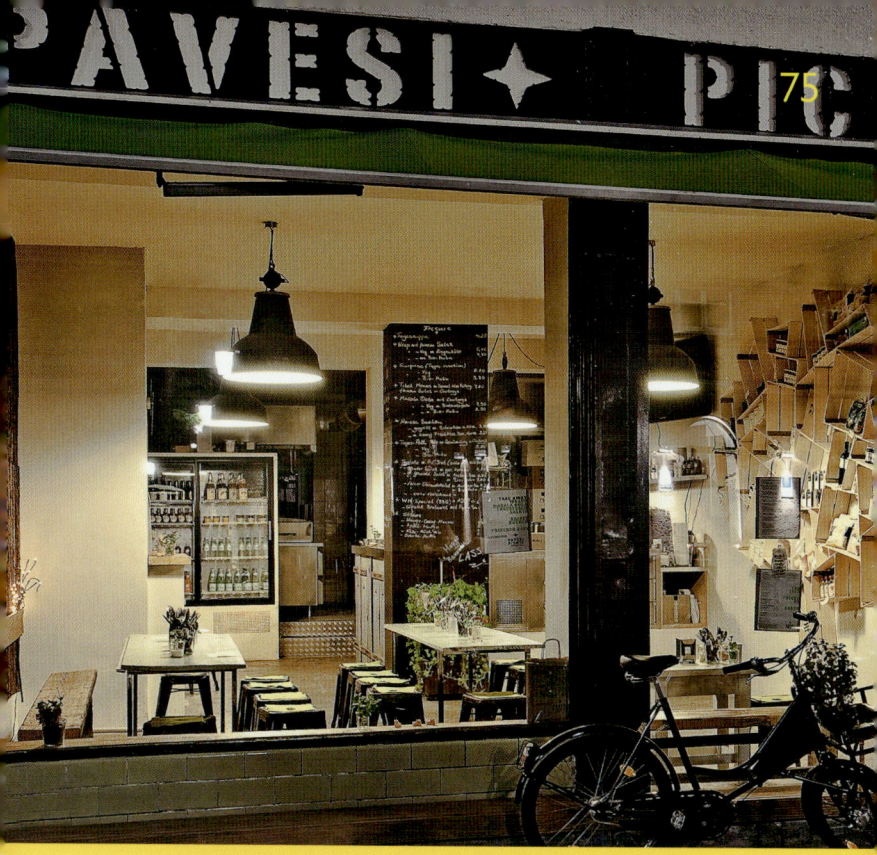

Pavesi Picnic klingt nach italienischen Panini, bietet jedoch eine indisch inspirierte Küche, die so gut tut, dass sie ärztlich verschrieben sein sollte. Die Momos z. B. beweisen eindrucksvoll, dass gesund und lecker sich nicht ausschließen. Die Produkte kommen je nach Saison aus der Region und werden mit hausgemachten Masala-Gewürzmischungen zu bekömmlichen Gerichten verarbeitet. „Picnicen macht glücklich", behaupten Markus Härle und Martin Küttner. Recht haben sie.

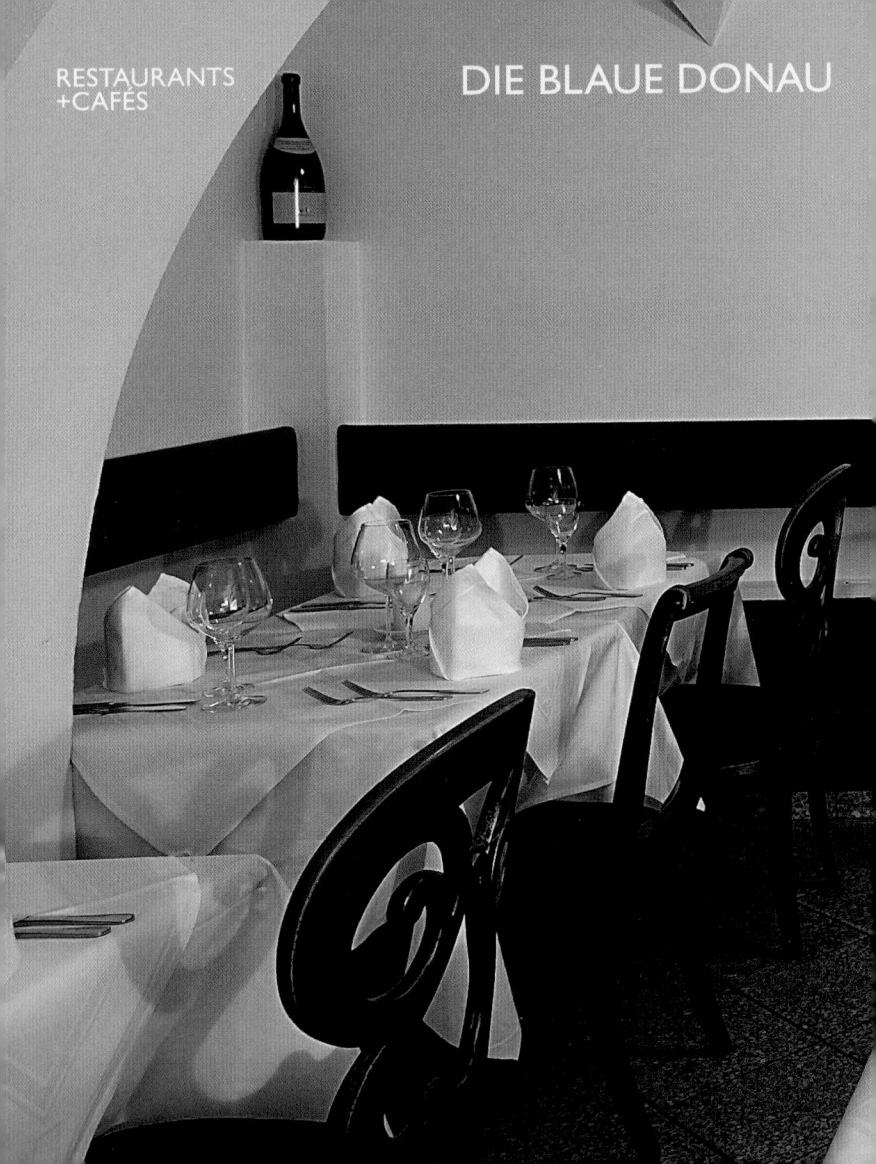

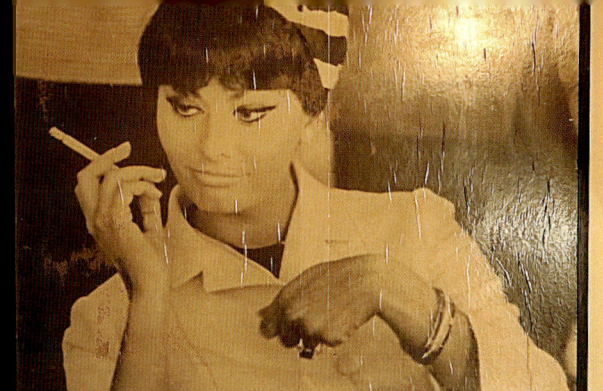

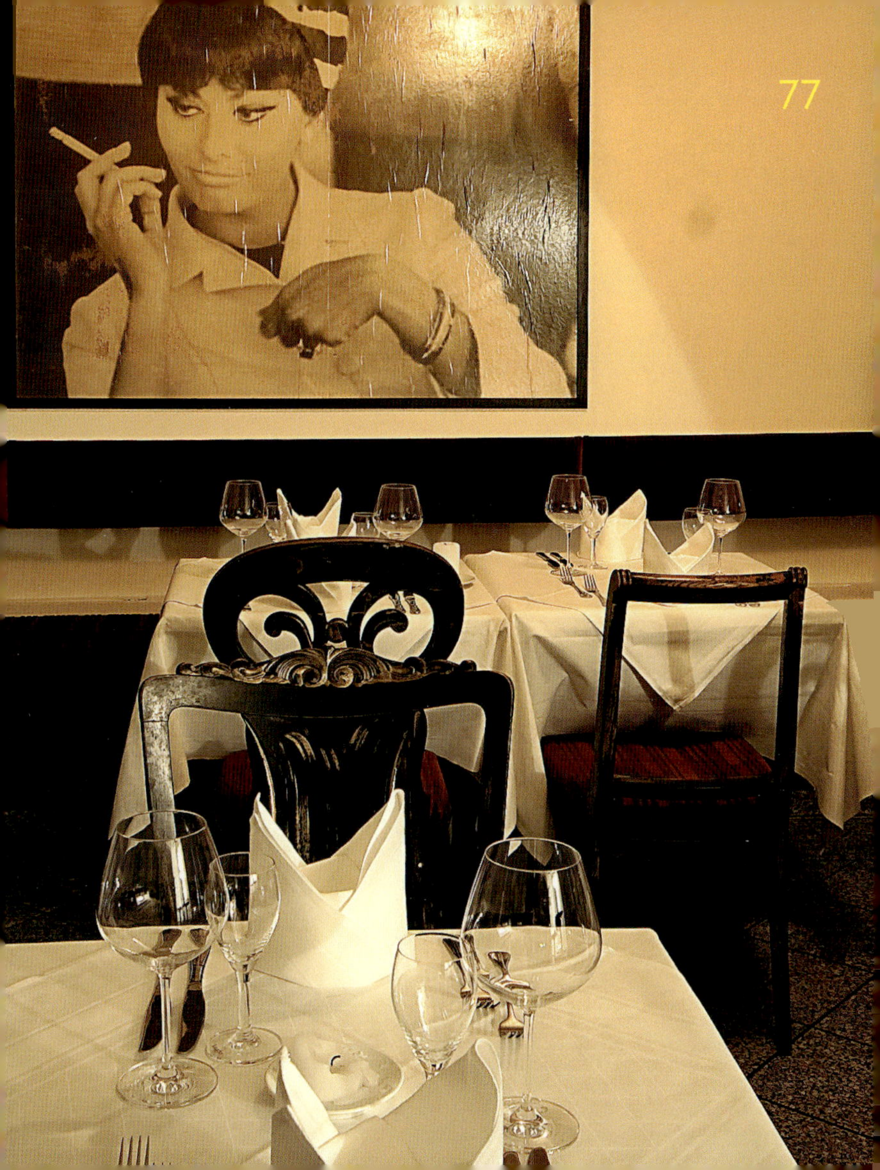

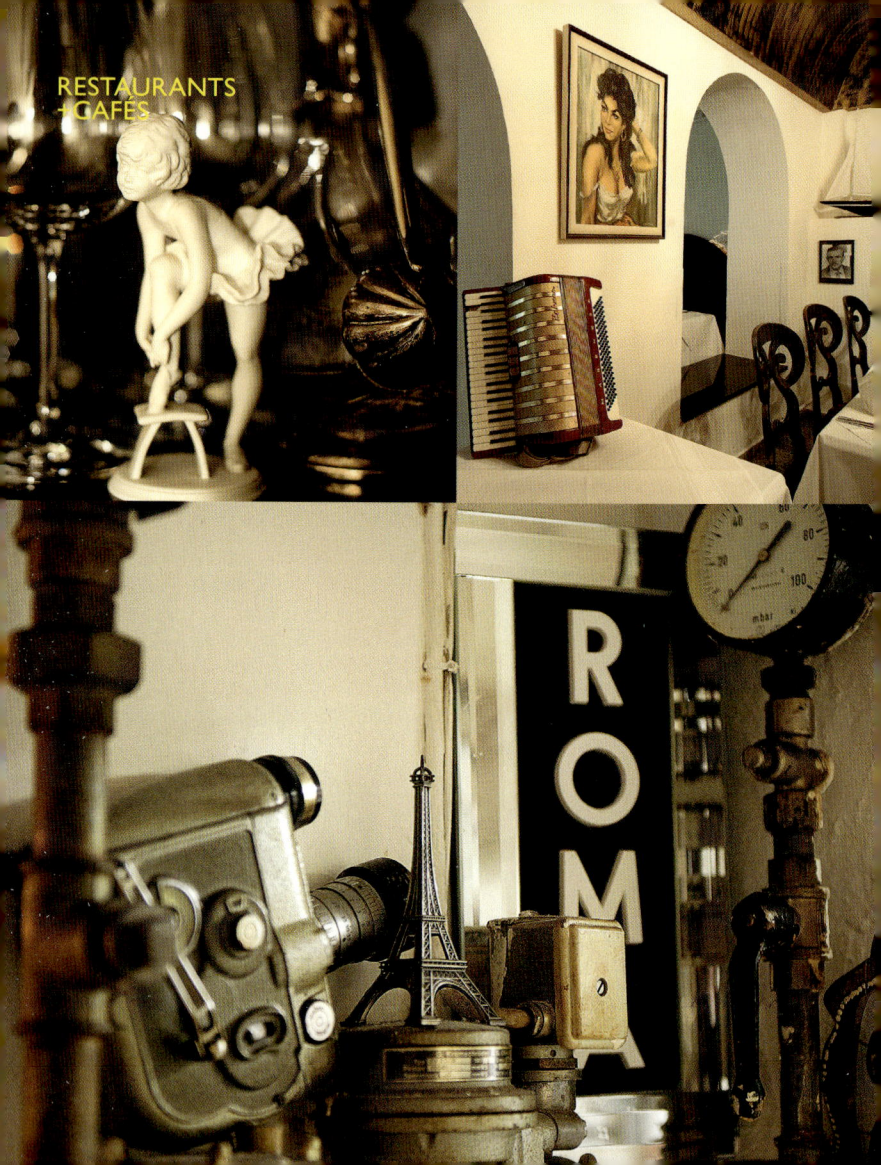

DIE BLAUE DONAU

Elisabethstraße 12 // Schwabing
Tel.: +49 (0)89 27 27 22 01
www.die-blaue-donau.de

Tue–Sat 7 pm to 1 am

Tram 27 Elisabethplatz
U2 Josephsplatz

Prices: $$
Cuisine: German-Austrian

KAREN WEBB'S SPECIAL TIP
Ask for the manager's wine recommendation—he is an expert!

"Die Blaue Donau is like a David Lynch film: you don't understand anything, but you like it." That's according to the self-description of the city's coolest upscale restaurant. Under Thomas Hertlein, manager and wine god, all guests are treated equally—that is to say pampered to the nth degree with rock music playing in the background. In addition to the delicious varying three- and four-course menus, there is a wine selection worthy of genuflection. Reservation recommended.

„Die Blaue Donau ist wie ein David Lynch-Film: Man versteht nichts, aber es gefällt einem." Soweit die Selbstauskunft des coolsten gehobenen Restaurants der Stadt. Bei Thomas Hertlein, Geschäftsführer und Weingott, werden alle Gäste gleich behandelt – nämlich auf höchstem Niveau verwöhnt, mit Rockmusik im Hintergrund. Neben den köstlichen, wechselnden Drei- oder Viergängemenüs gibt es eine Weinauswahl zum Niederknien. Es empfiehlt sich zu reservieren.

SCHÖNTAG

Herzogstraße 86 // Schwabing
Tel.: +49 (0)89 39 29 39 22
www.cafe-schoentag.de

Tue–Fri 8.30 am to 6 pm
Sat–Sun 9.30 am to 5 pm
weather permitting

U2, Tram 12, 27 Hohenzollernplatz

Prices: $
Cuisine: Breakfast

MAP N° 32

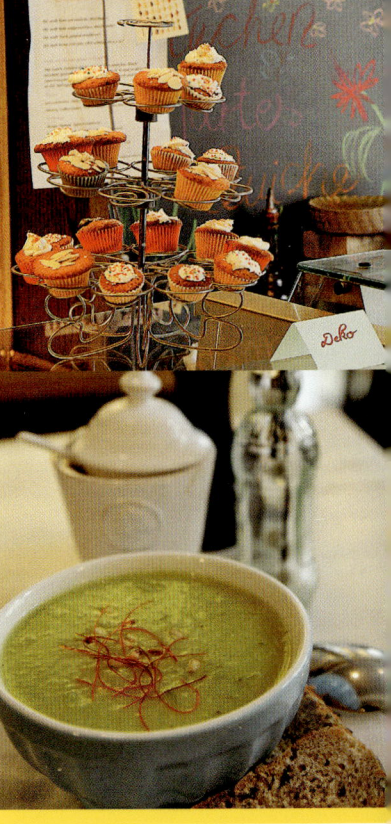
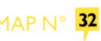

When Solveigh Maurice opened her "little eatery" in January 2010, she wouldn't have dared dream that people would ride in from the country-side surrounding Munich just to eat her homemade cakes. The off-center (in a good way) little shop in Schwabing has long since gained a devoted following. Not least thanks to Chef Inge who conjures up wonderful egg dishes and healthy creations. In a hurry? Get your individual mix to go at the organic muesli bar.

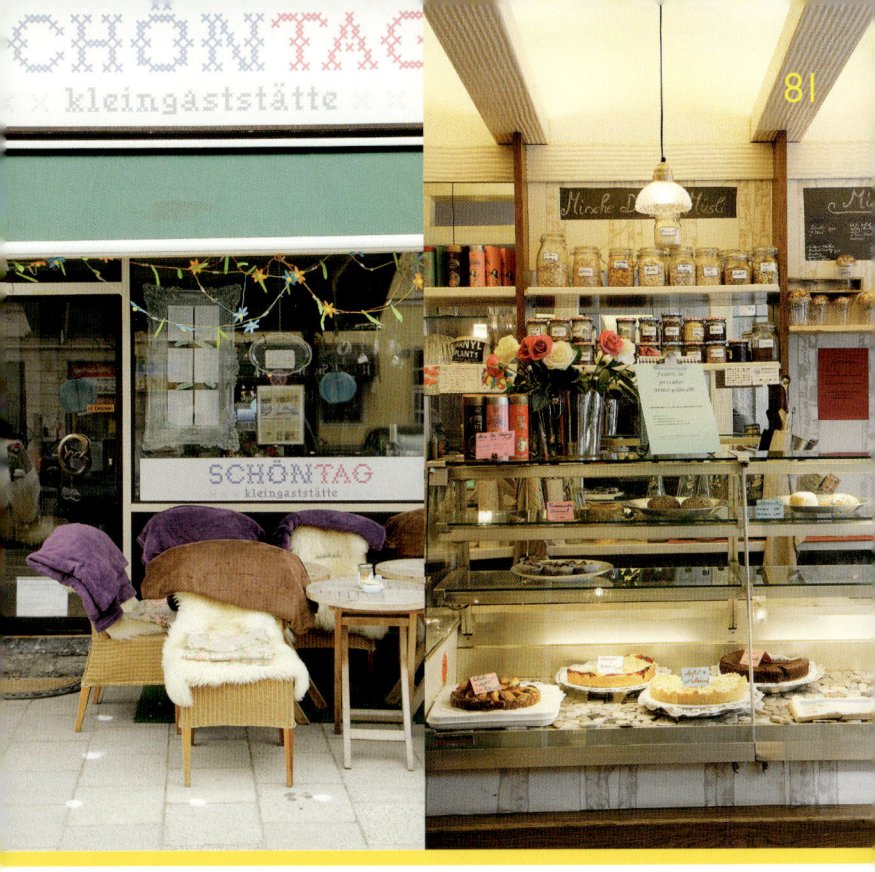

Als Solveigh Maurice im Januar 2010 ihre „Kleingaststätte" eröffnete, hätte sie sich nicht träumen lassen, dass Kunden aus dem Münchner Umland anreisen, eigens um bei ihr selbstgemachten Kuchen zu essen. In Schwabing ist der kleine, im besten Sinne schräge Laden längst heiß geliebt. Nicht zuletzt dank Köchin Inge. Die zaubert tolle „Eiergschichten" oder was „Gsundes". Eilige holen sich an der Müslibar ihre individuelle Bio-Mischung für unterwegs.

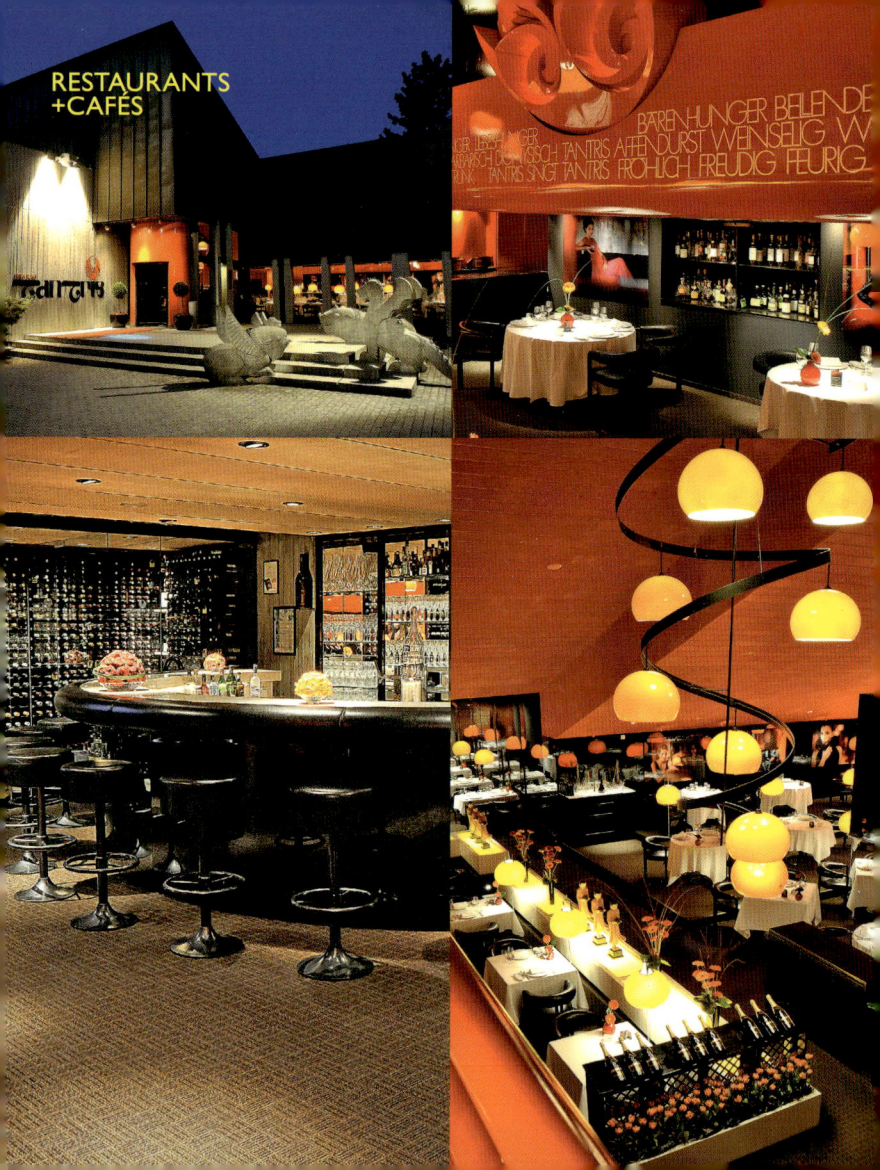

RESTAURANTS
+CAFÉS

TANTRIS

Johann-Fichte-Straße 7
Schwabing-West
Tel.: +49 (0)89 3 61 95 90
www.tantris.de

Tue—Sat noon to 3 pm
and 6.30 pm to 1 am

Tram 23 Parzivalplatz

Prices: $$$$
Cuisine: Fusion

Established in 1971, the restaurant with the promising name and two Michelin stars is one of Germany's best-known gourmet temples. This reputation was earned by Eckart Witzigmann followed by Heinz Winkler. Hans Haas has been head chef since 1991. The Tantris experience is not just culinary; the '70s remain the dominant style in the concrete building built by Justus Dahinden, with Far Eastern influences and a warm color palette.

Das 1971 gegründete Restaurant mit dem verheißungsvollen Namen und zwei Michelin-Sternen ist einer der bekanntesten Gourmettempel Deutschlands. Begründet hat diesen Ruf Eckart Witzigmann, ihm folgte Heinz Winkler. Seit 1991 ist Hans Haas Küchenchef. Nicht nur kulinarisch ist das Tantris ein Erlebnis: Im von Justus Dahinden gebauten Betonbau dominieren stilistisch immer noch die 70er, mit asiatischen Einschlägen und einem warmen Farbspiel.

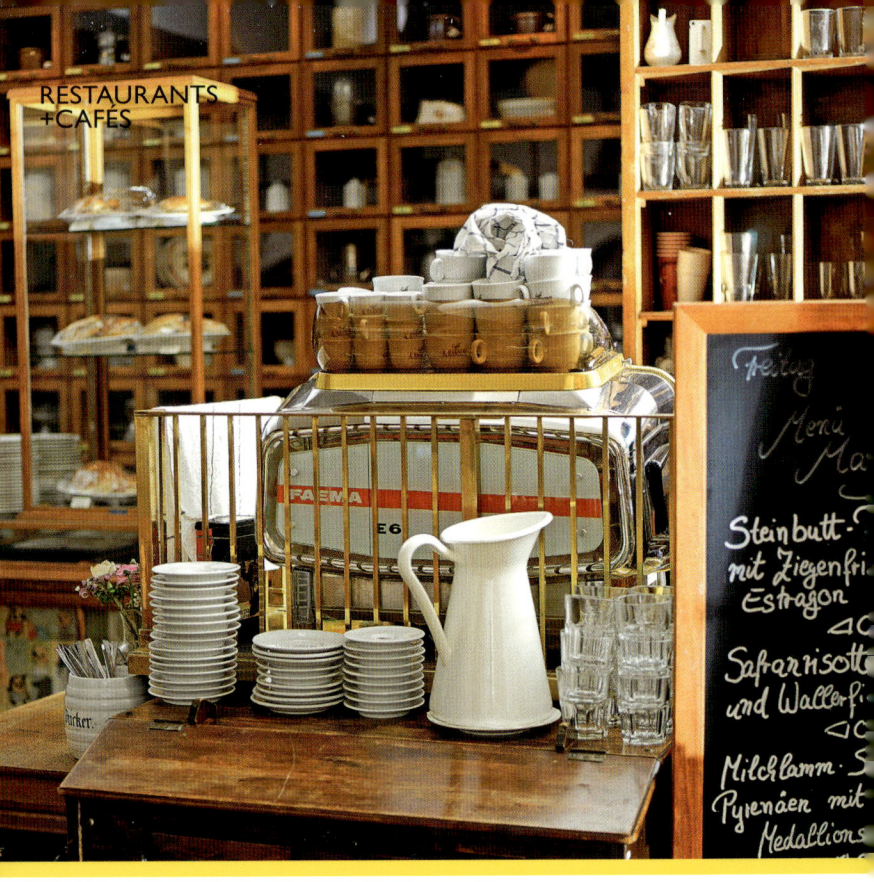

The Marais is pretty much the opposite of a cool, modern coffee bar.
For years an old-fashioned haberdashery was located here, and
the owners were wise to leave the wonderful interior decor as they
found it. You could hardly spend a nicer day in any café. The furnishings,
mainly from between 1900 and 1960, are mostly for sale. The same
goes for jewelry, toys, and other treasures.

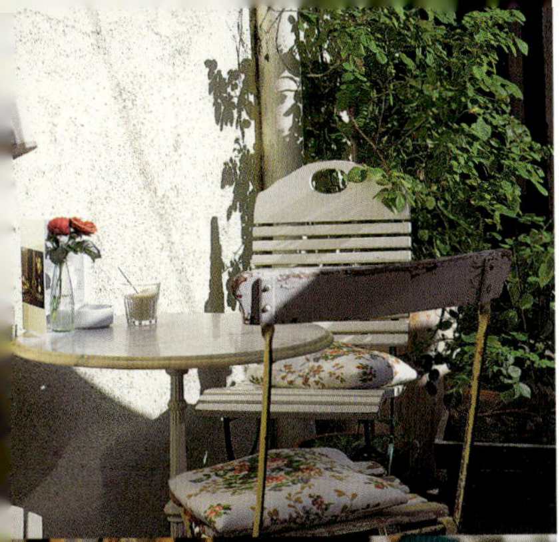

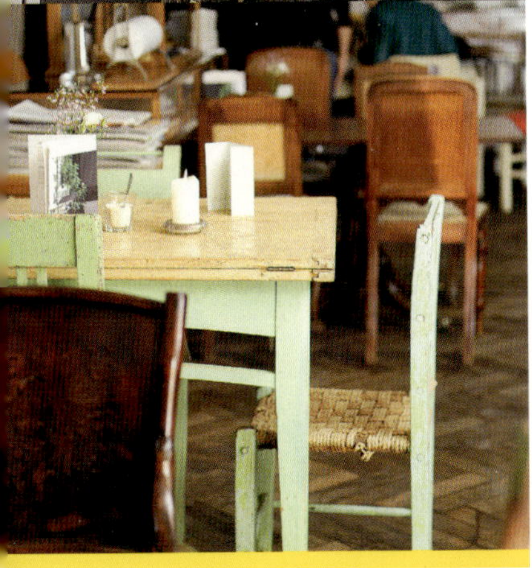

MARAIS

Parkstraße 2 // Schwanthalerhöhe
Tel.: +49 (0)89 50 09 45 52
www.cafe-marais.de

Tue–Sat 8 am to 8 pm
Sun 10 am to 6 pm

Tram 18, 19 Holzapfelstraße

Prices: $$
Cuisine: International

MAP N° 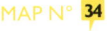 34

Das Marais ist so ziemlich das Gegenteil einer modern-kühl gestylten Kaffee-bar. Lange Zeit war hier ein altmodisches Kurzwarengeschäft untergebracht, und die Betreiberinnen haben gut daran getan, die wunderbare Inneneinrichtung so zu belassen, wie sie war. Schöner kann man einen Tag im Café kaum verbringen. Das Mobiliar, vornehmlich aus der Zeit 1900–1960, ist größtenteils verkäuflich, das gleiche gilt für Schmuck, Spielzeug und andere Kostbarkeiten.

JOSEFA

Westendstraße 29 // Schwanthalerhöhe
Tel.: +49 (0)89 28 97 91 83
www.josefa.eu

Mon–Fri 9 am to 11 pm
Sat–Sun 10 am to 5 pm

S1–8 Hackerbrücke
Tram 18, 19 Holzapfelstraße

Prices: $
Cuisine: Homemade

MAP N° **35**

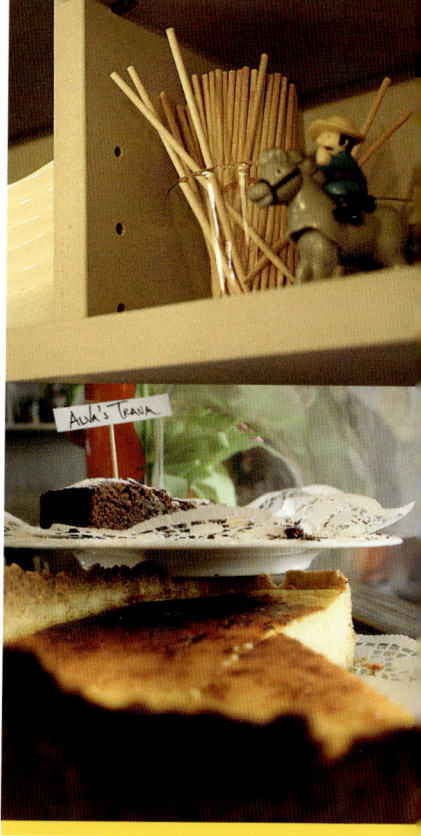

The pearl of the West End: despite the gold walls, Josefa comes across as unpretentious and just shamelessly likeable. It's Grit Idler and Judith Ramoser's fault, running the little place with abundant energy and passion and giving you the feeling you're at home with them—that's exactly how the tasty and reasonably priced lunch dishes taste. The evening concerts and readings take place in a charming salon atmosphere, complete with great cocktails.

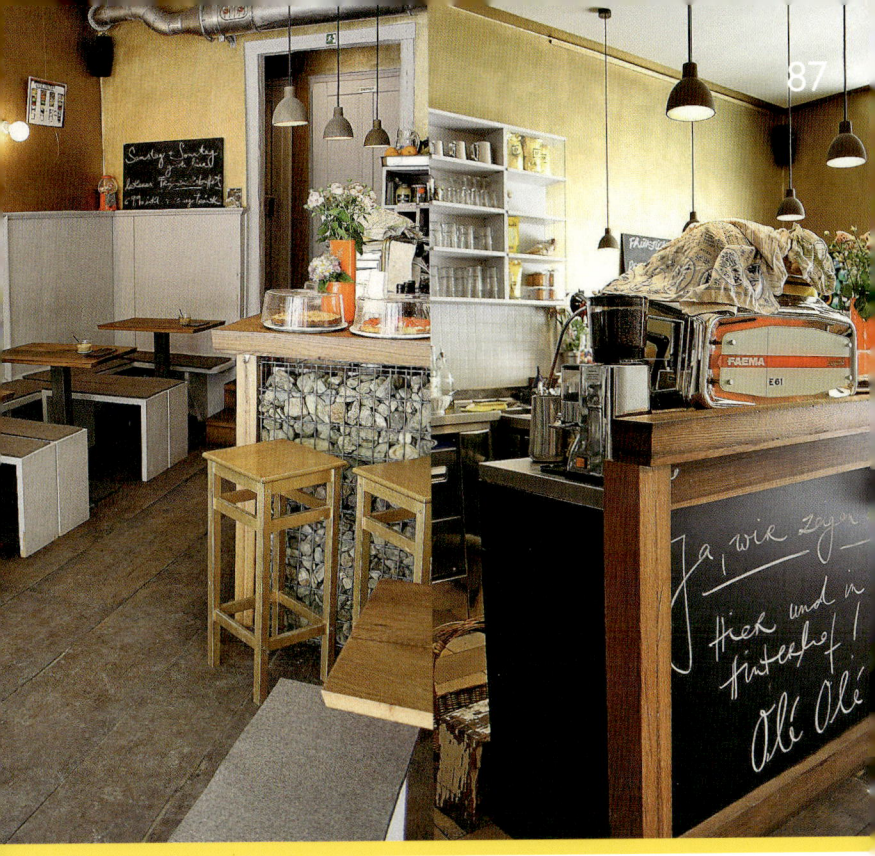

Die Perle im Westend: Trotz ihrer güldenen Wände kommt die Josefa unprätentiös und geradezu unverschämt sympathisch daher. Schuld daran sind Grit Idler und Judith Ramoser, die das kleine Lokal mit viel Energie und Herzblut führen und einem das Gefühl geben, bei ihnen zuhause zu sein – so schmecken auch die leckeren und günstigen Mittagsgerichte. Abends kann man in reizvollem Salon-Ambiente Konzerte und Lesungen genießen, dazu gibt es super Cocktails.

SHOPS

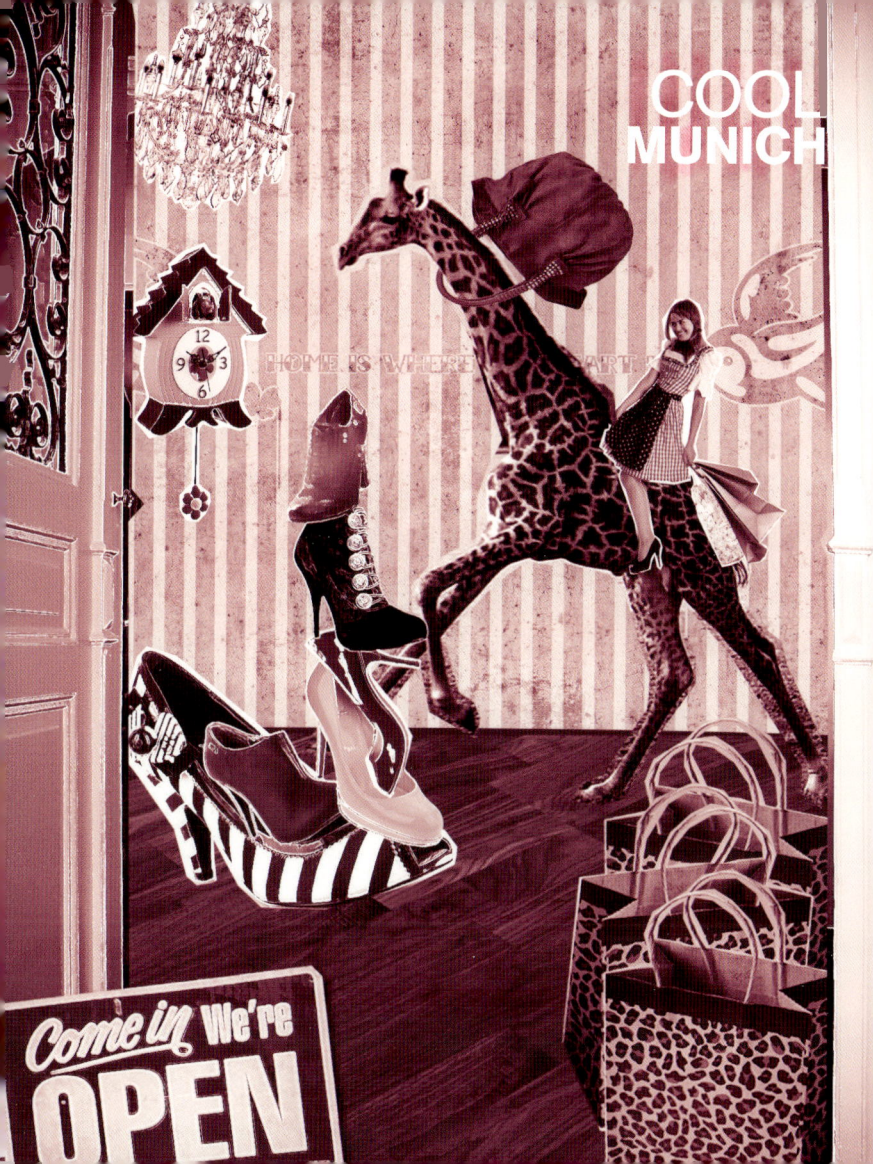

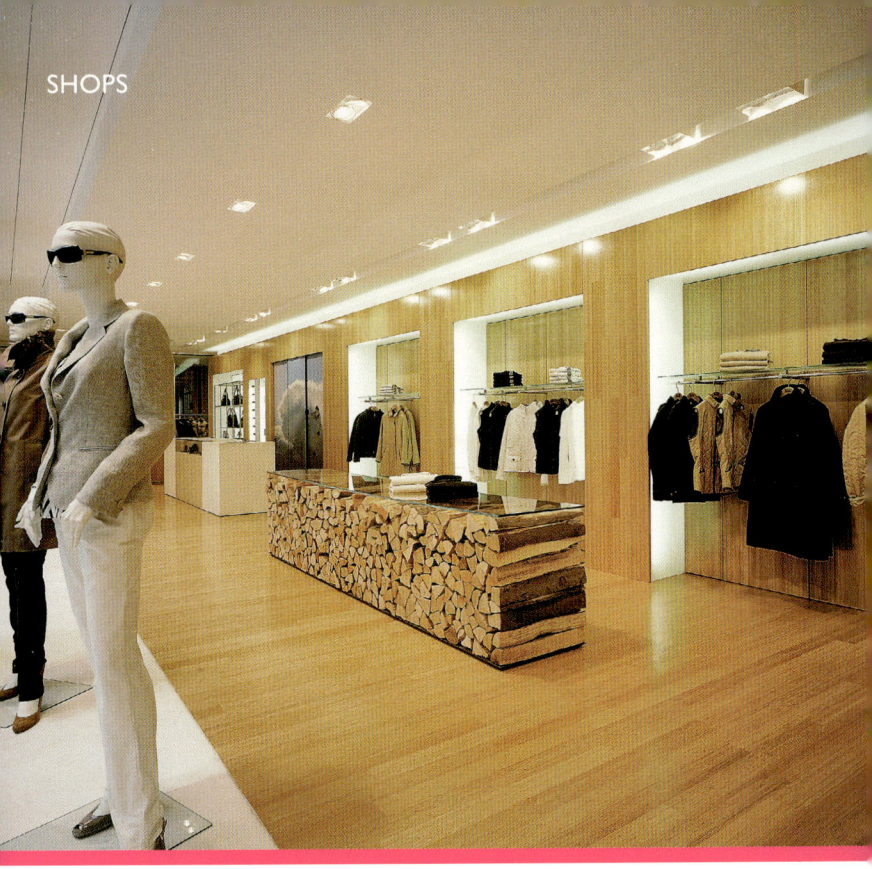

"If you don't want to chase the trends, you have to discover them in time and participate in their development" says Willy Bogner, who took part in various James Bond movies as a special cameraman. What he started in a backyard in 1932 is now an international brand for fashionable sportswear. 14,000 sq. ft. over three storeys are packed with goods ranging from business attire to ski clothing—all of which embody the corporate tradition of sportiness and elegance.

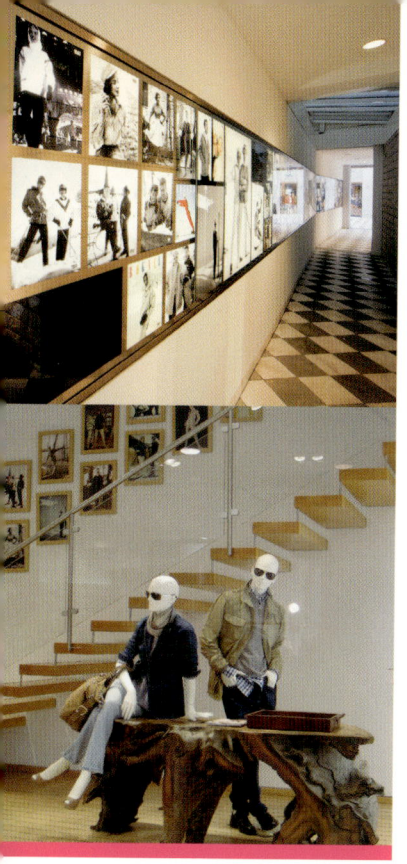

BOGNER

Residenzstraße 14–15 // Altstadt
Tel.: +49 (0)89 2 90 70 40
www.bogner.com

Mon–Fri 10 am to 7 pm
Sat 10 am to 6 pm

U3–6 Odeonsplatz
Tram 19 Nationaltheater

Prices: $$$$

„Wer Trends nicht hinterherlaufen will, muss sie rechtzeitig erkennen und aktiv mitgestalten", sagt Willy Bogner, der einst als Spezial-Kameramann an James Bond-Filmen mitwirkte. Was 1932 in einem Hinterhof begann, entwickelte sich zum internationalen Label für anspruchsvolle, modische Sportswear. Auf drei Etagen und 1 300 m² findet man ein Sortiment von Business- bis Skibekleidung, das gemäß der Firmentradition immer sportlich-elegant ist.

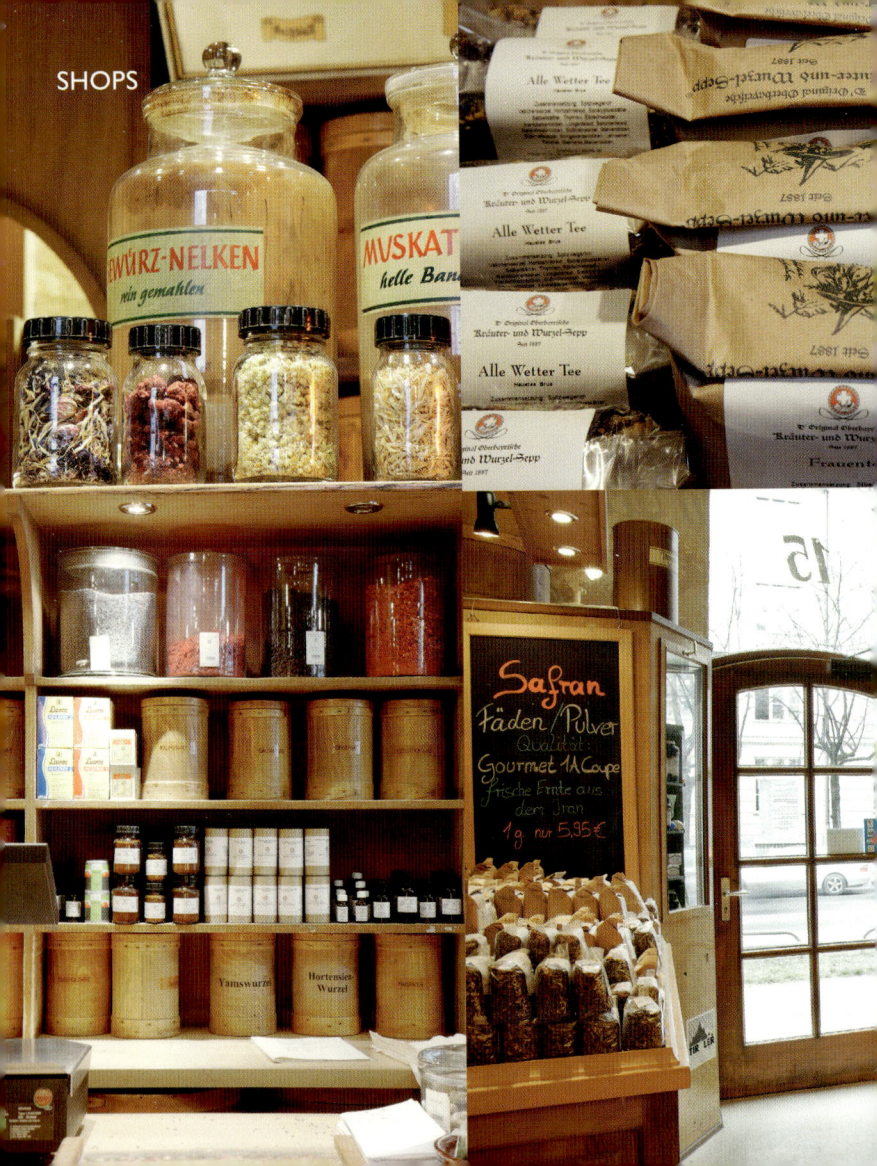

SHOPS

KRÄUTER- UND WURZELSEPP

Blumenstraße 15 // Altstadt
Tel.: +49 (0)89 26 57 26
www.phytofit.de

Mon–Fri 9 am to 6.30 pm
Sat 9 am to 1 pm

U1, U2, U3, U6, U7 Sendlinger Tor
Tram 16, 17, 18 Müllerstraße

Prices: $

First you're dazed by the herbal fragrance that greets you in this herb and spice emporium. Then you notice, astonished, that you've traveled at least 100 years into the past. Goods are filled from large barrels and tubs, weighed, and sold in paper cones like in an old general store. The wonderful and very popular shop has sold medicinal herbs, spices, teas, and natural cosmetics since 1887. Customers profit from this experience noticeably.

Zuerst ist man wie benommen von dem Kräuterduft, der einen empfängt. Dann stellt man verblüfft fest, mindestens 100 Jahre in die Vergangenheit gereist zu sein: Wie in einem alten Krämerladen wird aus großen Bottichen und Schütten das Gewünschte in Papiertüten abgefüllt, gewogen und verkauft. Seit 1887 führt der herrliche, stark frequentierte Laden Heilkräuter, Gewürze, Tees und Naturkosmetik. Als Kunde profitiert man spürbar von dieser Erfahrung.

LODENFREY

Maffeistraße 7 // Altstadt
Tel.: +49 (0)89 21 03 90
www.lodenfrey.com

Mon–Sat 10 am to 8 pm

S1–8, U3, U6 Marienplatz
Tram 19 Theatinerstraße

Prices: $$$$

KAREN WEBB'S SPECIAL TIP
Around the Oktoberfest it is very busy
here—you better be fashionably early!

MAP N° 38

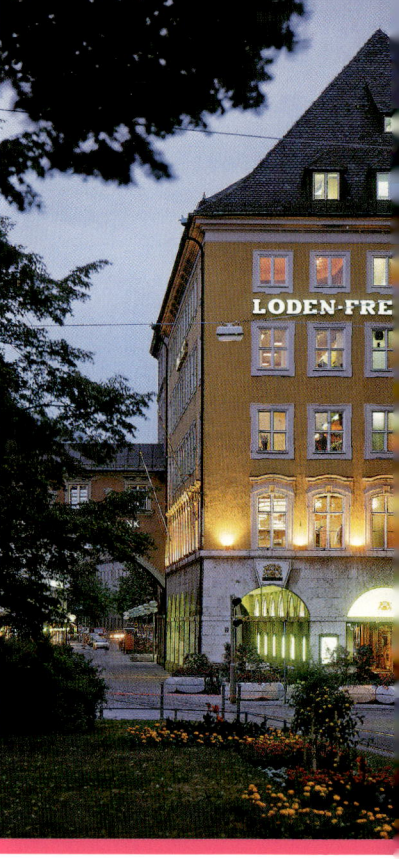

To the people of Munich, the name Lodenfrey is linked to exclusive
designer fashion and the newest collections around the Tracht.
Founded in 1842, the fashion house has been family-owned for six
generations and gained international fame with the invention of a
water-repellent loden cloth. The sales office with its superb location
in the old town area around the cathedral provides ladies and
gentlemen as well as kids with high-class garments for every occasion.

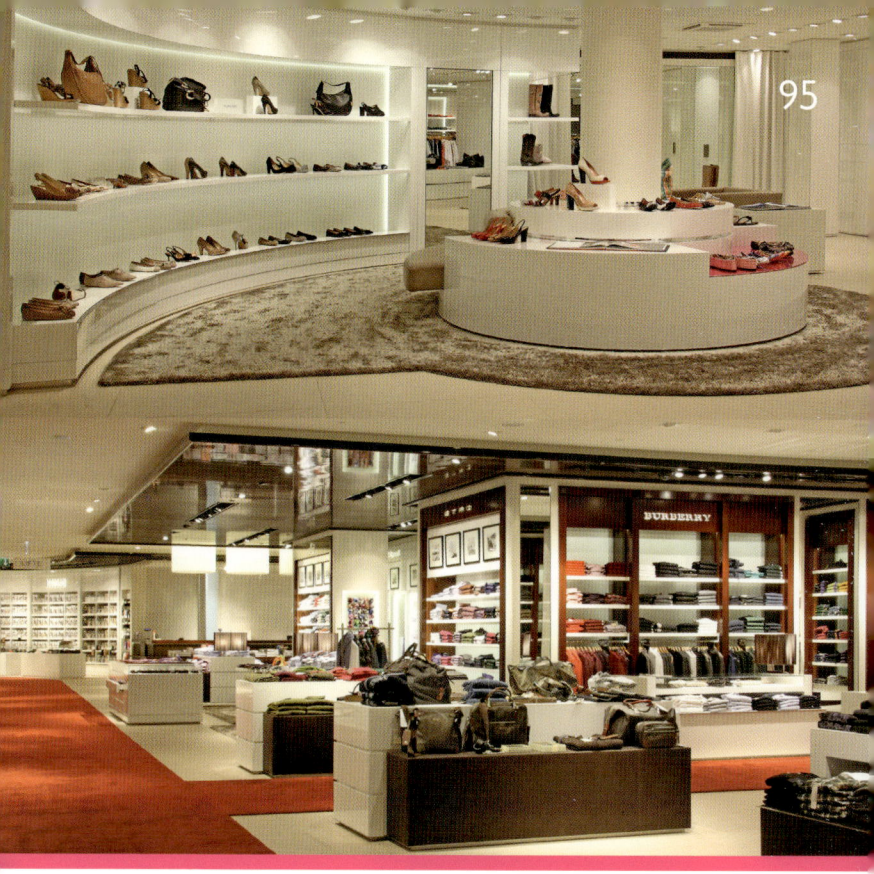

Mit dem Namen Lodenfrey verbinden Münchner exklusive Designermode und die neuesten Kollektionen rund um die Tracht. Seine internationale Berühmtheit verdankt das 1842 gegründete Bekleidungshaus, das seit sechs Generationen in Familienbesitz ist, der Erfindung eines wasserabweisenden Lodenstoffs. Das Verkaufshaus am Dom in bester historischer Altstadtlage kleidet Damen, Herren und Kinder ein – mit hochwertiger Mode für jeden Anlass.

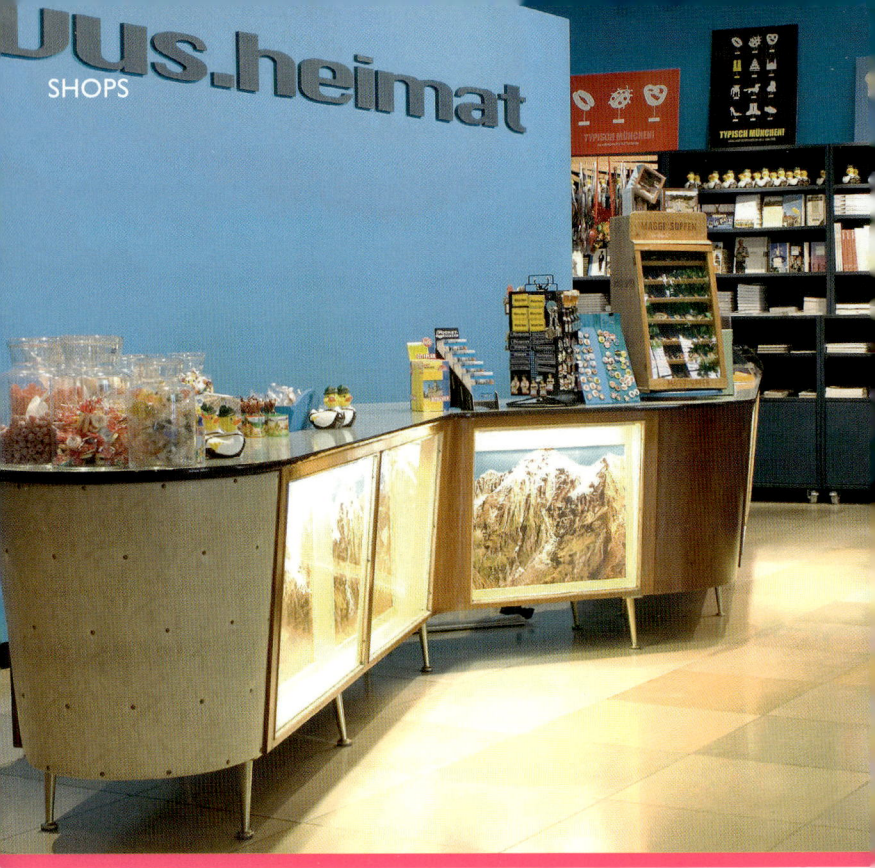

A rubber duck wearing leather trousers and the traditional "Gamsbart," various models of bobblehead dachshunds, a pink T-shirt with Empress Sissi's visage— the selection at "Munich's specialist for homeland and heartland" consists of surprisingly bearable (and often wearable) kitsch. Interesting reading materials, if you're fond of languages or cultural studies, include "Instructions for Use" for Munich and Bavaria and a Bavarian-to-German dictionary.

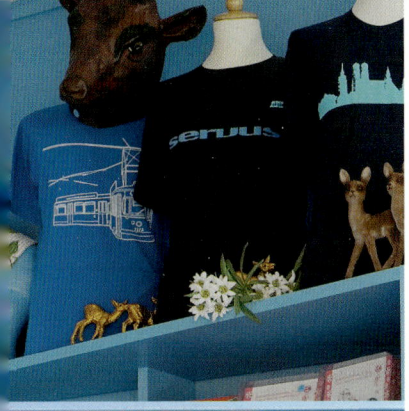

SERVUS.HEIMAT

Brunnstraße 3 // Altstadt
Tel.: +49 (0)89 24 29 47 80
www.servusheimat.com

Mon—Sat 10 am to 8 pm

U1, U2, U3, U6, U7
Tram 16, 17, 18, 27 Sendlinger Tor

Prices: $

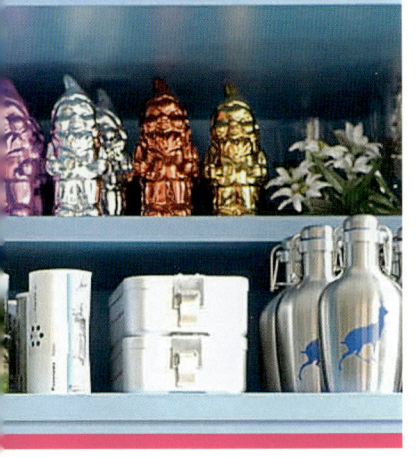

Eine in Lederhosen und Gamsbart gewandete gelbe Quietscheente, Wackeldackel in verschiedenen Ausführungen, ein rosafarbenes T-Shirt mit Sissis Konterfei darauf – das Sortiment des „Münchner Fachgeschäfts für Heimatliebe und Herzlichkeiten" ist erstaunlich gut erträglicher (oft sogar tragbarer) Kitsch. Interessante Lektüre für Sprachtalente und Kulturwissenschafter: die „Gebrauchsanweisungen" für München und Bayern und das Wörterbuch Bairisch-Deutsch.

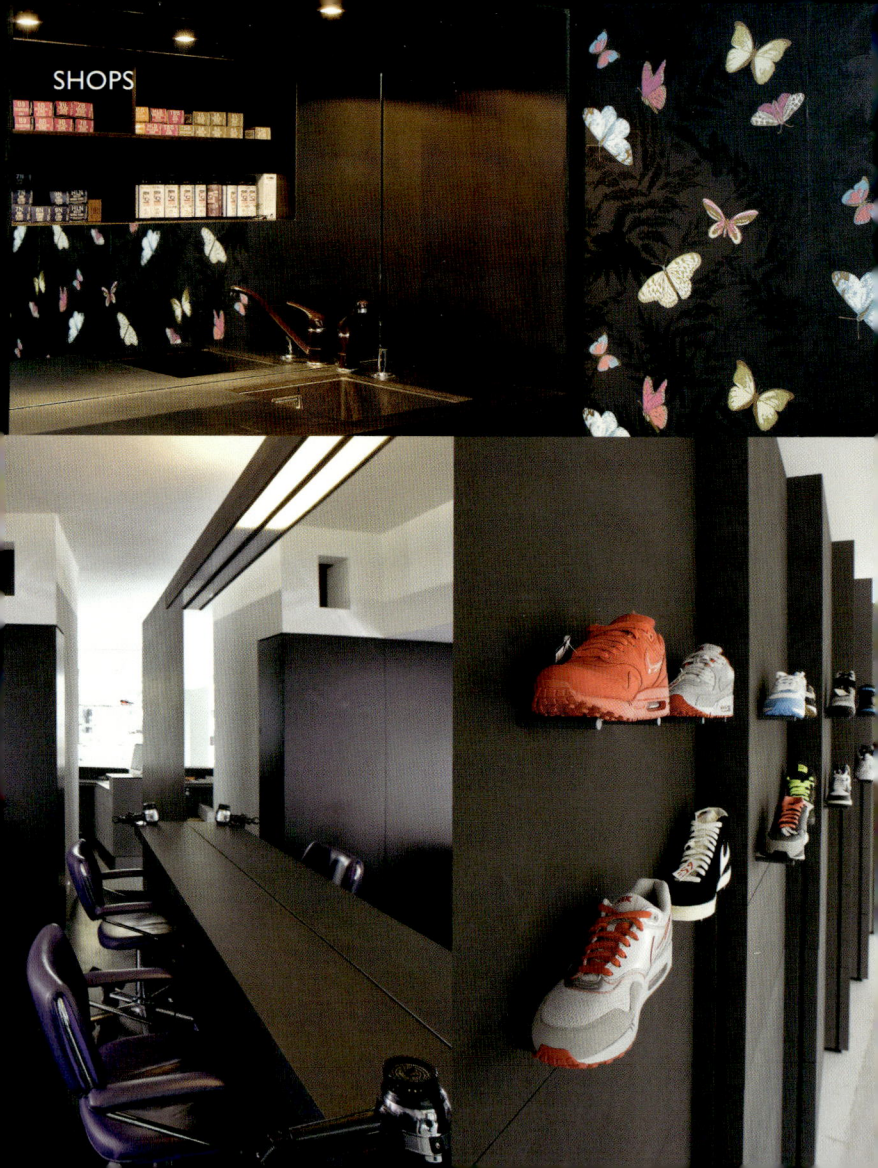

AMEN STORE

Corneliusstraße 1 // Isarvorstadt
Tel.: +49 (0)89 99 01 85 88
www.amen-store.com

Mon–Sat 11 am to 8 pm

S1–8, U3, U6 Marienplatz
U1, U2, U7 Fraunhoferstraße
Tram 16, 18 Reichenbachplatz

Prices: $$

As the name so subtly suggests, this minimalist shop is a mecca for all religious sneaker fans. Selected sneakers and fashion labels have been staged here like works of art since 2007. The wall of shoes by artist Paul Snowden where the shoe treasures lie (and behind which is a recommended hair salon) was added three years later. The people here are not only damn hip—they're also friendly. Amen!

Wie der Name subtil andeutet, ist der minimalistisch eingerichtete Laden ein Mekka für alle religiösen Sneaker-Liebhaber. Seit 2007 werden ausgesuchte Sneakers und Fashionlabels wie Kunstwerke in Szene gesetzt. Drei Jahre später kam die Schuhwand des Künstlers Paul Snowden hinzu, in der die Schuhschätze lagern und hinter der sich ein empfehlenswerter Friseursalon verbirgt. Hier ist man nicht nur verdammt hip, sondern auch noch freundlich. Amen!

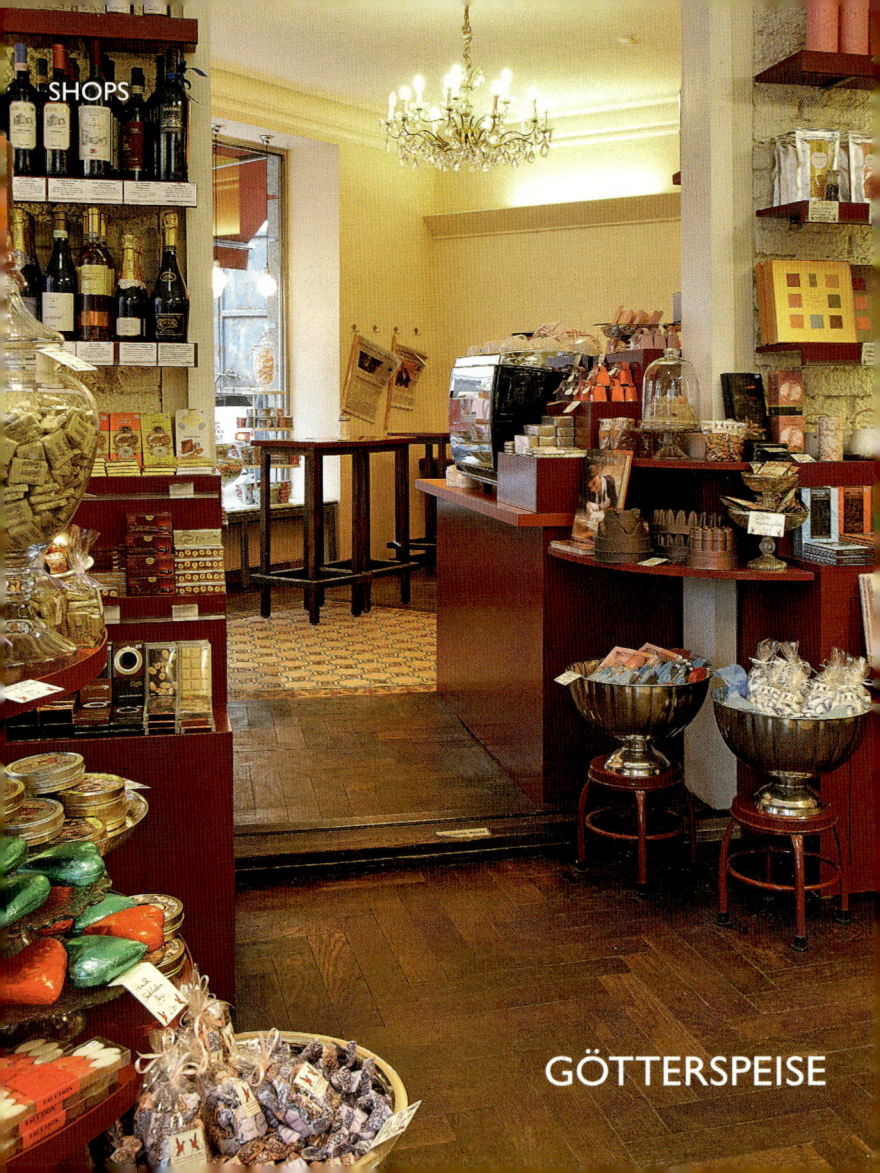

GÖTTERSPEISE

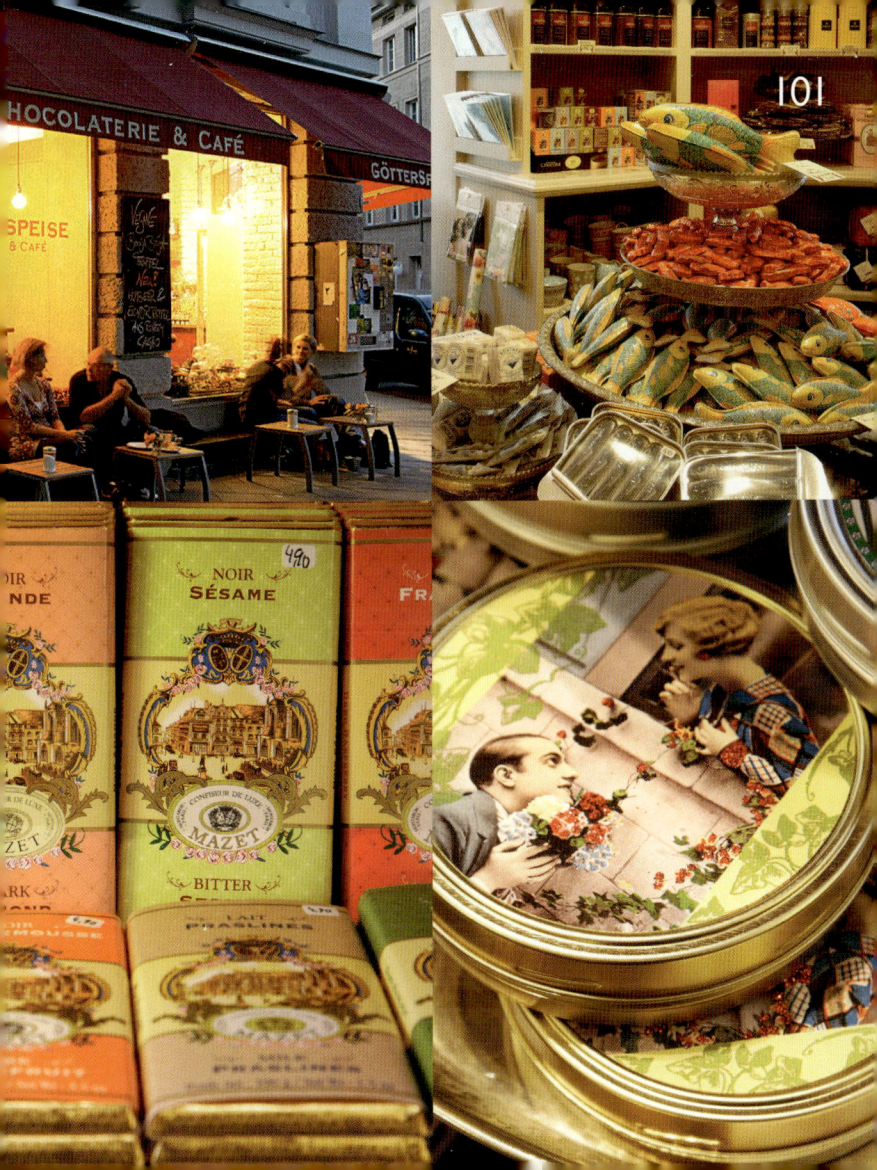

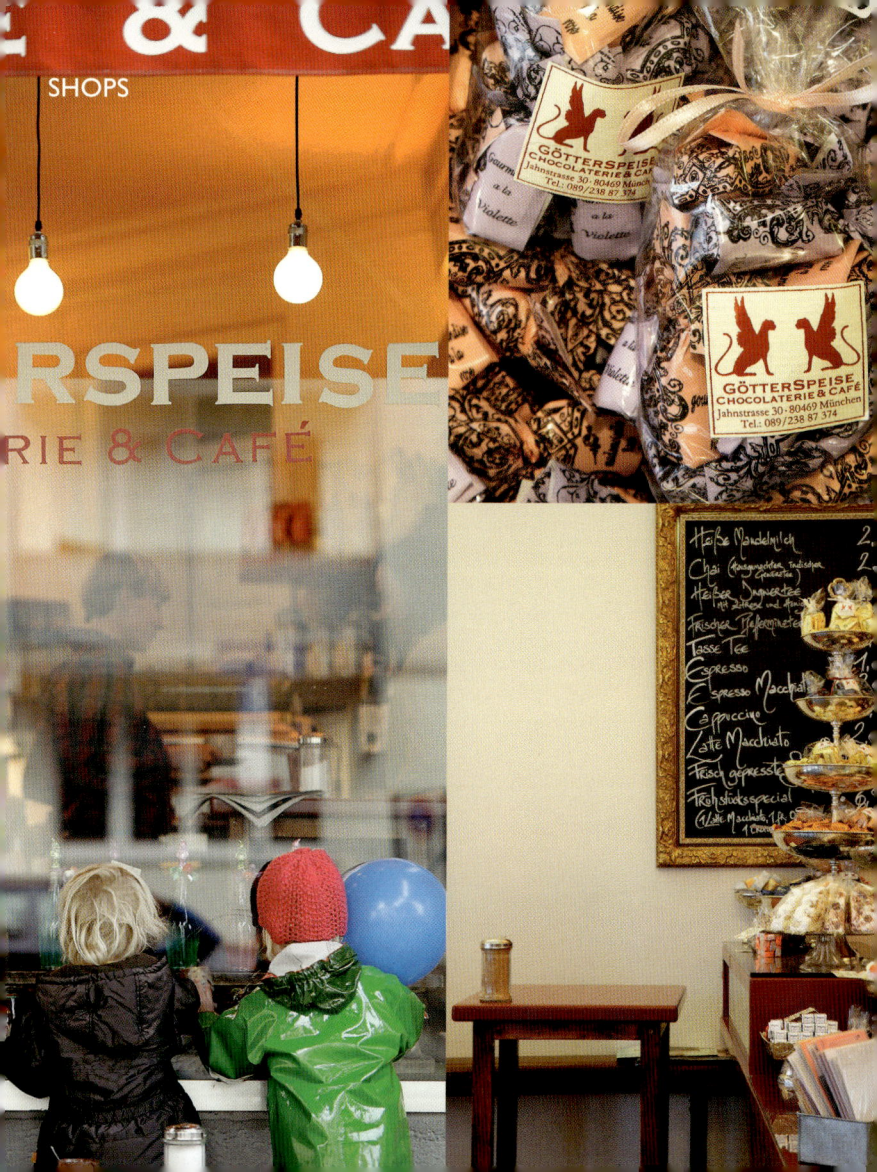

GÖTTERSPEISE

Jahnstraße 30 // Isarvorstadt
Tel.: +49 (0)89 23 88 73 74
www.goetterspeise.info

Mon–Fri 8 am to 7 pm
Sat 9 am to 6 pm

U1, U2, U7 Fraunhoferstraße
Tram 16, 17, 18 Müllerstraße

Prices: $$

KAREN WEBB'S SPECIAL TIP
This shop is always a (sweet) fatal attraction!

This retail café puts you in a sweet rapture—you can quickly find yourself in a childish buying frenzy. Meanwhile, the opulent chocolate confections also stimulate an adult sensuality. All manner of chocolate jewels, books, teas, ceramics and enamelware, wines, and much more conjure up a fairytale setting. Ultimately it is shop owner Priti Henseler and her team that make Götterspeise an absolute favorite.

Dieses Ladencafé versetzt einen in süße Verzückung, und man verfällt schnell in einen kindlichen Kaufrausch. Gleichzeitig beflügelt die opulente Chocolaterie auch die erwachsene Sinnlichkeit. Schokoladenpreziosen jeglicher Art, Bücher, Tees, Keramik- und Emailleobjekte, Weine und vieles mehr bilden ein märchenhaftes Arrangement. Nicht zuletzt sind es Inhaberin Priti Henseler und ihr Team, die die Götterspeise zu einem absoluten Lieblingsplatz machen.

MAP N° 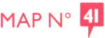 41

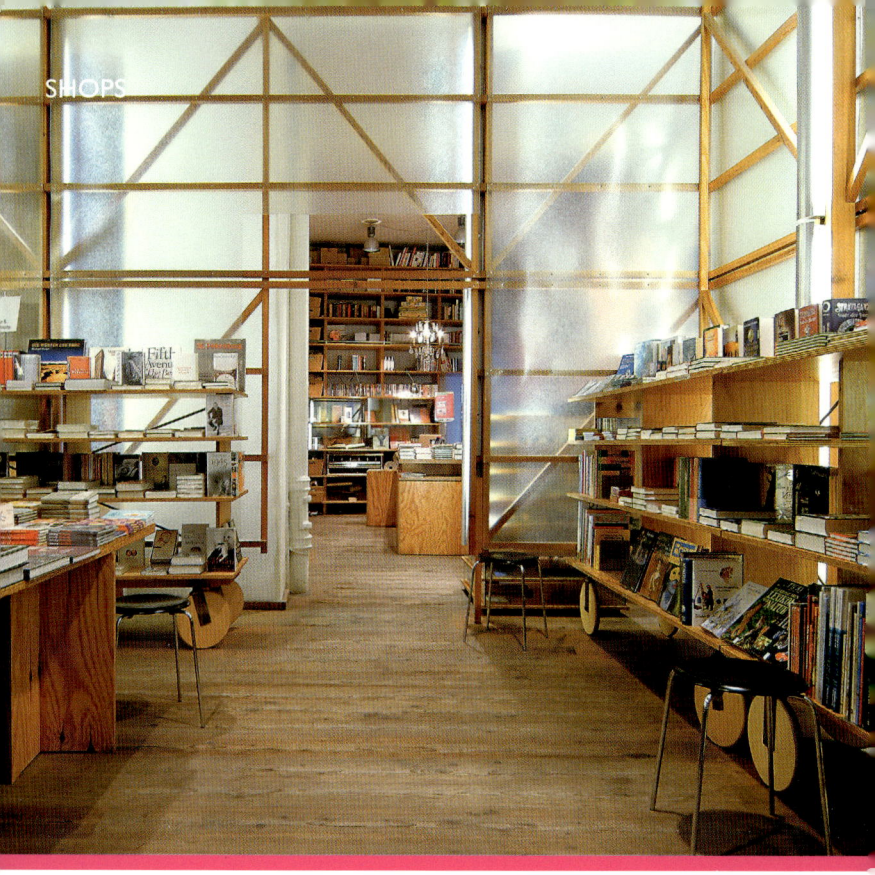

Regina Moths's store in the Gärtnerplatzviertel is a bookworms' and aesthetes' dream. With its creative display windows, lofty interior, and of course the competent staff above all, it is considered by many to be Munich's best and most beautiful bookstore. Literatur Moths carries thrilling new publications, classics, curiosities, and recently added a cookbook section, as well. Regular readings and exhibits extend the spectrum and broaden the participants' horizon.

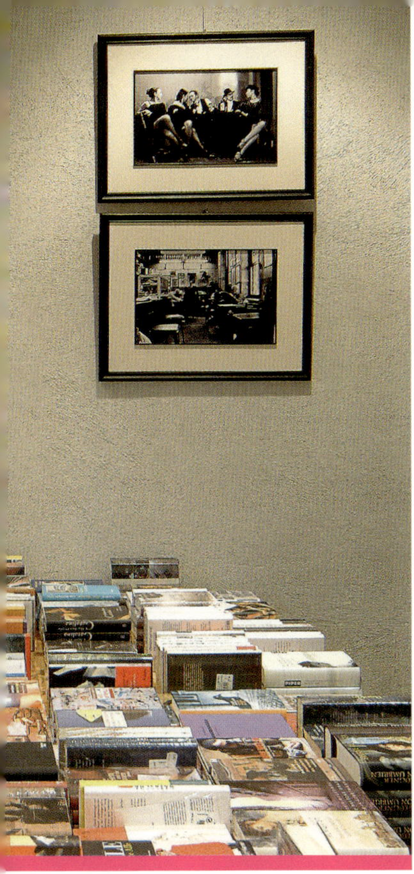

LITERATUR MOTHS

Rumfordstraße 48 // Isarvorstadt
Tel.: +49 (0)89 29 16 13 26
www.li-mo.com

Mon–Fri 10 am to 7 pm
Sat 10 am to 4 pm
During school holidays:
Mon–Fri 11 am to 6 pm
Sat 11 am to 2 pm

S1–8
Tram 16, 18 Isartor

Prices: $$

Regina Moths' Laden im Gärtnerplatzviertel ist ein Traum für Bücherwürmer und Ästheten. Wegen der phantasievollen Schaufenstergestaltung, dem loftigen Interieur und vor allem natürlich der sachkundigen Beratung gilt er vielen als schönste und beste Buchhandlung Münchens. Bei Literatur Moths findet man spannende Neuerscheinungen, Klassiker, Kurioses und seit Kurzem auch ein Kochbuchkabinett. Regelmäßige Lesungen und Ausstellungen erweitern das Spektrum und den Horizont.

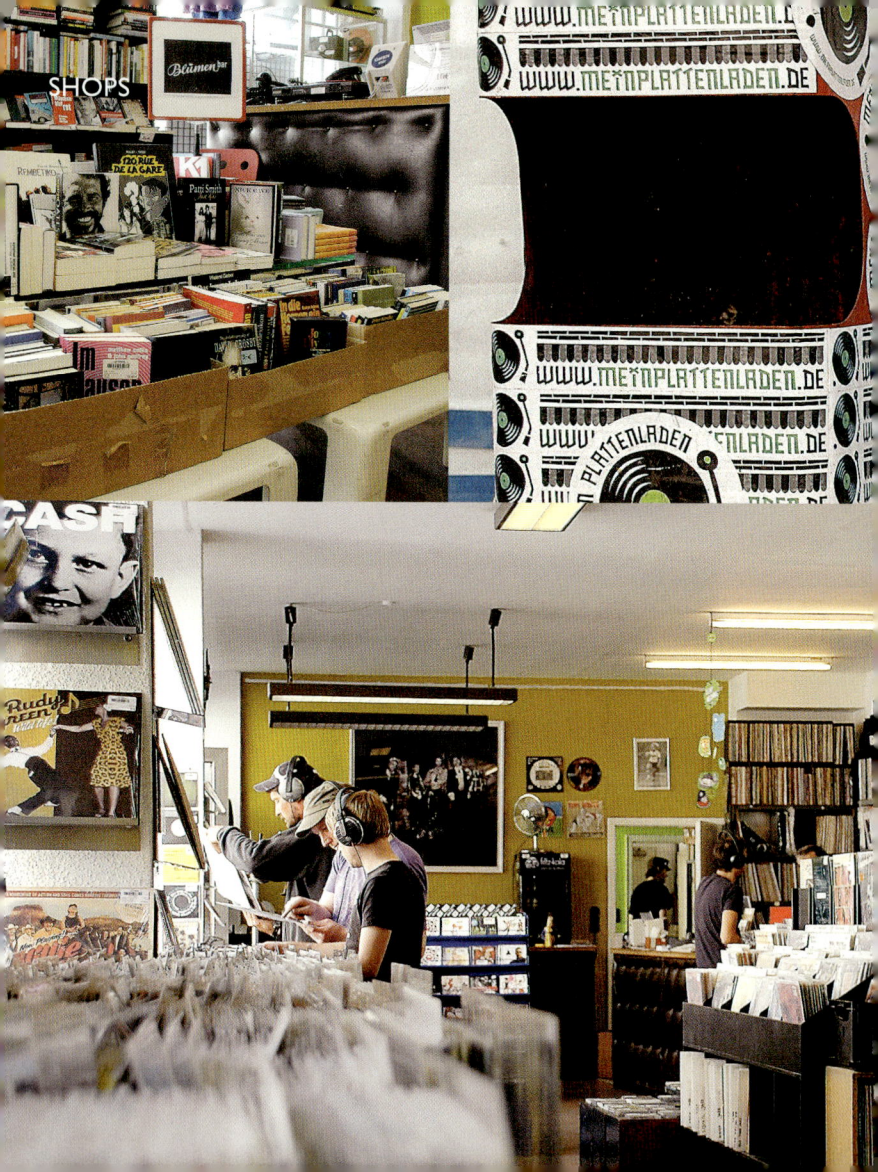

OPTIMAL

107

Kolosseumstraße 6 // Isarvorstadt
Tel.: +49 (0)89 26 81 85
www.optimal-records.com

Mon–Fri 11 am to 8 pm
Sat 11 am to 5.30 pm

U1, U2, U7 Fraunhoferstraße
Tram 16, 17, 18 Müllerstraße

Prices: $$

This is where the local music scene hangs—Optimal has been a central destination for the many Munich labels, musicians, DJs, and music lovers since 1982. Countless international artists, too, have visited and paid tribute to this institution. What's special about it is the enormous breadth of genres; nearly any record can be ordered. The major magazines and a great selection of literature are also available.

Hier tummelt sich die lokale Musikszene – das Optimal ist für die vielen Münchner Labels, Musiker, DJs und Musikliebhaber seit 1982 eine zentrale Anlaufstelle. Aber auch unzählige internationale Künstler haben diese Institution bereits besucht und ihr Respekt gezollt. Das Besondere ist die riesige Bandbreite an Genres; nahezu jede Platte kann bestellt werden. Zusätzlich gibt es hier die wichtigsten Magazine und eine feine Auswahl an Literatur.

MAP N° 43

RUBY STORE

Reichenbachstraße 37 // Isarvorstadt
Tel.: +49 (0)89 I 89 05 06 74
www.facebook.com/ruby.store

Mon–Fri II am to 7 pm
Sat 10.30 am to 7 pm

UI, U2, U7
Tram I7 Fraunhoferstraße

Prices: $$$

KAREN WEBB'S SPECIAL TIP
I like the decent perfection of the
interior design of the store that also
reflects in the fashion.

MAP N° 44

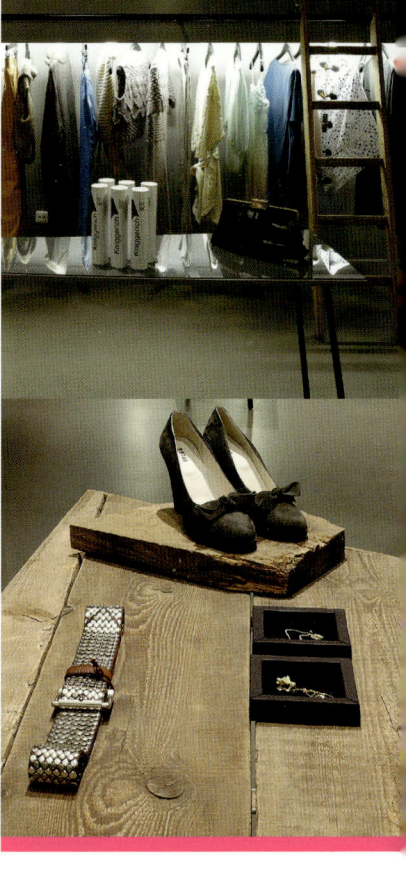

With Ruby Store, busy Mary Monschizada has set down roots at least a
little bit; she brings amazing things back from her—still frequent—travels,
usually in the form of exquisite labels (including Acne, Best Behavior,
Malene Birger, Mads Nørgaard), much to the delight of the fashion-
conscious public around Gärtnerplatz. Designed by the llot llov collec-
tive, the shop is a gray jewel—but definitely not the right thing
for a gray mouse.

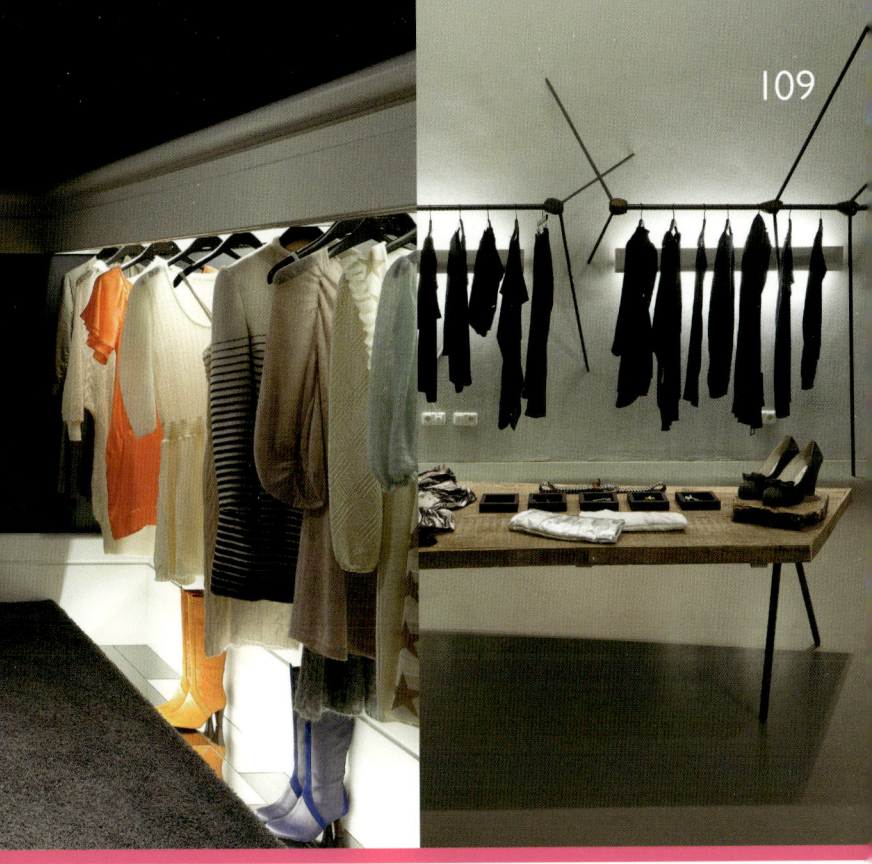

Mit dem Ruby Store hat sich die umtriebige Mary Monschizada wenigstens ein bisschen niedergelassen; von ihren immer noch zahlreichen Reisen bringt sie tolle Sachen mit, meistens in Form von exquisiten Labels (unter anderem Acne, Best Behavior, Malene Birger, Mads Nørgaard). Sehr zur Freude des modeaffinen Publikums rund um den Gärtnerplatz. Der vom Design-Kollektiv Ilot Ilov gestaltete Laden ist ein graues Juwel, aber sicher nichts für graue Mäuse.

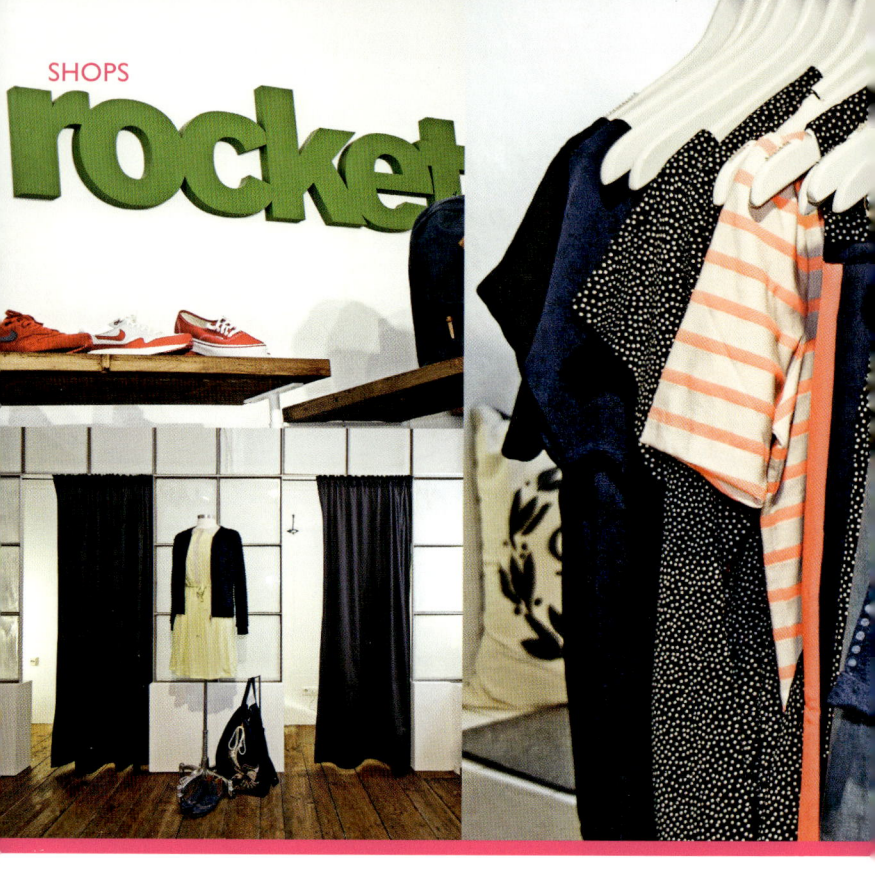

rocket

This relaxed concept store housed in an old building advertises the "finest premium streetwear". A visit holds the promise of inspiration and cool discoveries. Creaky floorboards meet trendy trainers and Scandinavian brands, and exquisite accessories such as iPad bags or TomShot jewellery round off the range. rocket's little brother also lives in the "street. art. stuff." building. It is called "Grey. with a little bit of red."

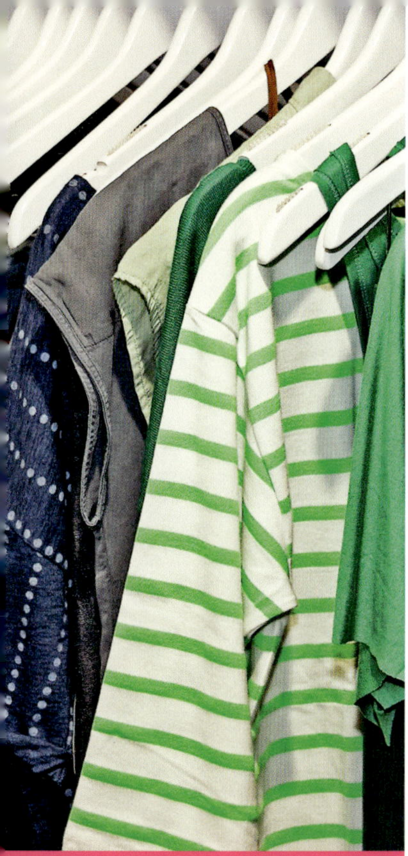

ROCKET.

Reichenbachstraße 41 // Isarvorstadt
Tel.: +49 (0)89 18 95 59 12
www.rocket-store.de

Mon–Sat 11 am to 7 pm

U1, U2, U7, Tram 17 Fraunhoferstraße

Prices: $$

„Finest premium streetwear" kündigt dieser entspannte Concept Store in Altbau-Ambiente an. Ein Besuch verspricht Inspiration und coole Entdeckungen. Knarzende Holzdielen treffen auf angesagte Sneakers und skandinavische Marken, exquisite Accessoires wie iPad-Taschen oder Schmuck von TomShot vervollständigen das Sortiment. Mit in der „street. art. stuff."-WG wohnt jetzt auch rocket's kleiner Bruder. Der trägt den klingenden Namen „Grey. with a little bit of red".

WASH & COFFEE

Klenzestraße 1 // Isarvorstadt
Tel.: +49 (0)89 21 66 78 44
www.wash-coffee.com

Mon 8 am to 9 pm
Tue, Wed, Fri 11 am to 9 pm
Sat–Sun 10 am to 6 pm

S1–8
Tram 16, 18 Isartor

Prices: $

MAP N° 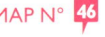 46

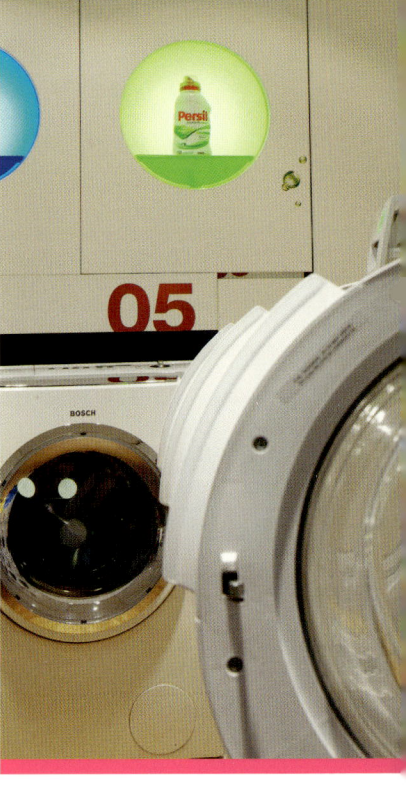

There's a real chance here for the mythical laundry-based flirt. A diverse cross-section of the population avails itself of this unique opportunity to wash their dirty laundry in public while contentedly working on their laptops, surfing the Internet, reading, drinking coffee—or starting a conversation. Familiar sponsors provide high-quality washing machines and detergents, and the staff offers competent laundry advice.

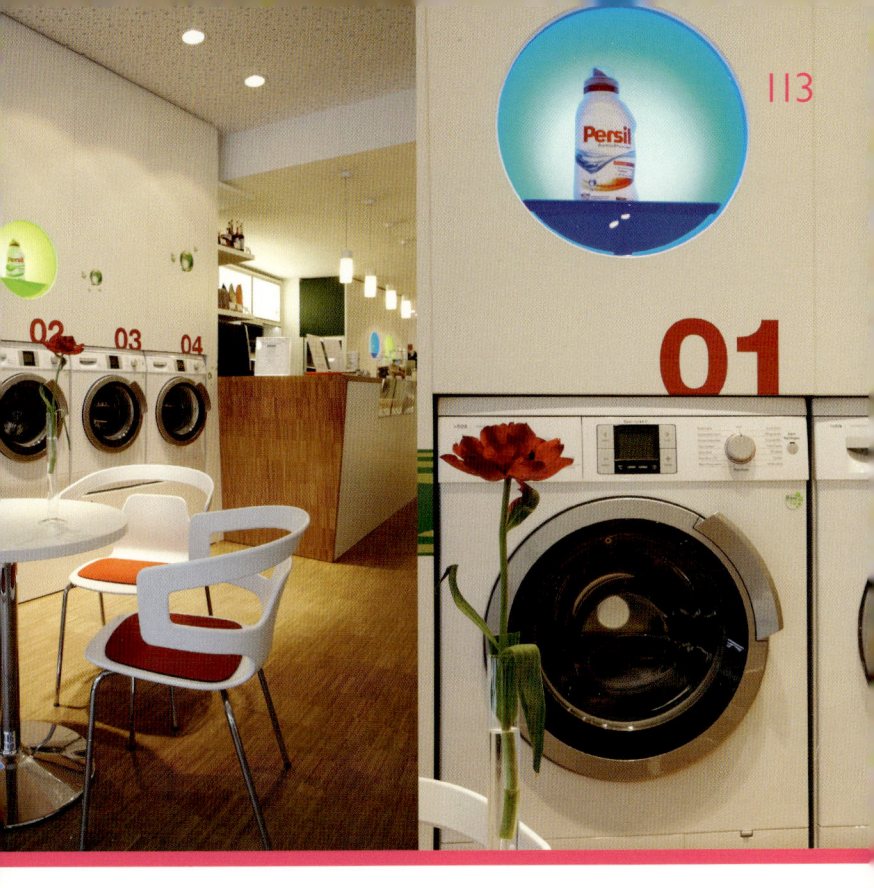

Hier hat der Mythos vom Flirt im Waschsalon eine reelle Chance. Denn ein bunter Querschnitt durch die Bevölkerung nutzt das einzigartige Angebot, seine schmutzige Wäsche in der Öffentlichkeit zu waschen und dabei gemütlich am Laptop zu arbeiten, im Internet zu surfen, zu lesen, Kaffee zu trinken – oder eben ins Gespräch zu kommen. Bekannte Sponsoren sorgen für hochwertige Maschinen und Waschmittel, die Mitarbeiter bieten eine kompetente „Wäscheberatung".

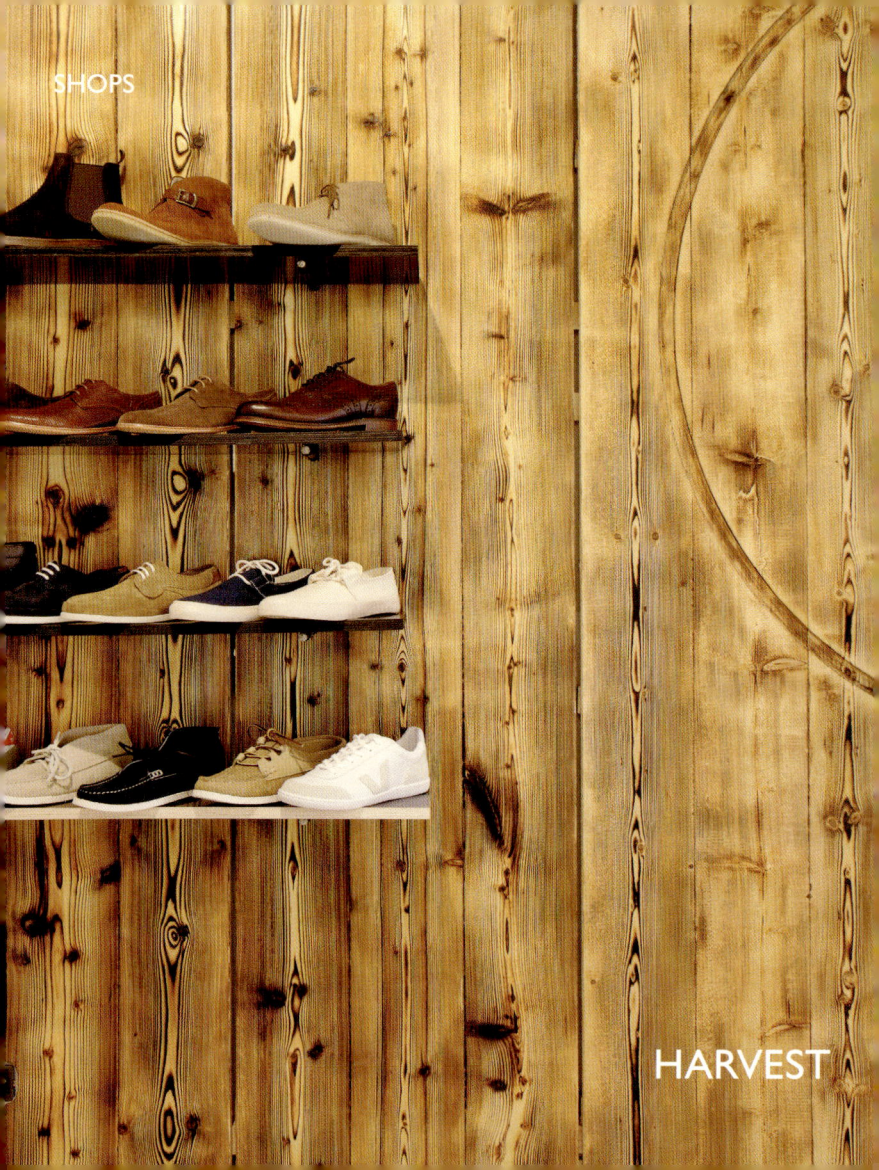

HARVEST

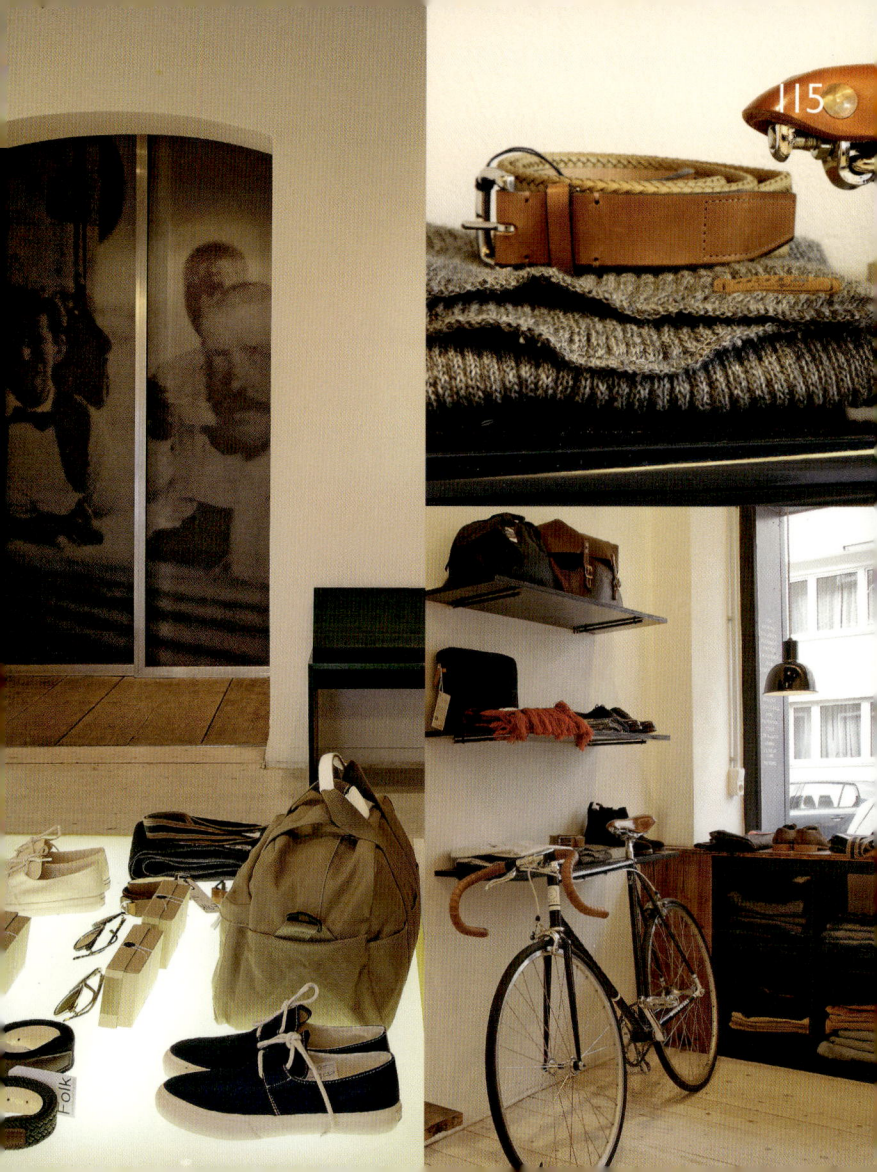

Folk

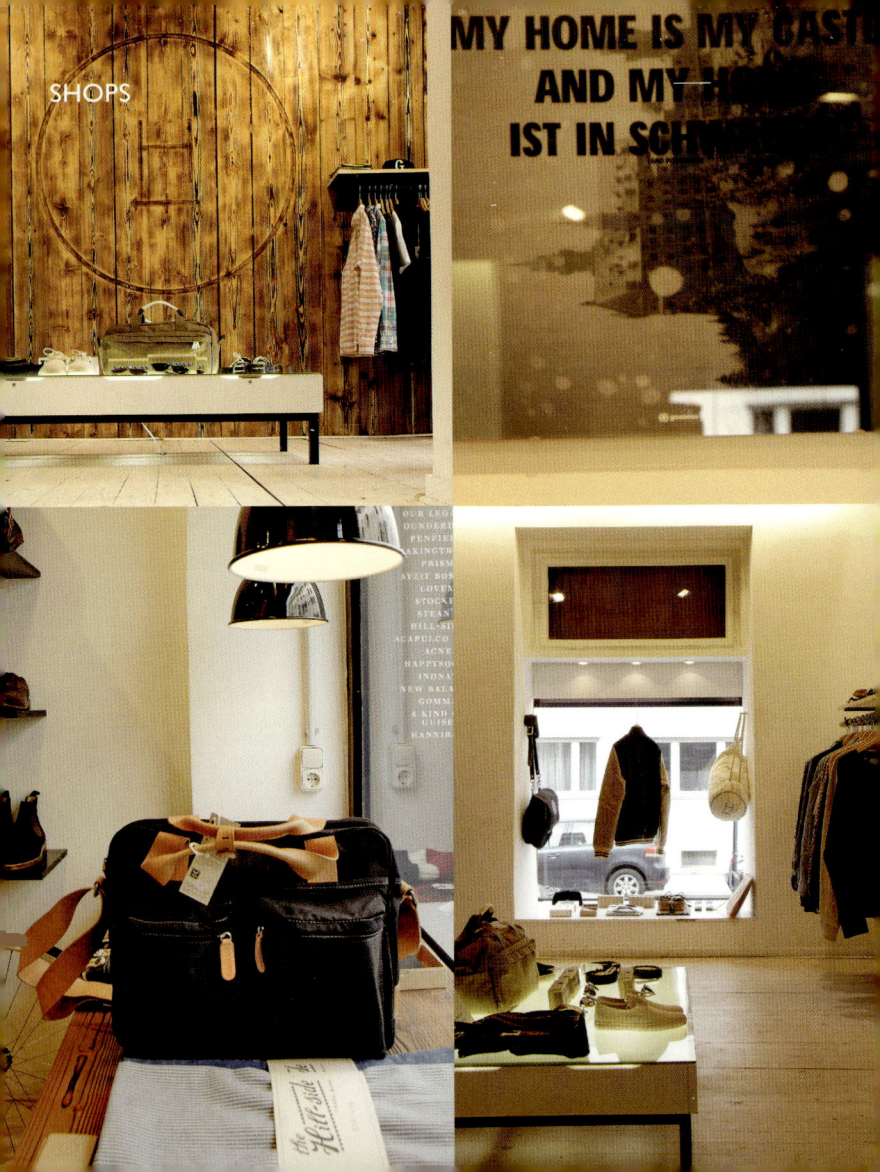

SHOPS

MY HOME IS MY CASTLE
AND MY H...
IST IN SCHN...

HARVEST

Zieblandstraße 5 // Maxvorstadt
Tel.: +49 (0)89 45 24 41 81
www.harvest-shop.de

Mon-Fri 11 am to 7 pm
Sat 11 am to 6 pm

Tram 27 Schellingstraße

Prices: $$$

As a trend, men are at a clear disadvantage over women—at least when it comes to shopping selection and styles. By contrast, Harvest has the kind of clothes and accessories that help men—for a change—earn envious glances from both women and men. Envy aside, the shop designed and run by Philip Stolte is itself a feast for the eyes. To say nothing of the exclusive labels like A Kind of Guise.

Tendenziell ist man als Mann gegenüber Frauen ja deutlich benachteiligt – zumindest in Punkto Auswahl und Styles beim Shoppen. Harvest hingegen hat die Art von Kleidung und Accessoires, für die Männer zur Abwechslung sowohl von Frauen als auch von Männern neidische Blicke bekommen. Abgesehen davon ist der von Philip Stolte gestaltete und geführte Laden an sich schon eine Augenweide. Von den exklusiven Labels wie A Kind of Guise ganz zu schweigen.

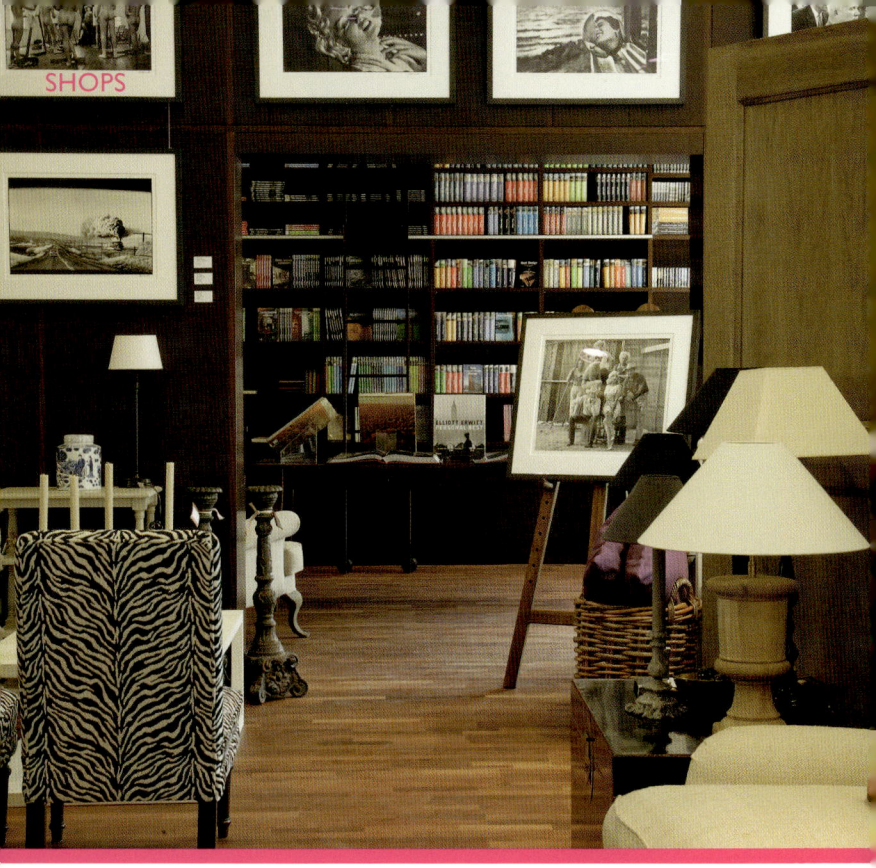

The teNeues bookstore at the corner of Brienner Straße and Oskar-von-Miller-Ring in Freso Home is tricky. Once you have become absorbed in one of the many photograph volumes it's easy to forget the time—and the fact that you're in a store. Designed in dark wood, the publishing house's reading corner seems more like a classy private library. The comfortable atmosphere lets you open yourself to inspiration about travel and design.

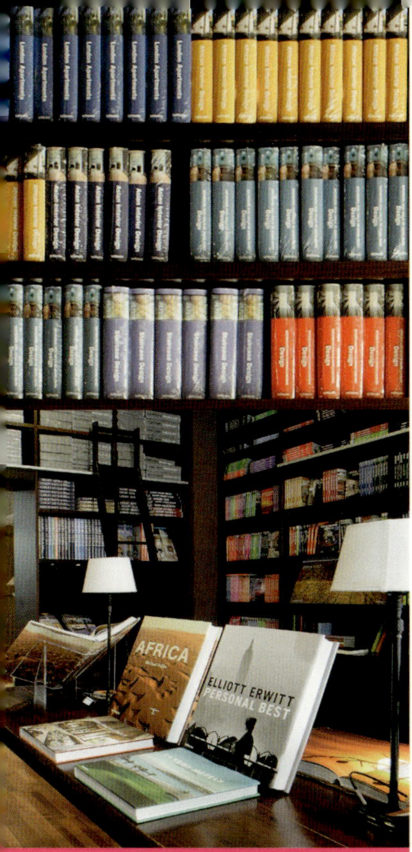

TENEUES STORE @ FRESO HOME

Brienner Straße 14 // Maxvorstadt
Tel.: +49 (0)89 22 80 79 76
www.fresohome.de

Mon–Fri 10 am to 6 pm
Sat 11 am to 3 pm

U3–6 Odeonsplatz

Prices: $$$

Der Buchladen von teNeues an der Ecke Brienner Straße/Oskar-von-Miller-Ring bei Freso Home ist tückisch. Wenn man sich erstmal in einen der vielen Fotobände vertieft hat, vergisst man leicht die Zeit – und die Tatsache, dass man sich in einem Geschäft befindet. Die in dunklem Holz gehaltene Lesecke des Verlags erinnert eher an eine stilvolle, private Bibliothek. In gemütlicher Atmosphäre kann man sich bestens rund um Reise und Design inspirieren lassen.

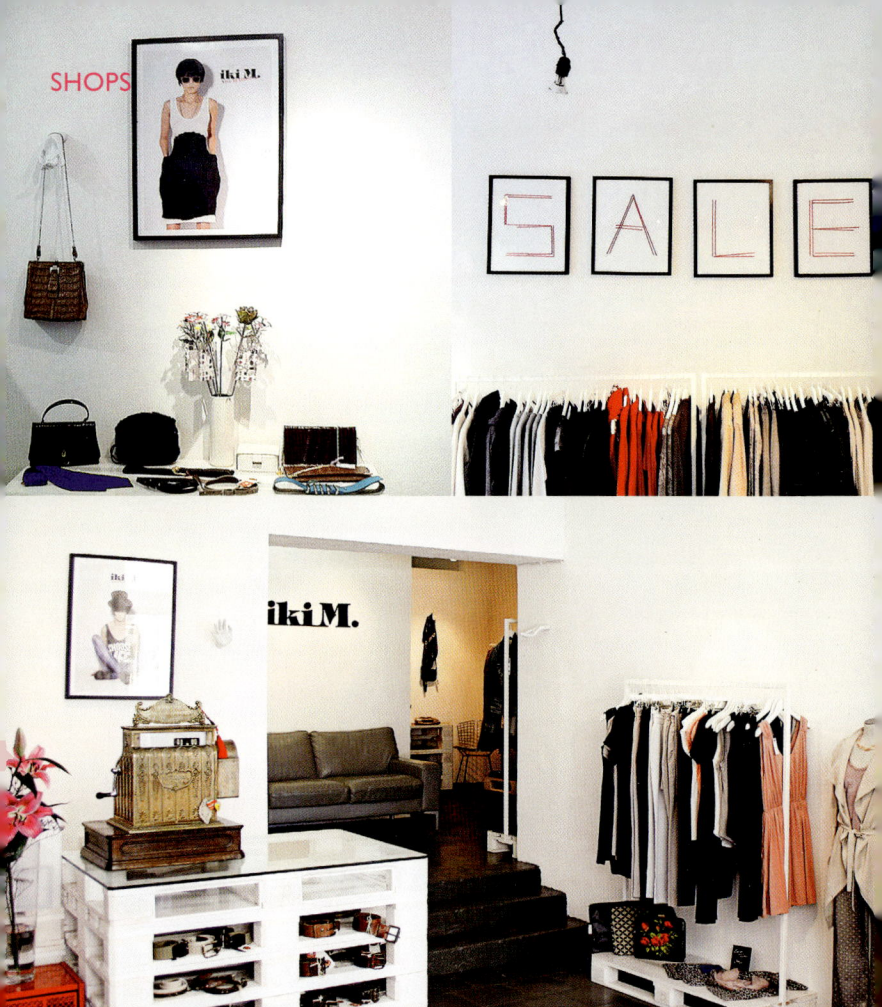

IKI M.

Fraunhoferstraße 8 // Isarvorstadt
Tel.: +49 (0)89 88 90 81 59
www.iki-m.de

Mon–Fri 11 am to 7 pm
Sat 10.30 am to 5.30 pm

U1, U2, U3, U6, U7 Sendlinger Tor
Tram 16, 17, 18 Müllerstraße

Prices: $$$

This is eco fashion without the tired old look: At iki M.,
which features brands such as Armed Angels, Kuyichi, and
Kami Organic, all the clothing is made from fair-trade and
organic materials. The assortment includes women's cloth-
ing as well as a selection of fashion for men and children.

Von Öko-Mief keine Spur, dabei wurden die Kleider von
Marken wie Armed Angels, Kuyichi und Kami Organic
durch die Bank weg aus ökologischen Materialien herge-
stellt und dazu noch fair gehandelt. Zum Sortiment gehört
neben Damenbekleidung auch eine Auswahl an Herren-
und Kindermode.

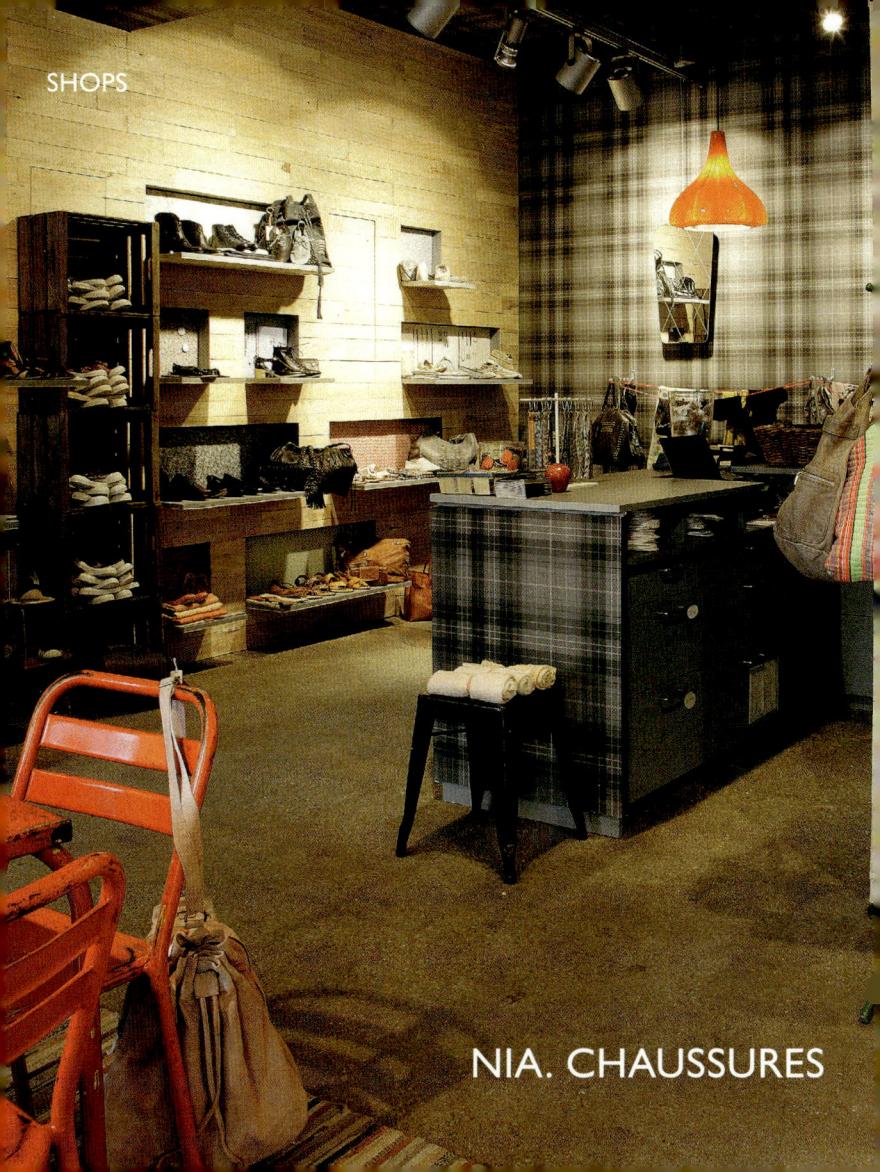

NIA. CHAUSSURES

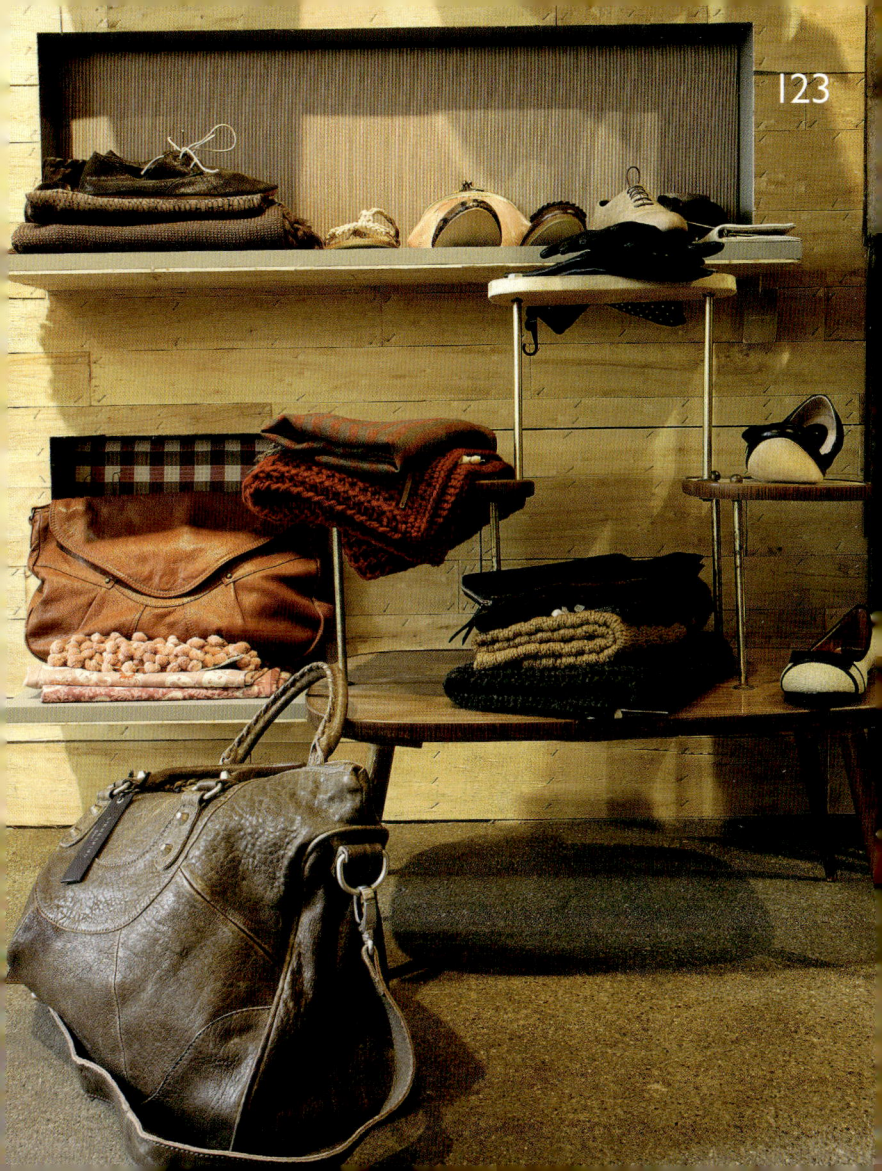

NIA. CHAUSSURES

Barer Straße 55 // Schwabing
Tel.: +49 (0)89 39 29 09 55
www.nia-chaussures.de

Mon–Fri 10 am to 7 pm
Sat 10 am to 6 pm

Tram 27 Schellingstraße

Prices: $$$

MAP N° 50

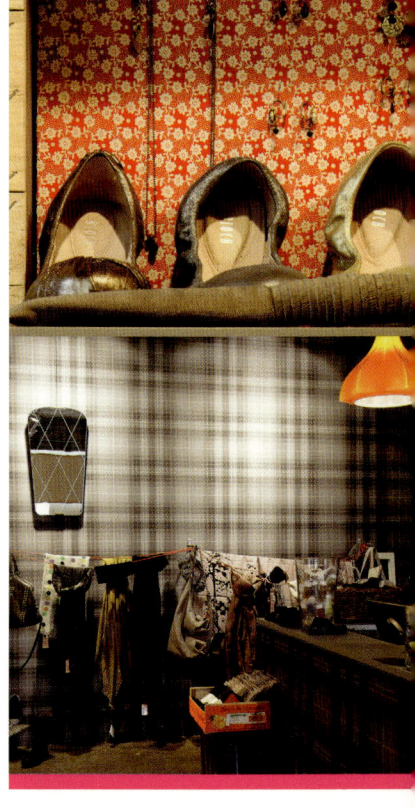

Caution: this store is extremely hazardous for women! The sight of the selections in the store on Barer Straße could cause one of them to faint, only to wake with several large shopping bags full of shoes and accessories, her credit card still drawn. But the pieces by labels such as Sessùn, Tatoosh, Bloch, or the Munich jewelry collective Jewelberry are arranged so tastefully, and the whole interior is just so seductive…

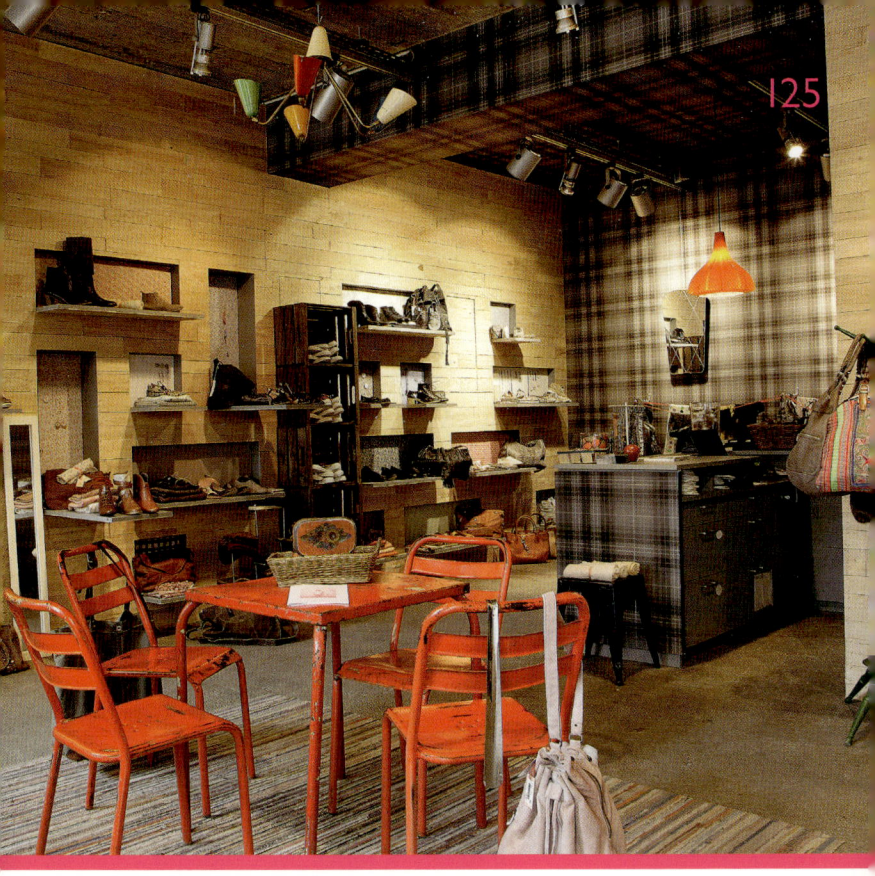

Achtung: Dieser Laden ist extrem gefährlich für Frauen! Beim Anblick des
Sortiments in der Barer Straße kann es sein, dass frau in Ohnmacht fällt
und erst wieder mit mehreren großen Einkaufstaschen voller Schuhe und
Accessoires erwacht, die Kreditkarte noch im Anschlag. Die Stücke von
Labels wie Sessùn, Tatoosh, Bloch oder dem Münchner Schmuck-Kollektiv
Jewelberry sind aber auch so geschmackvoll arrangiert, und das gesamte
Interieur verführt zum Kaufen…

CLUBS, LOUNGES +BARS

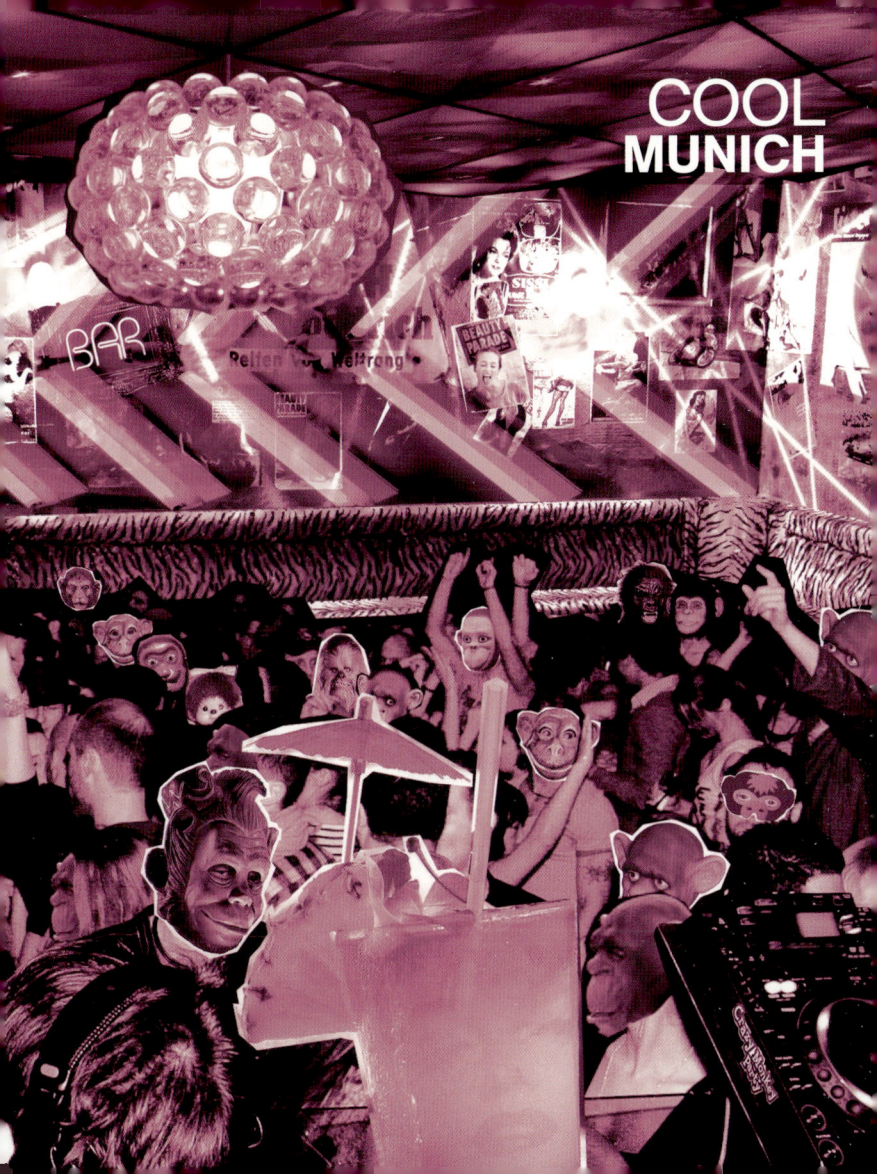

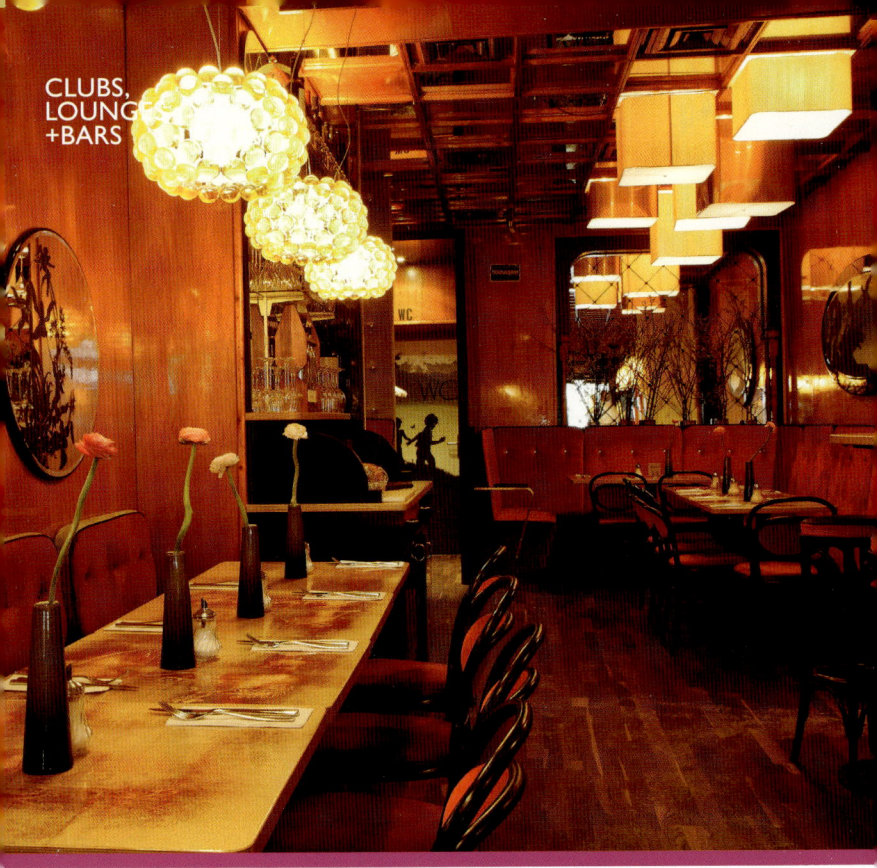

Even though Bar Lux belongs to the hotel of the same name (or rather the hotel belongs to the bar), it deserves its own entry. It is, after all, one of the city's best addresses for the refined art of the drink, thanks to Oliver von Carnap. The head bartender practices his craft with evident fervor while at the same time educating his guests in mixology with great affability. Snuggled into the warm, soft atmosphere of the room, no wish goes unfulfilled at Lux.

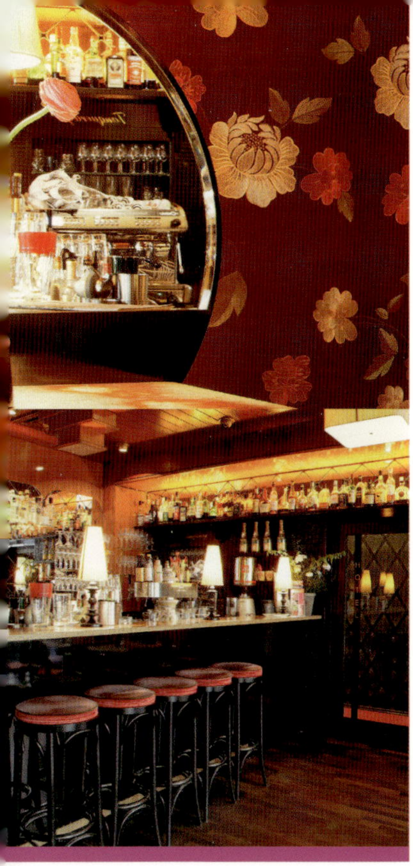

BAR LUX

Ledererstraße 13 // Altstadt
Tel.: +49 (0)89 45 20 73 00
www.hotel-lux-muenchen.de

Mon–Fri 7 am to 1 am
Sat–Sun 8 am to 1 am

S1–8, U3, U6 Marienplatz

Prices: $$

Obwohl die Bar Lux zum gleichnamigen Hotel gehört (bzw. das Hotel zur Bar) muss sie noch mal separat erwähnt werden. Denn sie gehört dank Oliver von Carnap zu den stadtbesten Adressen für gehobene Trinkkultur. Der Barchef ist mit einer offensichtlichen Inbrunst am Werk und bringt dem Gast nebenbei auf sehr sympathische Weise die Drinks auch theoretisch näher. Eingebettet in das warme, weiche Ambiente des Raums bleiben im Lux keine Wünsche offen.

JOSEF BAR

Klenzestraße 99 // Isarvorstadt
www.dasjosef.de

Tue–Wed 7 pm to 1 am
Thu 7 pm to 3 am
Fri–Sat 7 pm to 4 am

U1, U2, U7 Fraunhoferstraße

Prices: $$

MAP N° 52

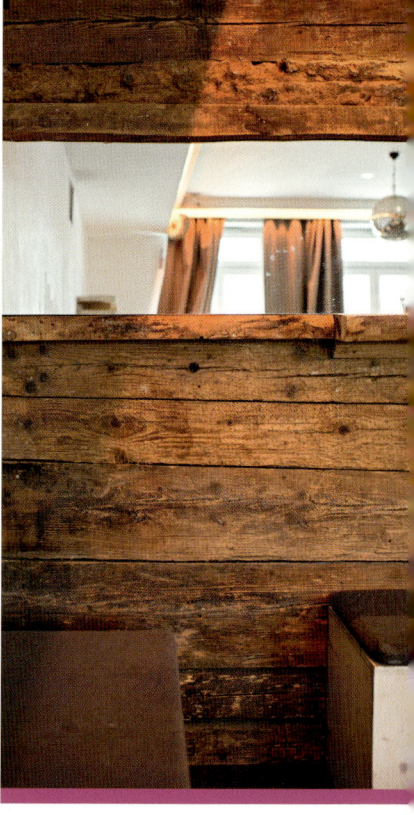

Even the Bible teaches us that Josef and Maria belong together. In the late evening hours, Josef Bar accommodates the guests of Café Maria from across the street. The furnishings strike a balance between a modern lodge and a blend of alpine and religious elements. The menu is also filled with contrasts: It offers typical Bavarian treats such as homemade meatballs and hearty sandwiches alongside mixed cocktails, all while the DJ plays very un-Bavarian music ranging from house to electro.

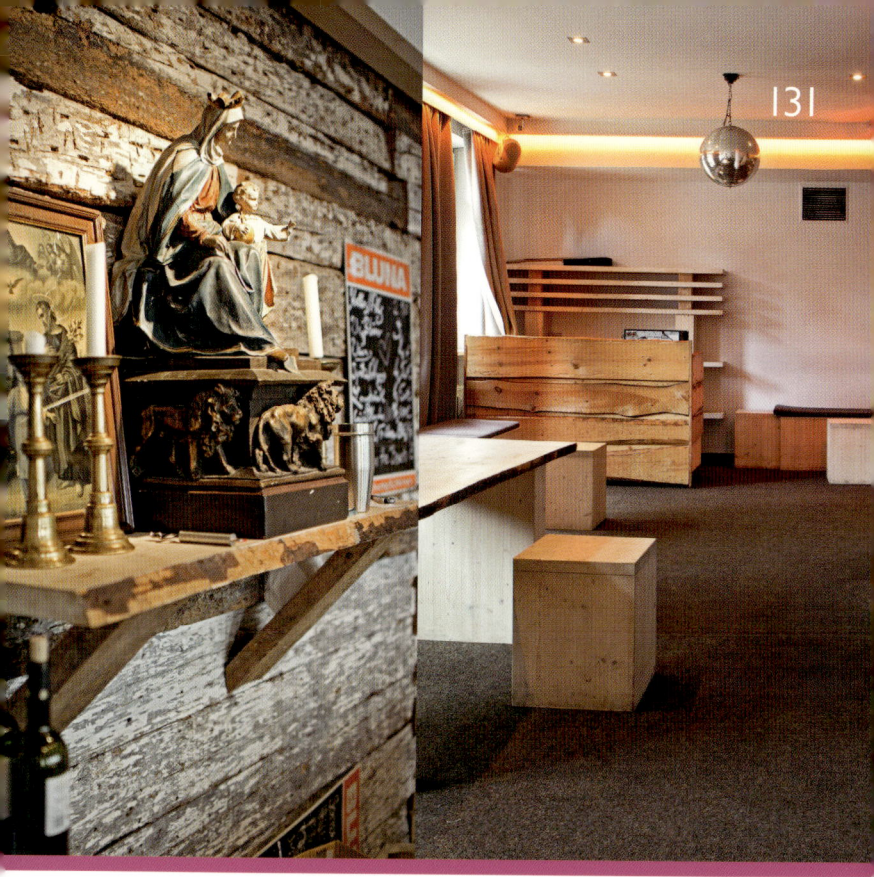

Schon aus der Bibel weiß man: Josef kommt nicht allein. Zu später Stunde löst die Josef Bar das Café Maria auf der gegenüberliegenden Straßenseite ab. Die Einrichtung schafft einen gelungenen Spagat zwischen moderner Lounge und alpin-sakraler Deko. Ebenso gegensätzlich die Karte: Es gibt typisch bayrische Schmankerl wie selbstgemachte Fleischpflanzerl oder herzhaft belegte Bauernbrote; dazu werden Cocktails gemixt und der DJ legt ganz un-bayrische Musik von House bis Electro auf.

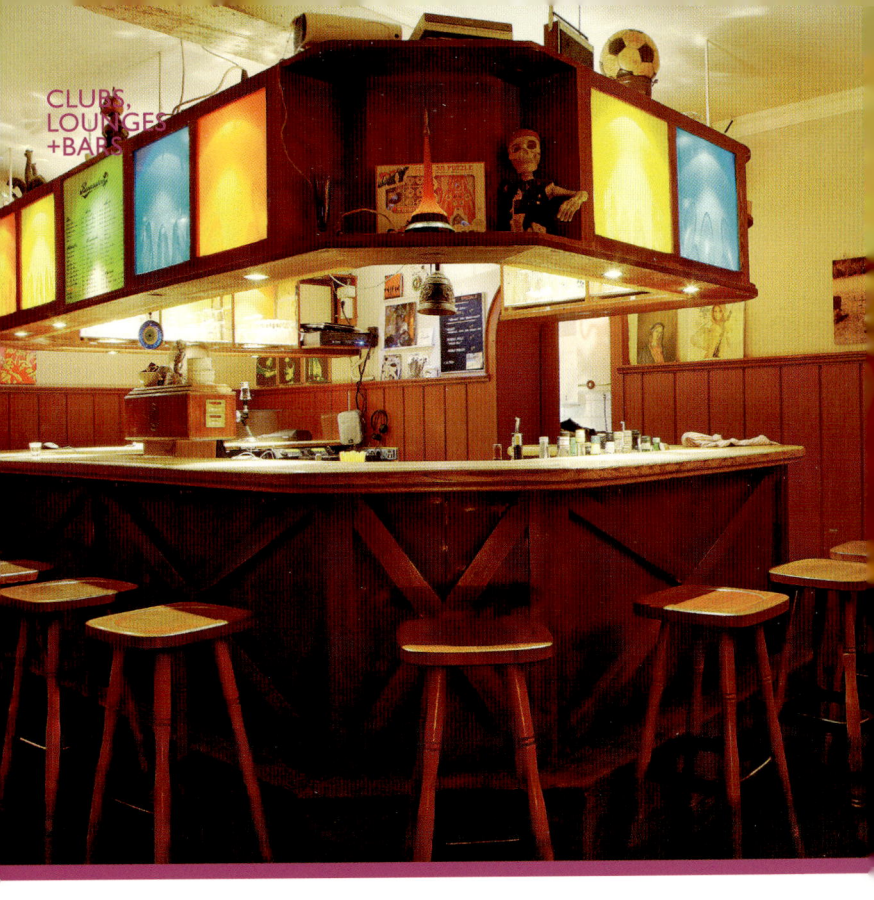

Authentic, long-established pubs are gradually going extinct. They are often forced to the wayside by ostentatiously over-styled or unstyled hotspots. Run by ten friends, the honorable Rennsalon lies right in the middle, in the pleasant zone. It retains its pub patina, merely enriched by this or that modern fetish. The music is diverse due in part to the operators' varying tastes.

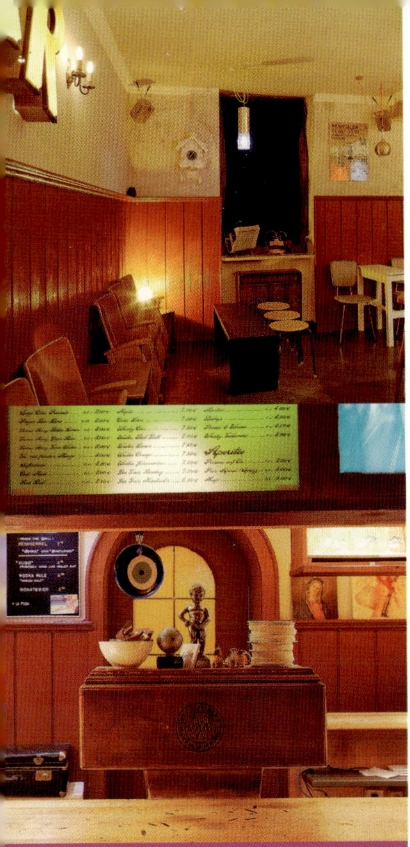

RENNSALON

Baldestraße 13 // Isarvorstadt
Tel.: +49 (0)176 38 32 37 34
www.rennsalon.de

Tue–Thu 8 pm to 1.30 am
Fri–Sat 8 pm to 3 am

U1, U2, U7 Fraunhoferstraße
U3, U6 Goetheplatz

Prices: $

53

Authentische, lang eingesessene Kneipen sterben nach und nach aus.
Oft müssen sie überstylten oder demonstrativ ungestylten „In-Locations"
weichen. Der von zehn Freunden betriebene, ehrliche Rennsalon liegt
genau dazwischen, im angenehmen Bereich. Die Kneipen-Patina wurde
ihm gelassen, nur hier und da mit modernem Fetisch angereichert.
Musikalisch ist viel Abwechslung geboten, auch bedingt durch die unter-
schiedlichen Geschmäcker der Betreiber.

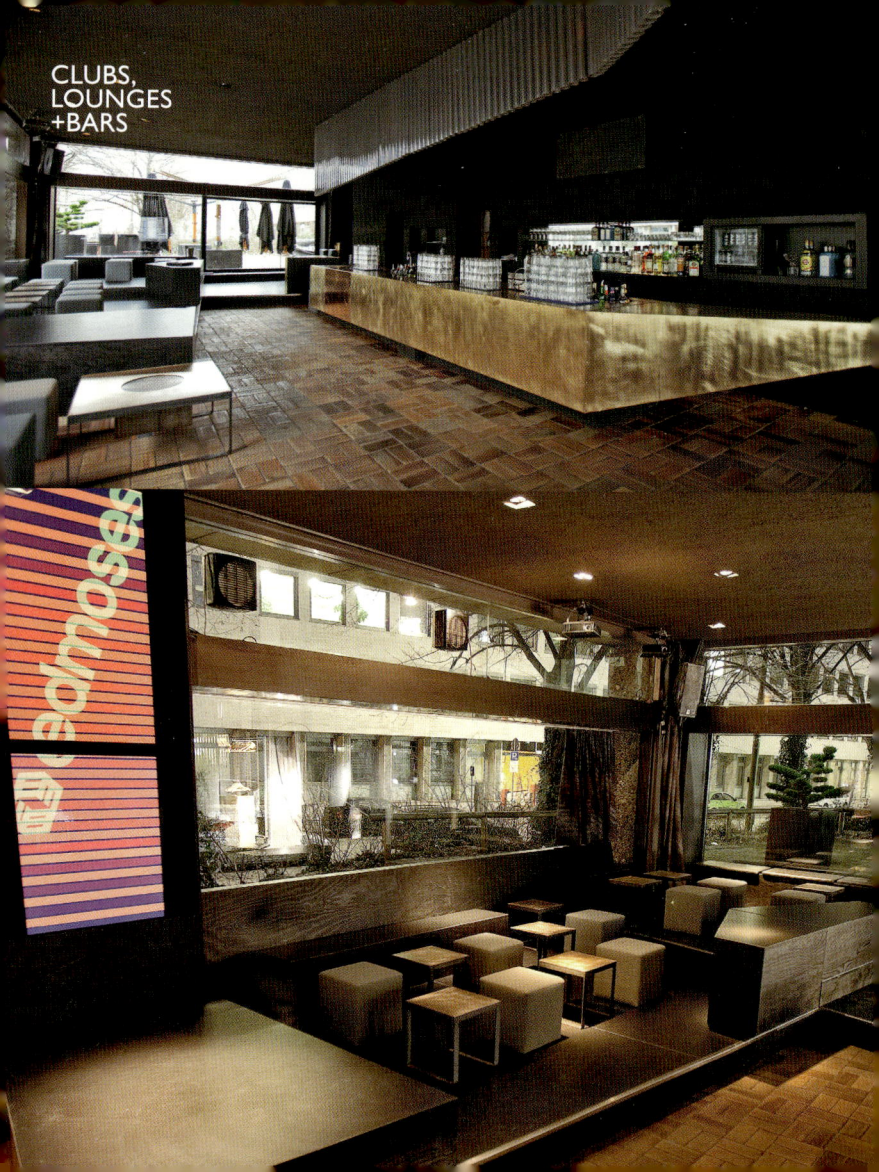

ED MOSES

Prinzregentenstraße 2 // Lehel
Tel.: +49 (0)177 2 54 74 76
www.edmosesbar.com

Fri–Sat 9 pm to 4 am

Tram 18 Nationalmuseum / Haus der Kunst

Prices: $$

With its outdoor patio, the Ed Moses is particularly lovely on warm summer nights. On the other hand, it's also nice in summer or winter to get sweaty inside in the aquarium when—as usual—a great DJ is spinning and the crowd gets wild. The crowd is young and attractive and relatively mixed. The lounge-like club bears the name of American track star Edwin Moses, who remained undefeated for ten years and always looked good crossing the finish line.

Besonders in lauen Sommernächten ist das Ed Moses mit seiner Terrasse reizvoll. Andererseits lohnt sich – sommers wie winters – das Schwitzen drinnen im Aquarium, wenn wie meistens ein großartiger DJ gebucht ist und die Menge wild wird. Das Publikum ist jung und schön und relativ durchmischt. Benannt ist der loungige Club nach dem US-Leichtathleten Edwin Moses, der in seiner Disziplin zehn Jahre ungeschlagen blieb und beim Siegen immer gut aussah.

GOLDENE BAR

Prinzregentenstraße 1 // Lehel
Tel.: +49 (0)89 54 80 47 77
www.goldenebar.de

Daily 10 am to 2 am
Sun until 8 pm

Tram 18 Nationalmuseum /
Haus der Kunst

Prices: $$

MAP N°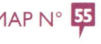

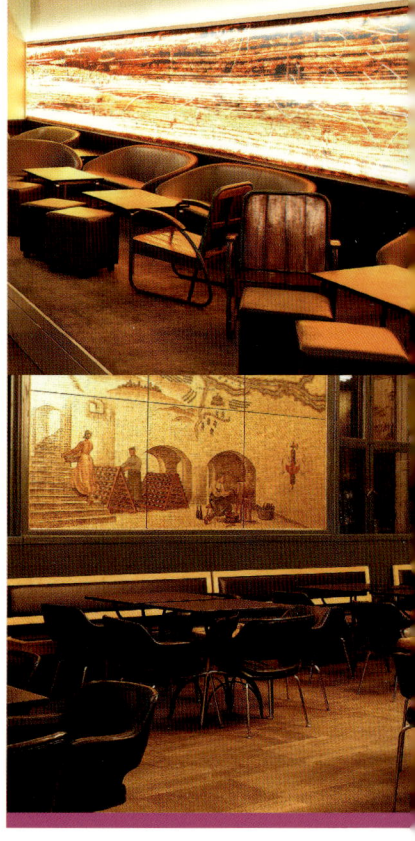

The first time you stumble upon Goldene Bar behind Haus der Kunst,
it's a bit like accidentally discovering the Czar's Amber Room. Except,
this is a temple of drink with historic "alcoholic" maps on the walls and a
back bar like an altar. Klaus St. Rainer, who runs the establishment with
Leonie Rainer, and his young recruits combine bartending perfection
with a relaxed nonchalance.

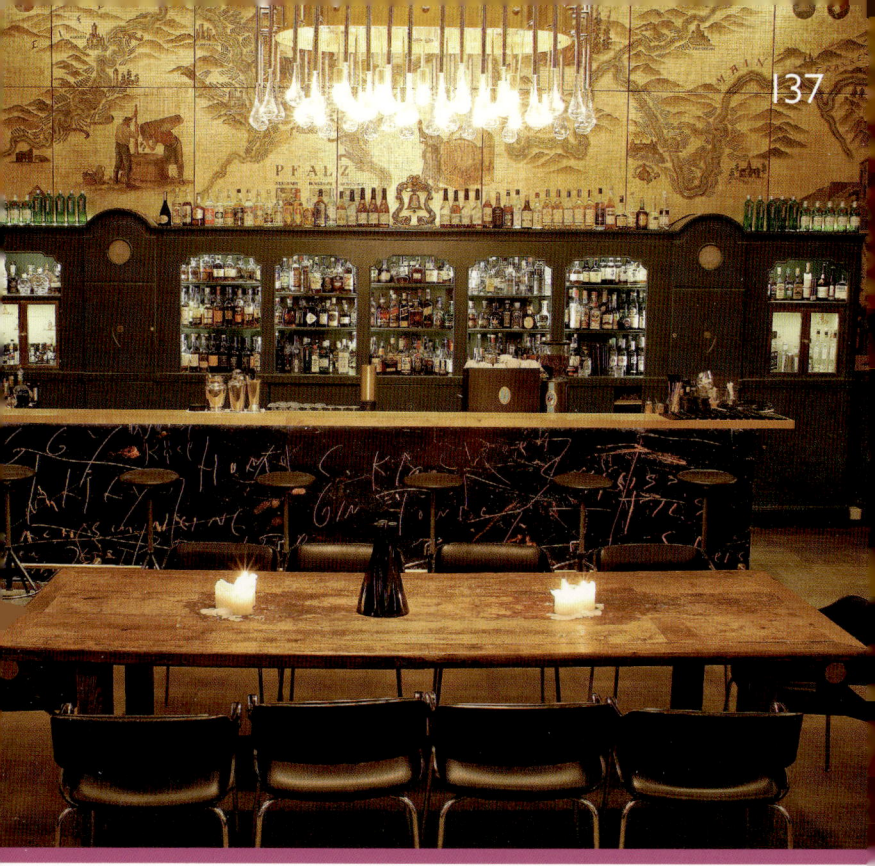

Wenn man sich zum ersten Mal in die Goldene Bar hinten im Haus
der Kunst verirrt, ist es ein wenig so, als ob man zufällig das Bernstein-
zimmer entdeckt hätte. Nur dass es sich um einen Trinktempel handelt,
mit historischen „alkoholischen" Landkarten auf den Wänden und
einer Backbar wie ein Altar. Klaus St. Rainer, der die Location mit
Leonie Rainer betreibt, und seine jungen Rekruten verbinden
Bartending-Perfektionismus mit einer entspannten Lässigkeit.

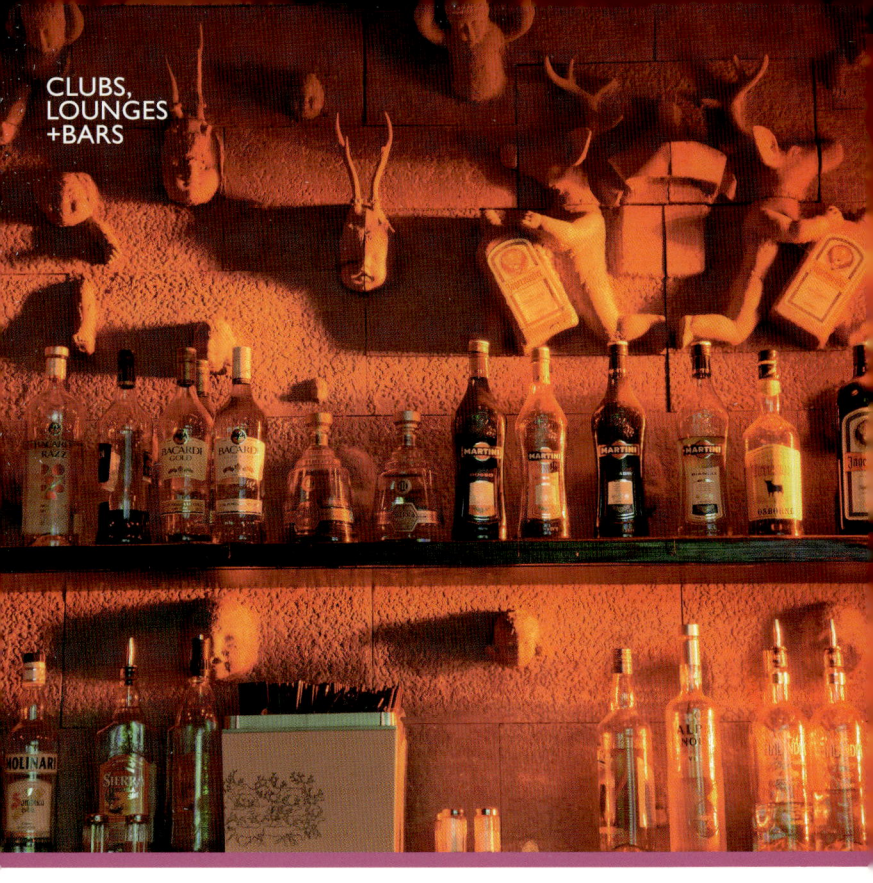

Turn into a passageway, go through a heavy metal door and a green gate, and you're in the heart of Harry Klein, the epicenter of electronic music in Munich. Harry Klein's heart is a freely vibrating concrete cube mounted on ginormous metal springs—guaranteed to be soundproof! None of this is noticeable to the ravers inside, unlike the ultra visuals that, along with the best basses in town, are the club's trademark.

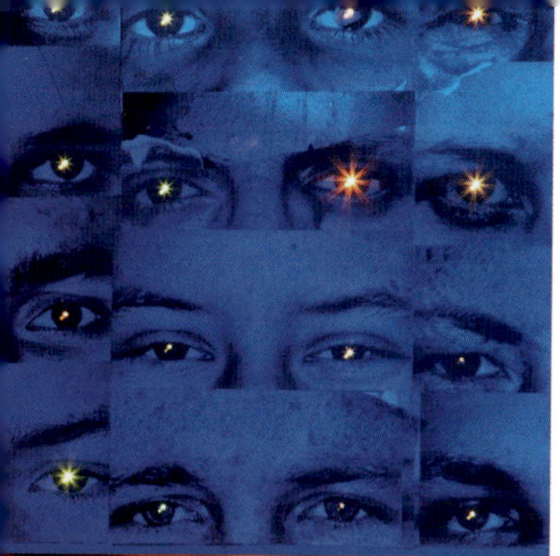

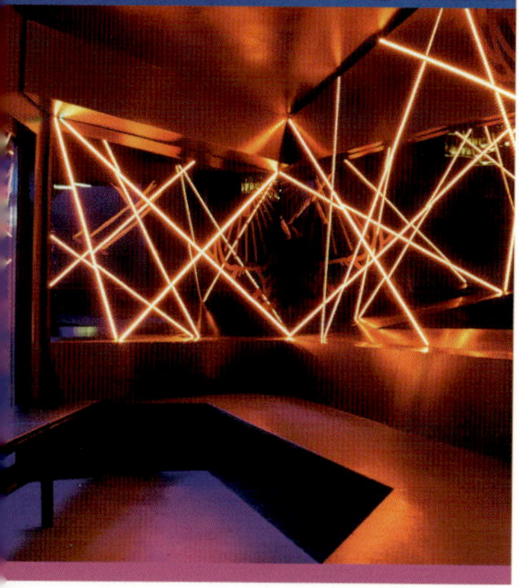

HARRY KLEIN

Sonnenstraße 8 // Ludwigsvorstadt
Tel.: +49 (0)89 40 28 74 00
www.harrykleinclub.de

Check website for program

S1–8, U4, U5
Tram 16–21, 27 Karlsplatz (Stachus)

Prices: $$

Man biegt in eine Passage ein, geht durch eine schwere Metalltür und eine grüne Schleuse – und befindet sich im Herzen von Harry Klein, dem Epizentrum der elektronischen Musik in München. Harry Kleins Herz ist ein auf monströsen Metallfedern aufgebrachter, frei schwingender Betonkubus – Schallschutz garantiert! Davon bemerkt der Raver im Inneren nichts, wohl aber die „ultra visuals", die neben den besten Bässen der Stadt das Markenzeichen des Clubs sind.

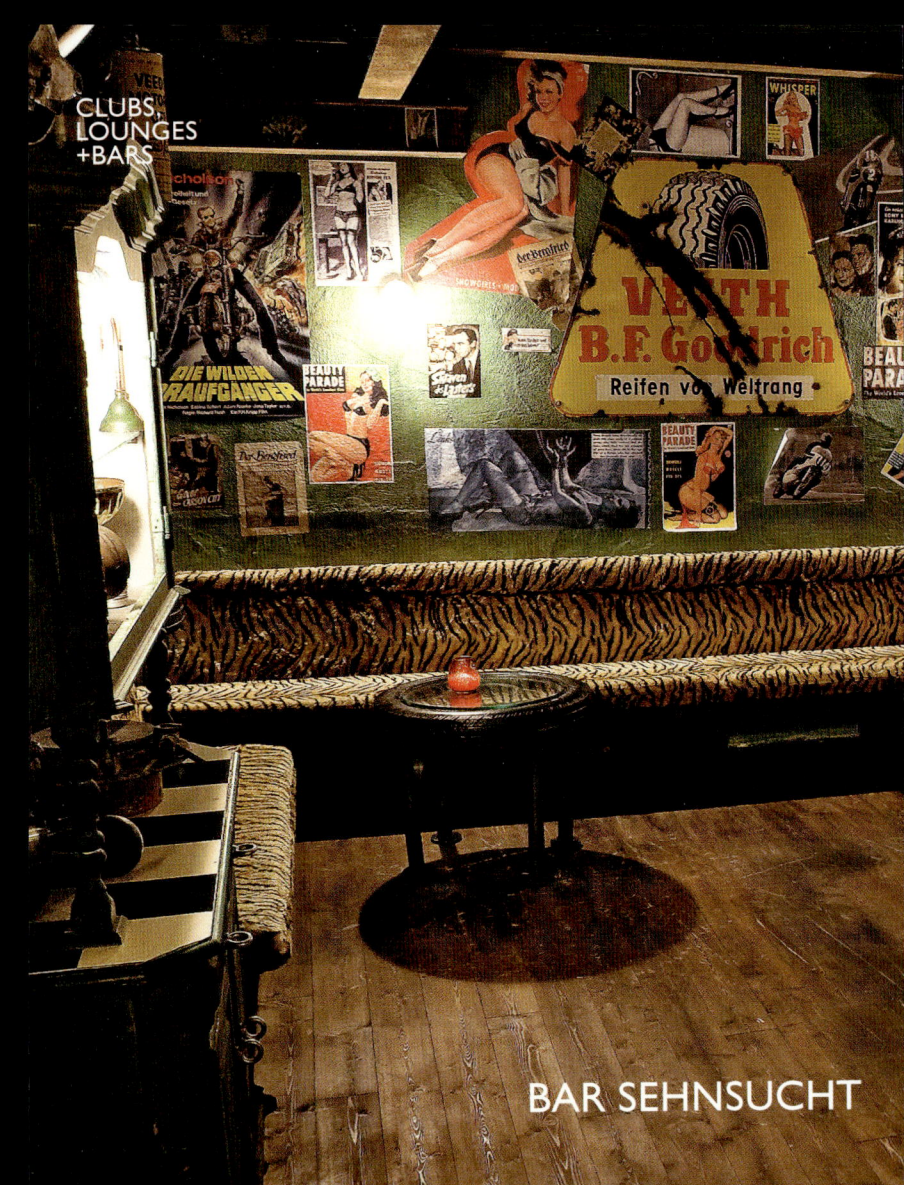

BAR SEHNSUCHT

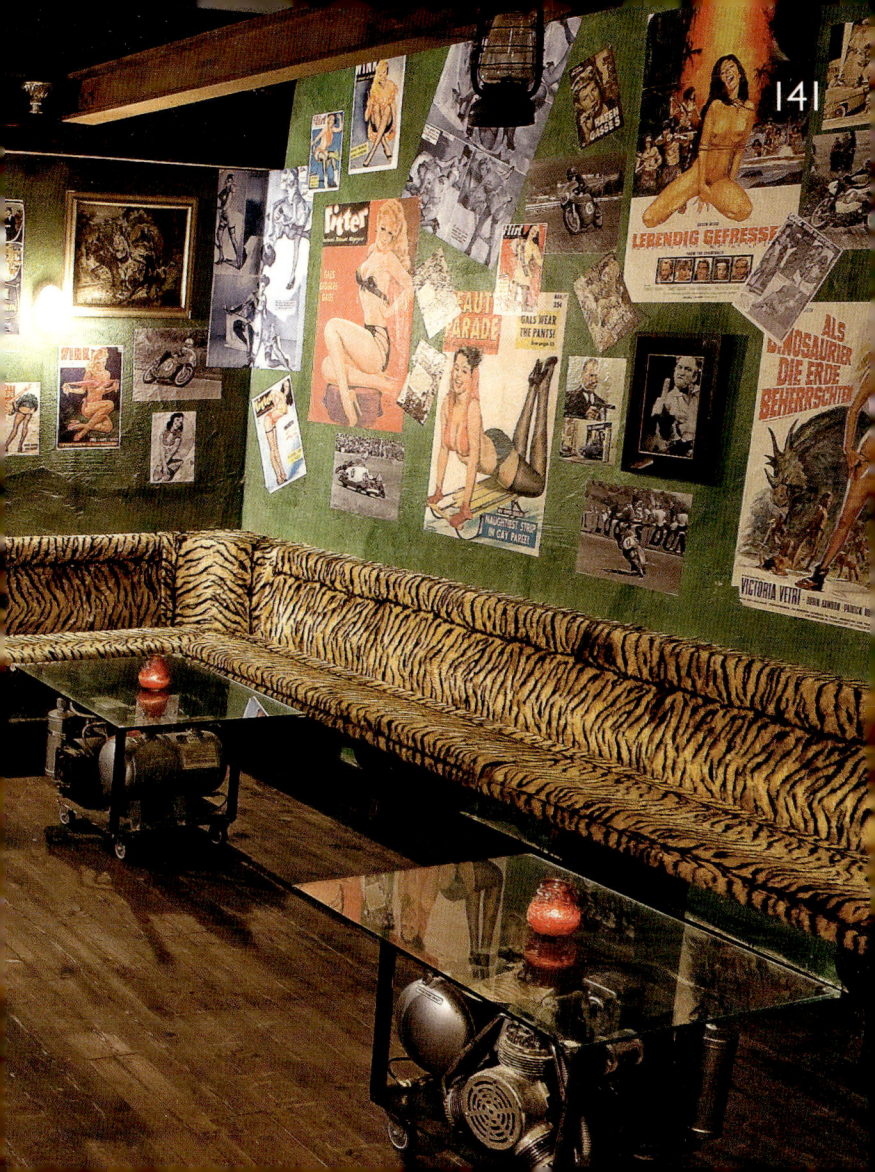

BAR
SEHNSUCHT

Amalienstraße 26 // Maxvorstadt
www.bar-sehnsucht.de
Tel.: +49 (0)89 28 75 50 88

Tue–Wed 7 pm to 2 am
Thu–Sat 7 pm to 3 am

U3, U6 Universität
U3–6 Odeonsplatz

MAP N° **57**

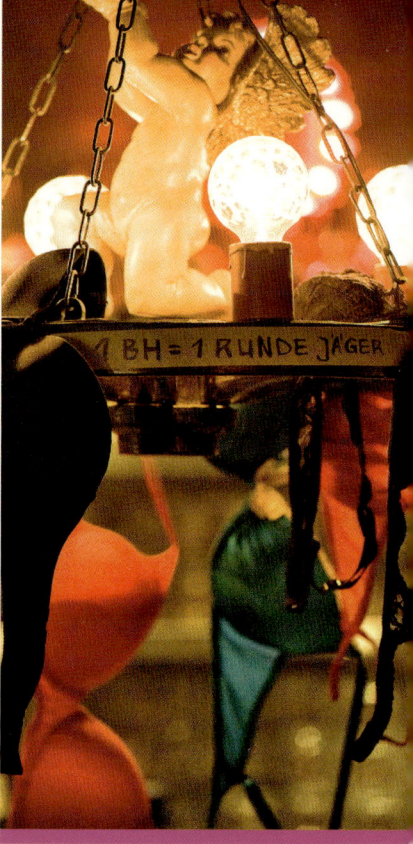

A bar that smells of sweat, testosterone, gasoline, and oil is a bar for manly men. The cigarette smoke has unfortunately been replaced by a fog machine since the authorities banned smoking here, too—depriving the rocker bar of some of its edge. Judging from the many bras hanging over the bar, women will occasionally peel off a layer or two here, as well. It's also demonstrated by the pinup girls in the Sehnsucht calendar, available at the bar.

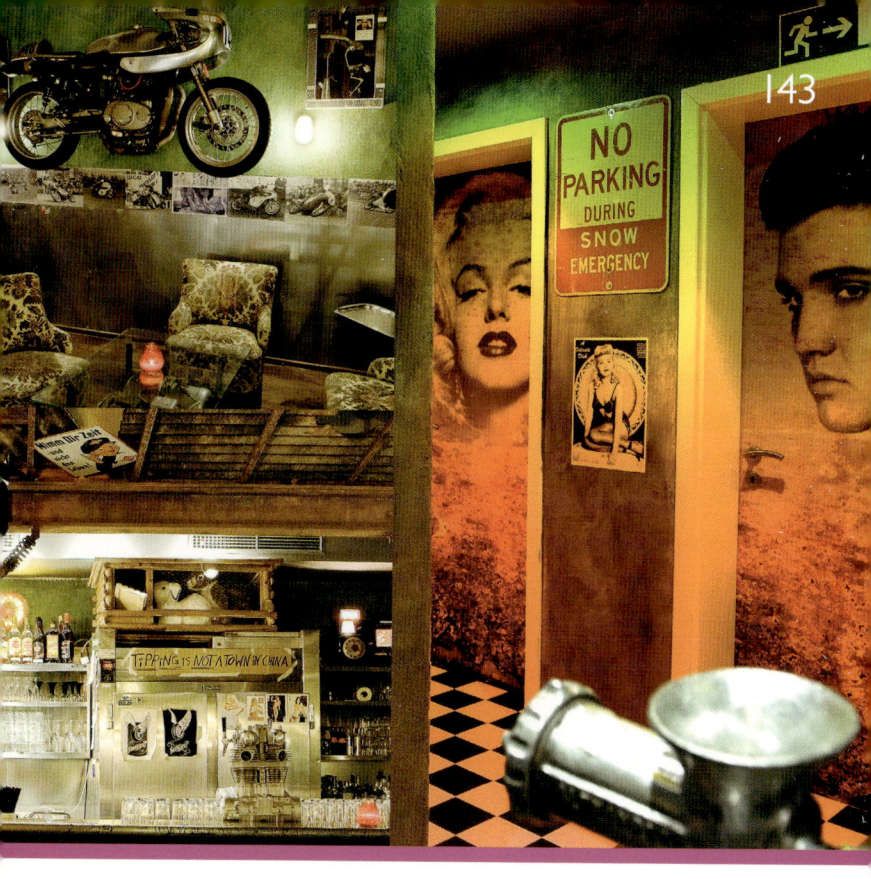

Ein Laden, der nach Schweiß, Testosteron, Benzin und Öl riecht – eine Bar für echte Kerle. Den Zigarettenqualm ersetzt leider die Nebelmaschine, seit die Behörden das Rauchverbot auch hier durchgesetzt und der Rockerkneipe damit ein Stück ihrer Subversivität gestohlen haben. Den zahlreichen BHs über der Bar nach zu urteilen, lassen hier auch Frauen gerne mal Federn. Wie es auch die Pin-Ups des in der Bar erhältlichen Sehnsucht-Kalenders demonstrieren.

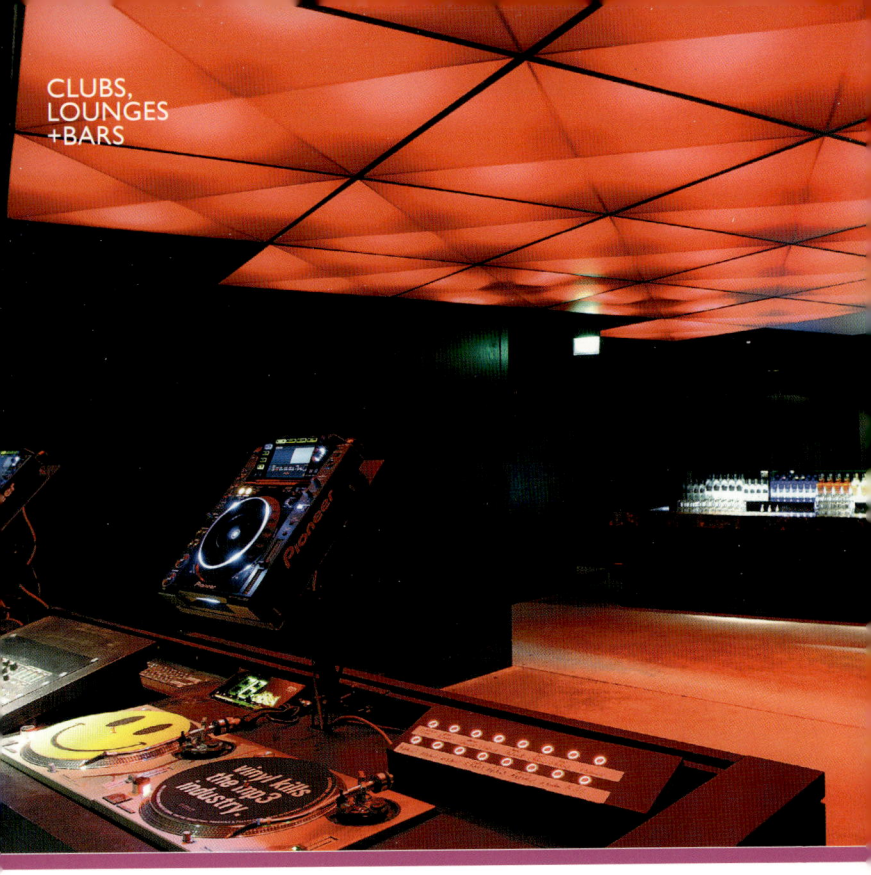

Rumor has it this place unites the best sound system with the city's best room acoustics. Either way, the wild younger brother of Ed Moses is very hot. His choice of music is more than ambitious and the interior, including the Fantomas light installation that hovers above the dancers and lifts them to new heights, is stimulating and gives the crowd party fever. Bob also likes to entertain on the patio on Sundays in the summer.

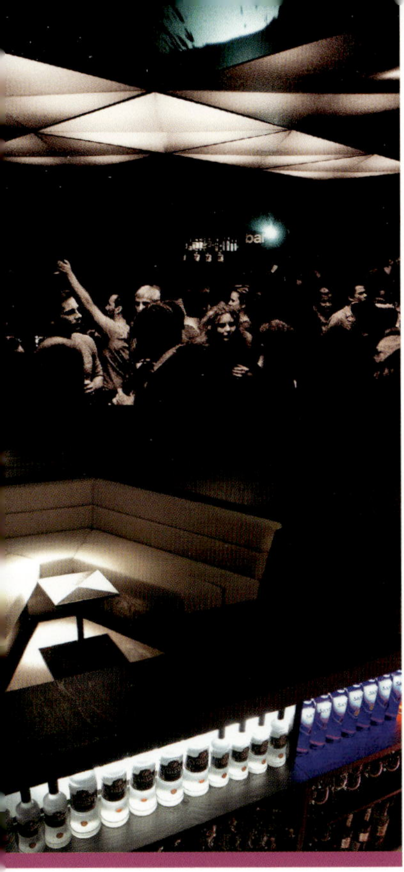

BOB BEAMAN

Gabelsbergerstraße 4 // Maxvorstadt
Tel.: +49 (0)177 2 54 74 76
www.bobbeamanclub.com

Fri–Sat from 11 pm

U3–6 Odeonsplatz

Prices: $$

Man munkelt, dass sich hier die beste Soundanlage mit der besten Raumakustik der Stadt verbindet. Auf jeden Fall ist der junge, wilde Bruder des Ed Moses ein ganz heißer Typ. Sein Musikprogramm ist mehr als ambitioniert, die Einrichtung mit der Lichtinstallation von Fantomas, die über den Tanzenden schwebt und sie in höhere Sphären zieht, ist stimulierend, und die Besucher sind feierwütig. Immer wieder empfängt Bob an Sommersonntagen auch auf der Terrasse.

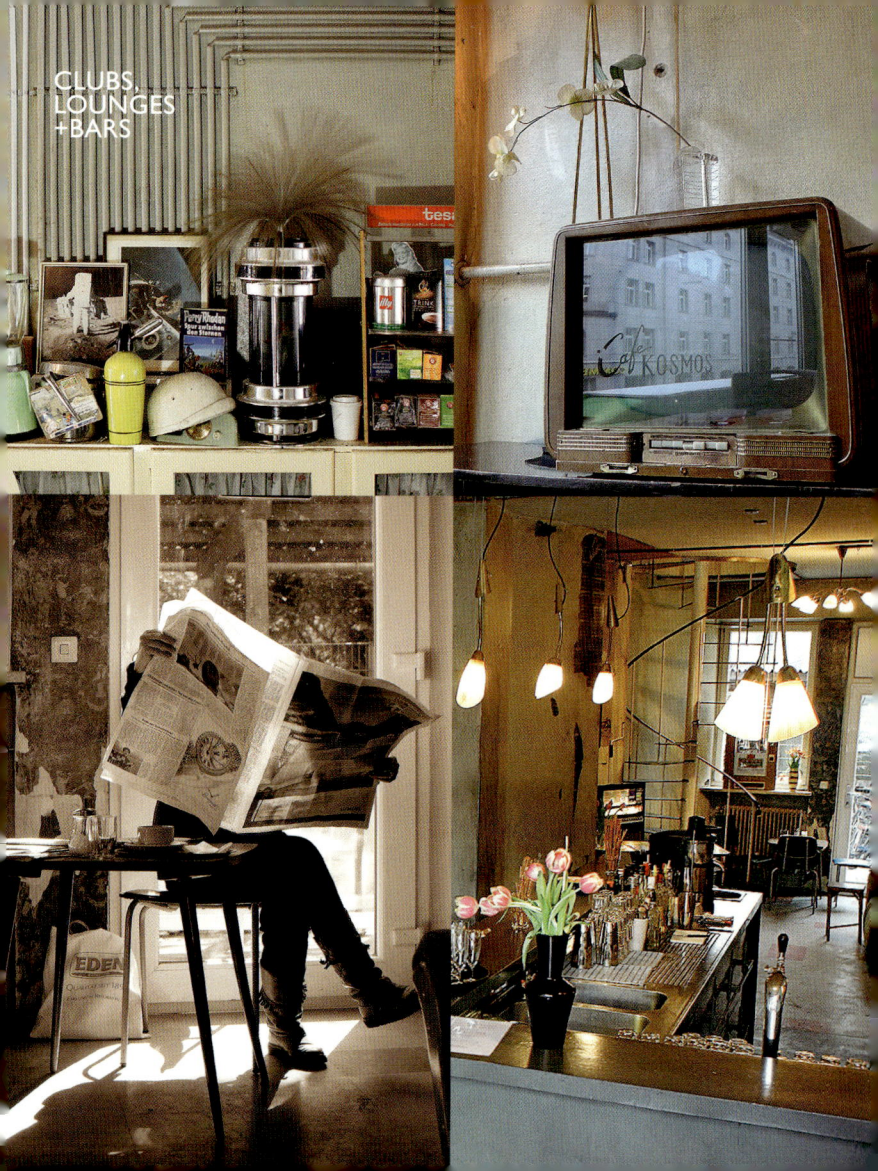

CAFÉ KOSMOS

Dachauer Straße 7 // Maxvorstadt
Tel.: +49 (0)89 55 29 58 67
www.cafe-kosmos.de

Mon–Fri noon to at least 1 am
Sat–Sun 6 pm to at least 3 am

S1–8, U1, U2, U4, U5, U7
Tram 16, 17, 19, 20, 21 Hauptbahnhof

Prices: $

Tucked in among the casinos and kebab joints around the train station is the wonderful Café Kosmos. On the whole it's not very "Munich-y," and not just because they serve beer from Hamburg (at a price that is more than fair). The spiral staircase and one-of-a-kind Vodkarella are trademarks of the establishment, which is always bursting at the seams. Regulars include suits, students, and anyone who doesn't mind involuntary body contact.

Im Bahnhofsviertel liegt zwischen Spielhöllen und Dönerbuden das wunderbare Café Kosmos. Es ist insgesamt sehr „unmünchnerisch", und das nicht nur, weil unter anderem Hamburger Bier ausgeschenkt wird, zu einem mehr als fairen Preis. Die Wendeltreppe und die einzigartige Vodkarella sind Markenzeichen des immer aus allen Nähten platzenden Lokals. Anzugträger und Studenten, und alle, die nichts gegen unfreiwilligen Körperkontakt haben, sind hier Stammgäste.

CLUBS,
LOUNGES
+BARS

EAT THE RICH

Heßstraße 90 // Maxvorstadt
Tel.: +49 (0)89 18 59 82
www.eattherich.de

Tue–Thu 7 pm to 1 am
Fri–Sat 7 pm to 3 am

U2 Theresienstraße

Prices: $$

MAP N° **60**

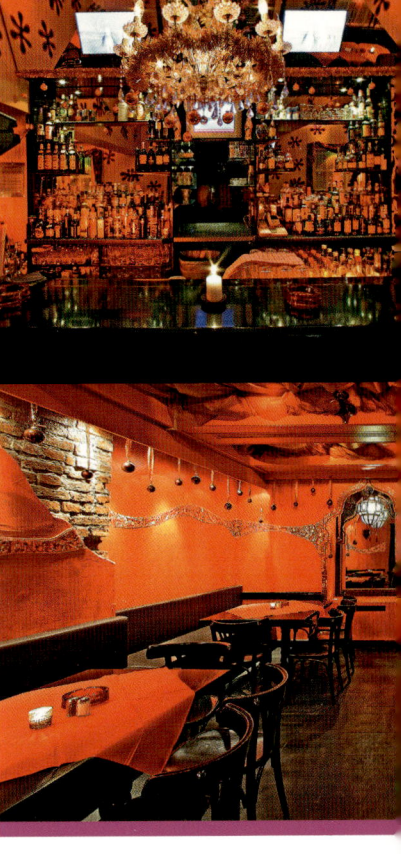

The things these wildly decorated walls have seen: romantic dinner dates, wild parties, legendary post-Oktoberfest bashes. The Eat, as the bar is affectionately called, is an institution in Munich's nightlife. It has been jam-packed every weekend for 15 years, with the atmosphere kicking into high gear by midnight. Once you've made it inside, you don't want to leave—and that's due in large part to the always-cheerful wait staff and bartenders.

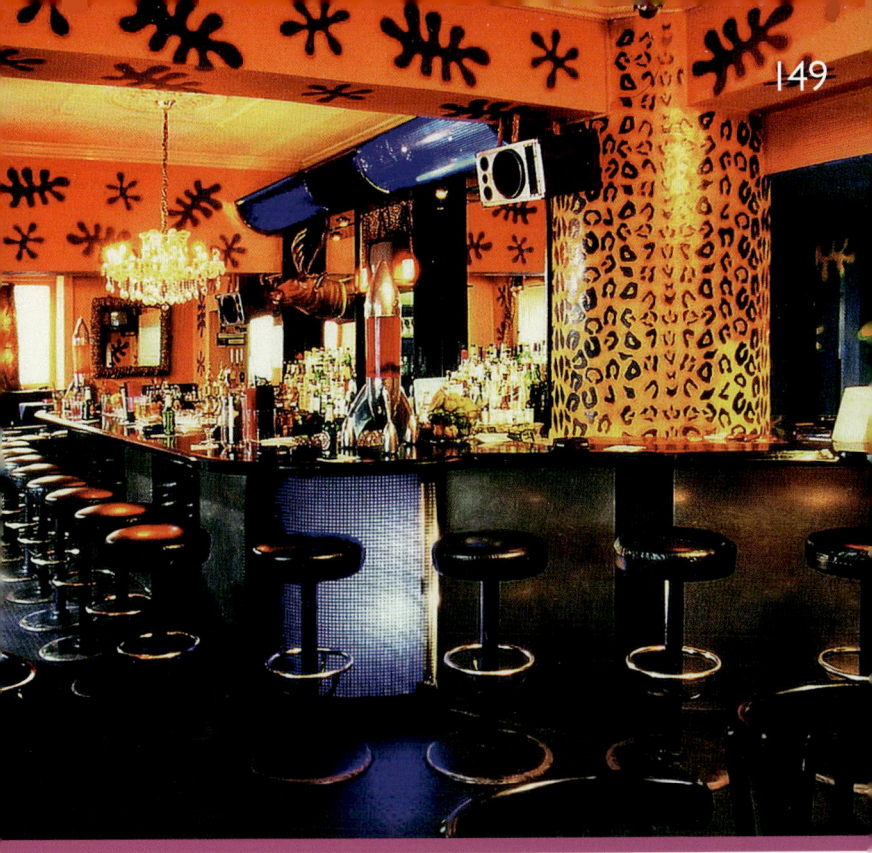

Was haben die wild dekorierten Wände nicht schon alles gesehen: romantische Dinner-Dates, wilde Partys, legendäre After-Wiesn-Sausen. Das Eat, so wird die Bar liebevoll genannt, ist eine Institution im Münchner Nachtleben. Seit über 15 Jahren ist es hier Wochenende für Wochenende gerammelt voll, die Stimmung gegen Mitternacht am Siedepunkt. Wer einmal drin ist, mag nicht mehr gehen. Und das liegt vor allem an den immer gut gelaunten Kellnern und Barmännern.

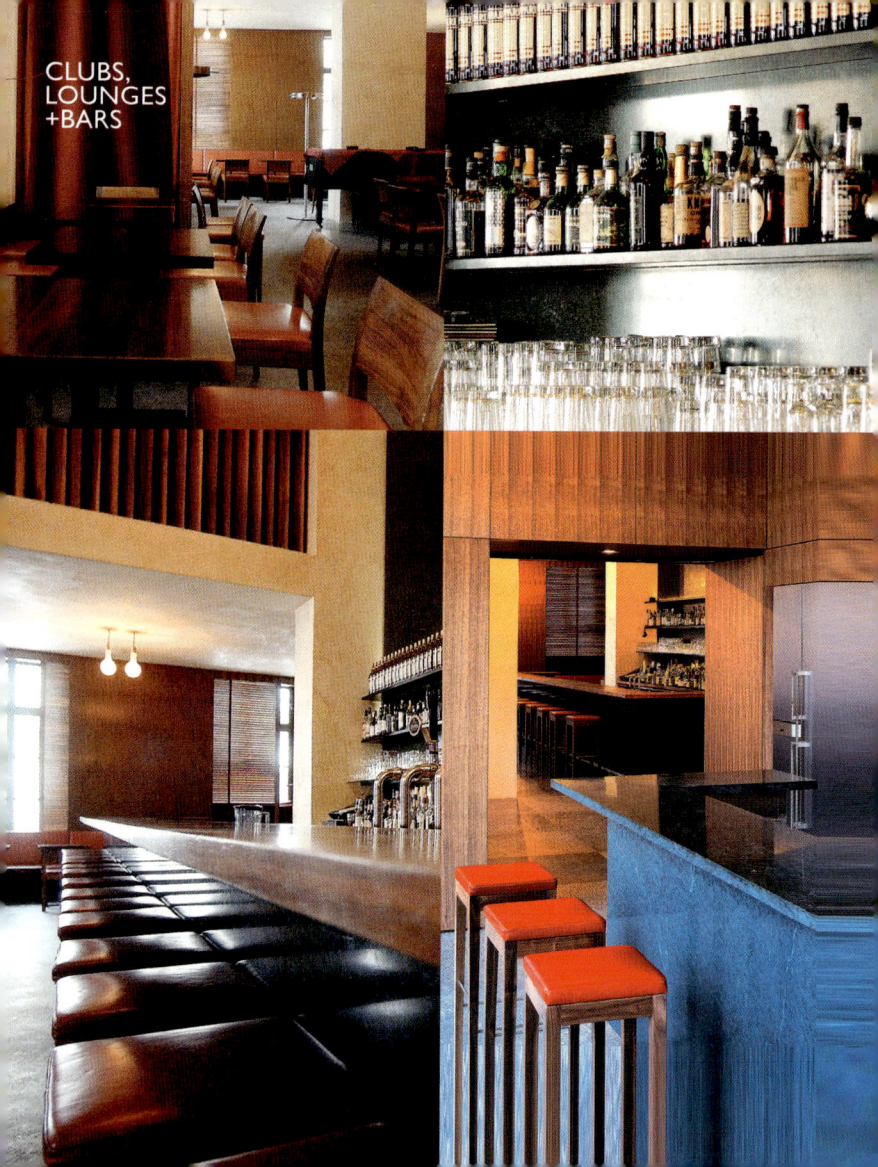

CLUBS,
LOUNGES
+BARS

SCHUMANN'S BAR
AM HOFGARTEN

Odeonsplatz 6–7 // Maxvorstadt
Tel.: +49 (0)89 22 90 60
www.schumanns.de

Mon–Fri 8 am to 3 am
Sat–Sun 6 pm to 3 am

U3–6 Odeonsplatz

Prices: $$$

KAREN WEBB'S SPECIAL TIP
Some call it the cliché of a bar—for me it is one of the best in the city!

Charles Schumann is the coolest cat in town. There's no other way to put it. The legendary bartender of international fame stands for old-school (cocktail) refinement. This makes his bar at the Hofgarten an absolute must for any status-conscious connoisseur. Early on, Schumann's was a regular gathering place for intellectuals, while today it is frequented by high society. A visit to this institution is an experience in itself.

Charles Schumann ist die coolste Sau der Stadt. Anders kann man es nicht ausdrücken. Die international bekannte Barkeeper-Legende steht für (Trink-)Kultur der alten Schule. Seine Bar am Hofgarten gehört daher zum Pflichtprogramm für alle standesbewussten Genießer. In seinen Anfängen war das Schumann's ein ausgemachter Intellektuellentreff, heute gibt sich hier die High Society die Klinke in die Hand. Ein Besuch in dieser Institution ist ein Erlebnis.

MAP N° 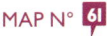 61

HIGHLIGHTS

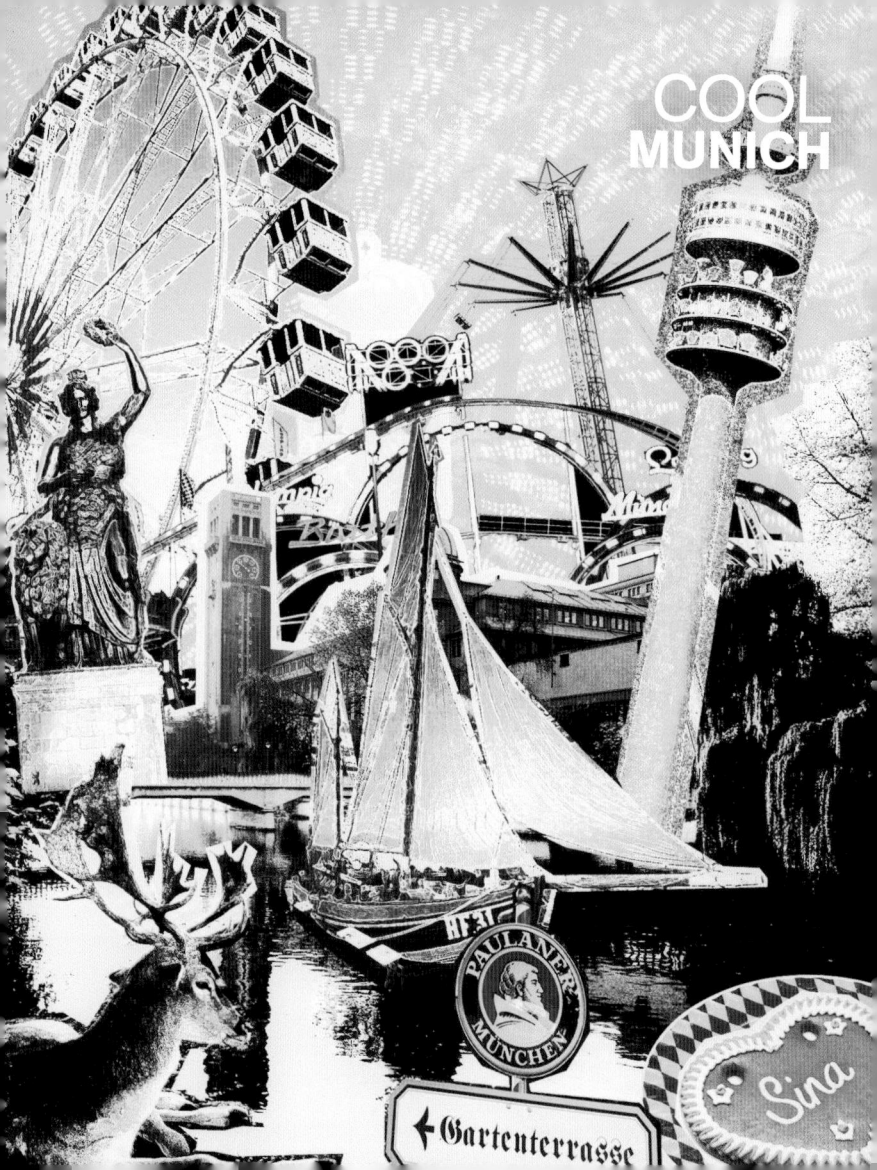

COOL
MUNICH

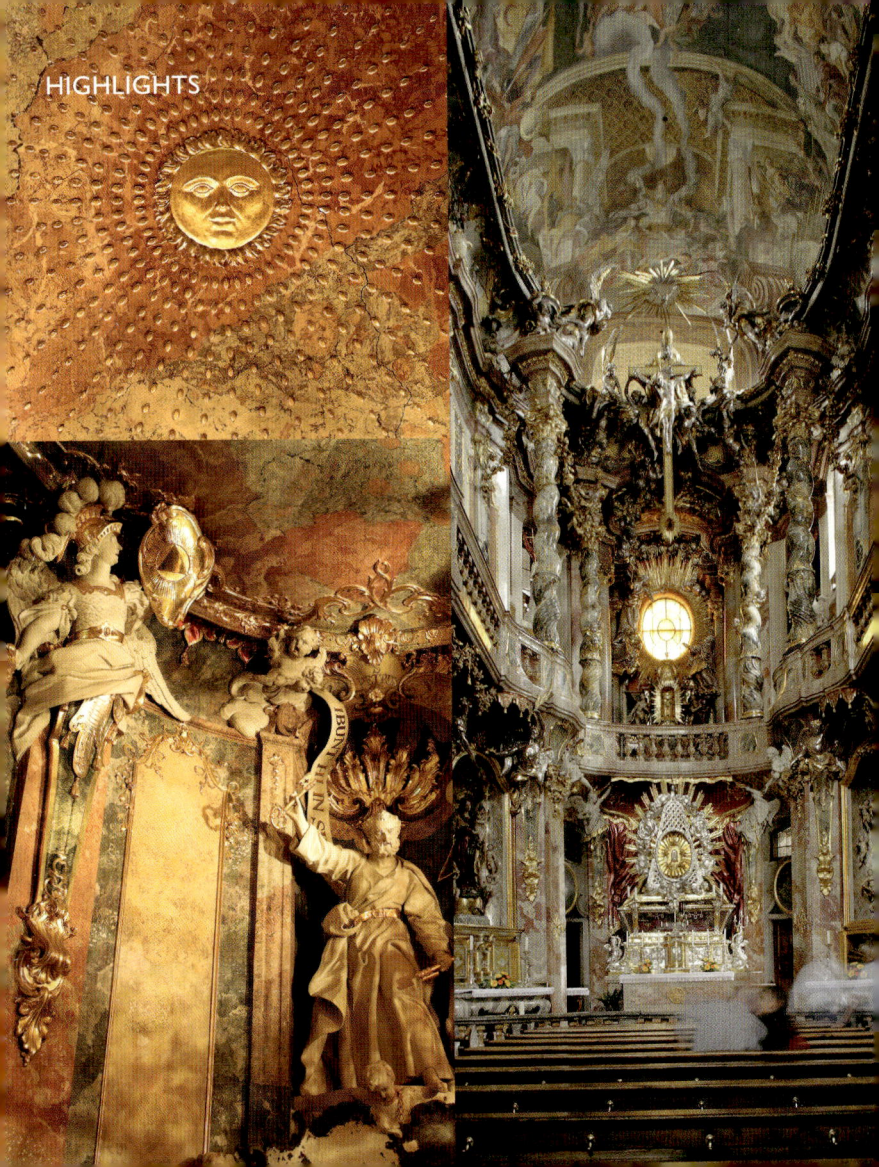

ASAMKIRCHE

Sendlinger Straße 34 // Altstadt
Tel.: +49 (0)89 23 68 79 89

U1, U2, U3, U6, U7
Tram 16, 17, 18, 27 Sendlinger Tor

If the Asam brothers had had their way, the church originally called
St. Johann Nepomuk, built between 1733 and 1746, would be a private
chapel. From their house on the neighboring property they could look
directly at the high altar. But they yielded to protests and opened the
Late Baroque wonder to the public, after all. Integrated into the line of
house fronts, to this day the little church with the grandiose interior is
something very special.

Nach dem Willen der Gebrüder Asam sollte die 1733–1746 von
ihnen in Eigeninitiative erbaute Kirche (ursprünglich St. Johann
Nepomuk genannt) eine Privatkapelle sein. Von ihrem Wohnhaus
auf dem angrenzenden Grundstück konnten sie direkt auf den
Hochaltar blicken. Nach Protesten machten sie das spätbarocke
Wunderwerk doch der Öffentlichkeit zugänglich. Bis heute ist diese
in die Häuserfassaden integrierte Kirche mit dem pompösen
Innenleben etwas ganz Besonderes.

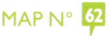 MAP N° 62

VALENTIN-KARLSTADT-MUSÄUM

Tal 50 // Altstadt
Tel.: +49 (0)89 22 32 66
www.valentin-musaeum.de

Mon–Tue, Thu 11.01 am to 5.29 pm
Fri–Sat 11.01 am to 5.59 pm
Sun 10.01 am to 5.59 pm
Special program:
every first Fri, open until 9.59 pm

S1–8, Tram 16, 18 Isartor

MAP N° 63

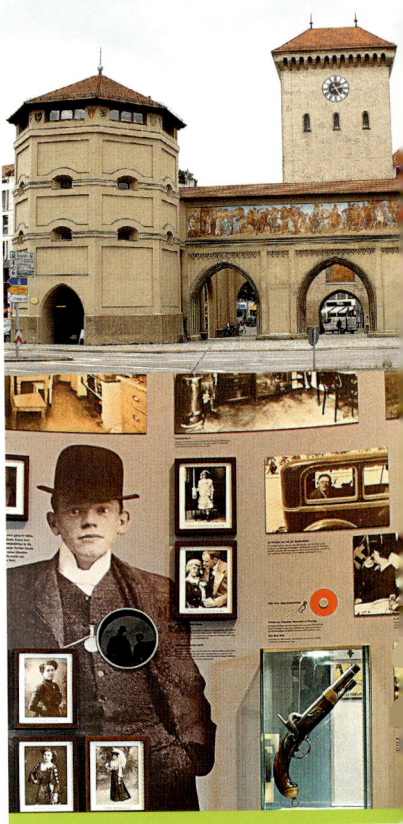

This wonderful museum is dedicated to one of Munich's most brilliant sons and his stage partner of many years, Liesl Karlstadt. The career of multimedia satirist, cabaret artist, and actor Karl Valentin is played out in the towers of the Isartor. During Valentin's lifetime Bertolt Brecht, Kurt Tucholsky, and Thomas Mann were fans of his acerbic humor. Don't miss the turret room on the 3rd floor, done up in turn-of-the-century style!

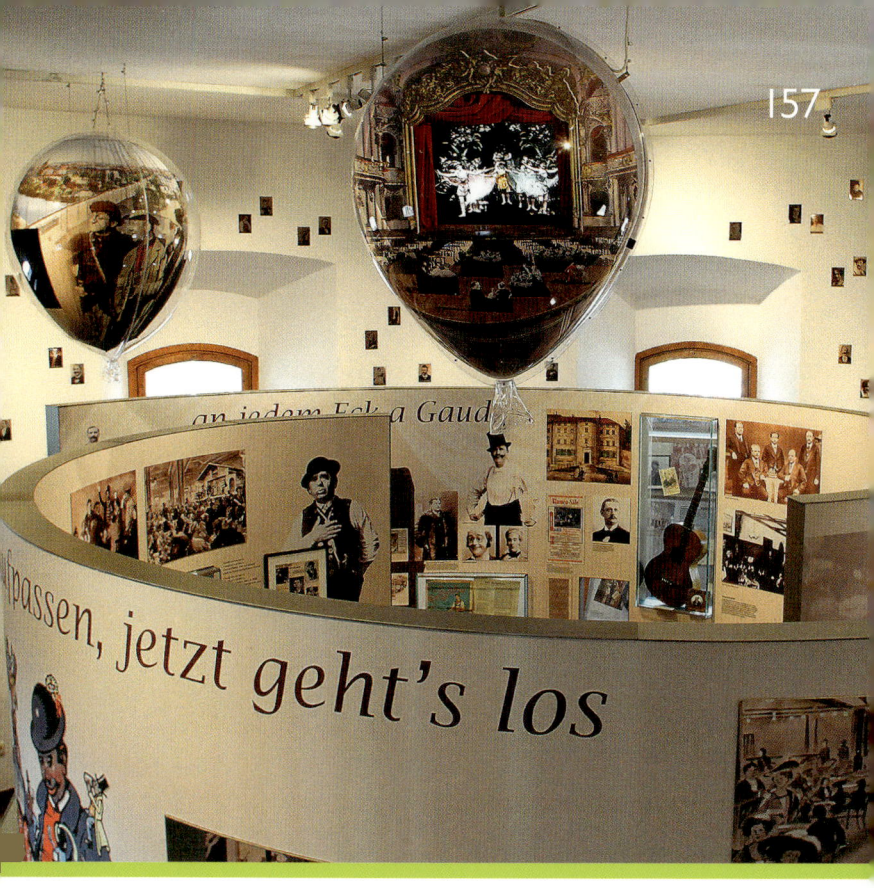

Dieses wunderbare Museum ist einem der genialsten Söhne der Stadt und seiner langjährigen Bühnenpartnerin Liesl Karlstadt gewidmet. In den Türmen des Isartors wird die Laufbahn des multimedialen Satirikers, Kabarettisten und Schauspielers nachvollzogen. Bertolt Brecht, Kurt Tucholsky und Thomas Mann waren zu Lebzeiten Fans von Valentins schneidendem Humor. Das im Stil der Jahrhundertwende eingerichtete Turmstüberl im 3. Stock muss man gesehen haben!

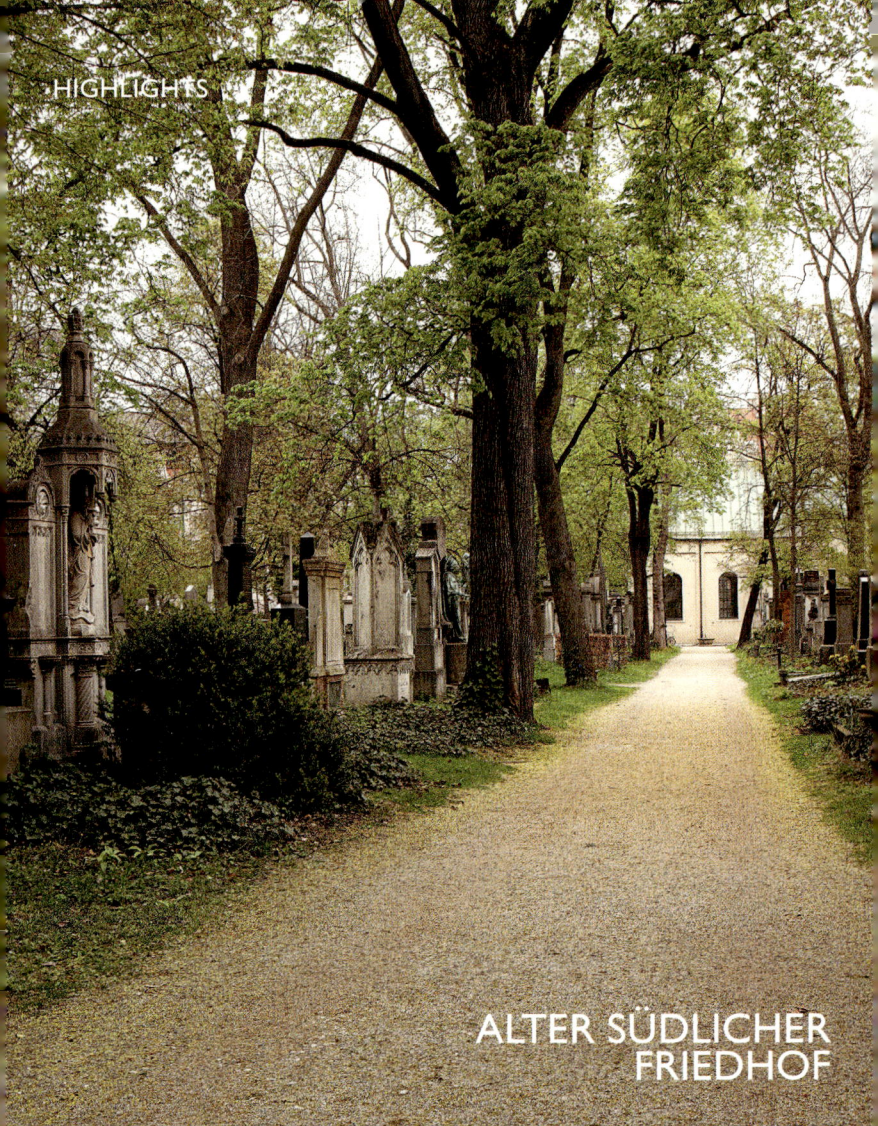

ALTER SÜDLICHER
FRIEDHOF

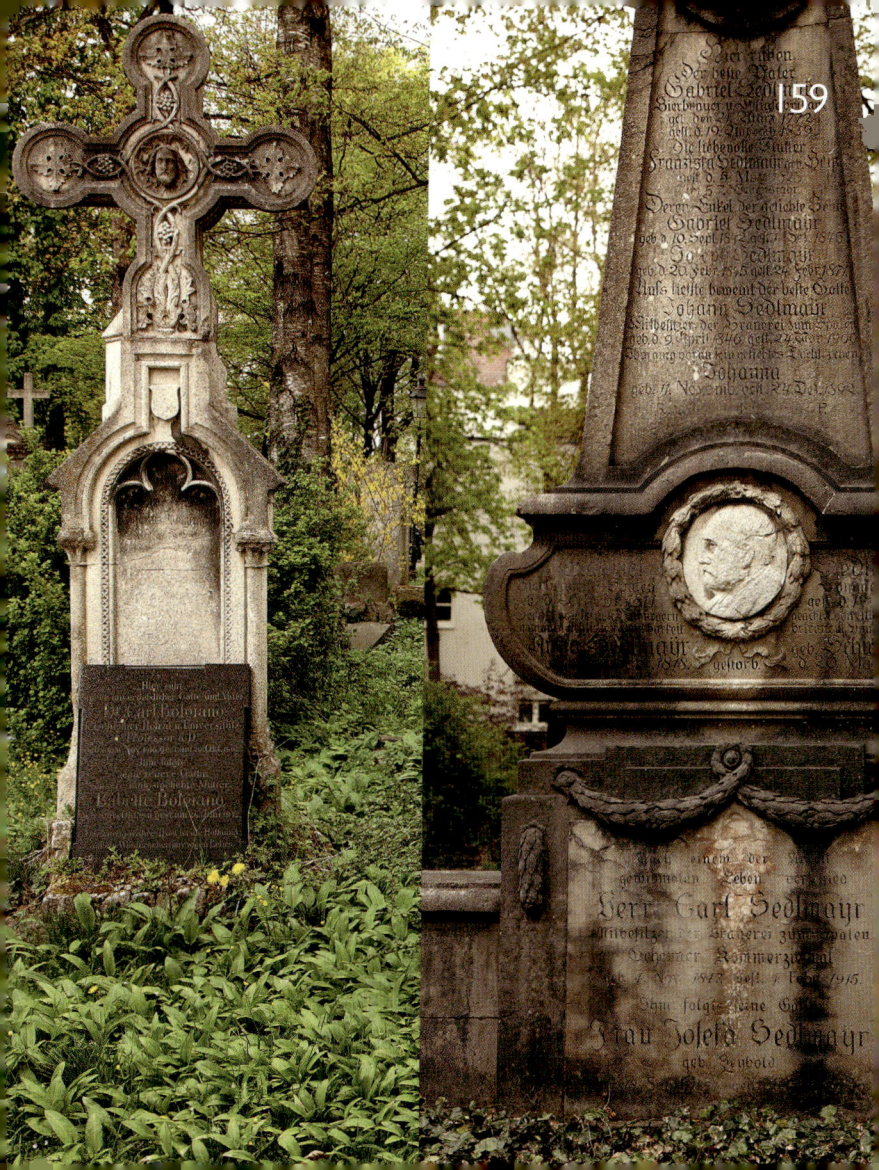

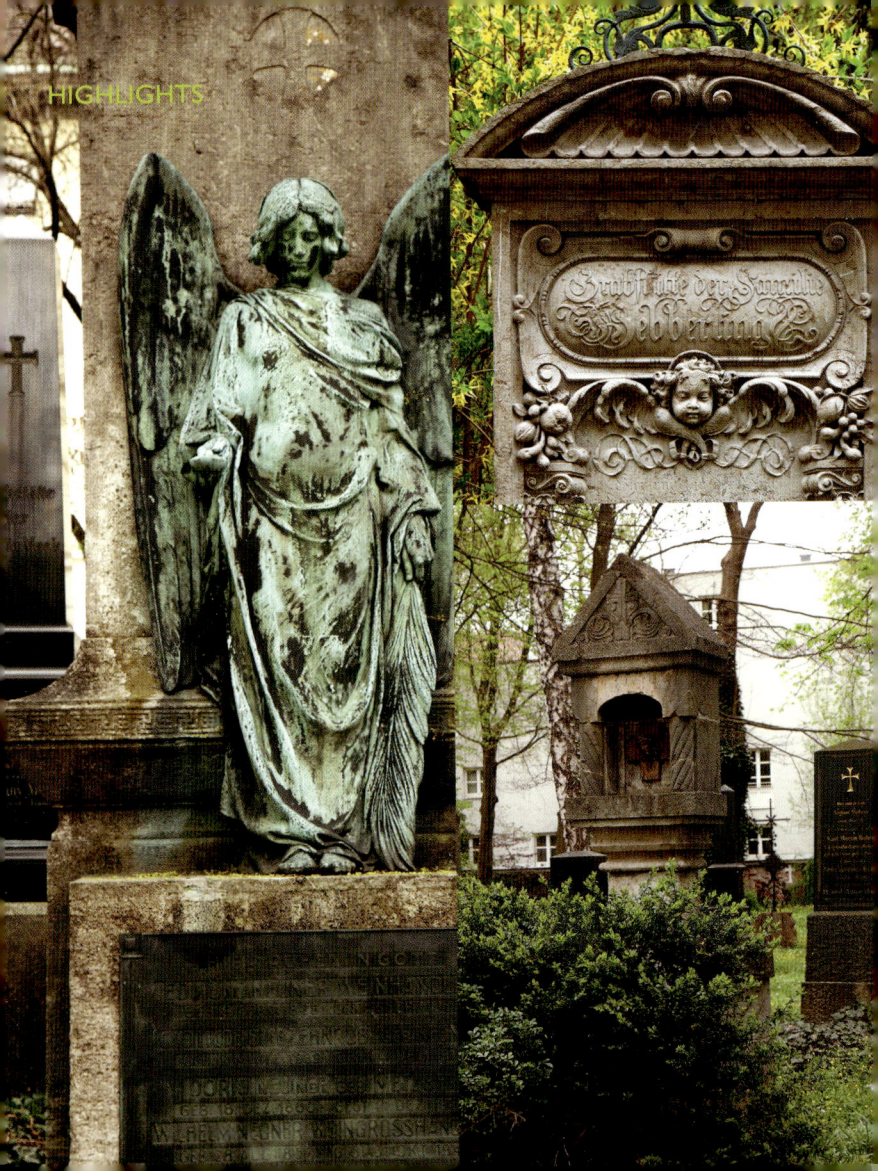

ALTER SÜDLICHER FRIEDHOF

Thalkirchnerstraße // Isarvorstadt

U1, U2, U3, U6, U7
Tram 16, 17, 18, 27
Sendlinger Tor

A magical place with special charm: the Plague Cemetery. That's what Duke Albrecht V ordered built beyond the gates of the city in 1563. No one has been buried in the old cemetery with the coffin-shaped outline since 1944. Many prominent residents of Munich are buried here, including Leo von Klenze, Friedrich von Gärtner, and Carl Spitzweg. Weathered and overgrown in places, the graves are hauntingly beautiful, historically interesting, and often entertaining.

Ein magischer Ort mit besonderem Charme: der Pestfriedhof. Als solchen ließ ihn Herzog Albrecht V. 1563 vor den Toren der Stadt anlegen. Auf dem alten Friedhof mit dem sargförmigen Grundriss wird seit 1944 nicht mehr bestattet. Viele prominente Münchner liegen hier begraben: Leo von Klenze, Friedrich von Gärtner oder Carl Spitzweg. Die teilweise überwucherten, verwitterten Grabstätten sind verwunschen schön, historisch interessant und oft unterhaltsam.

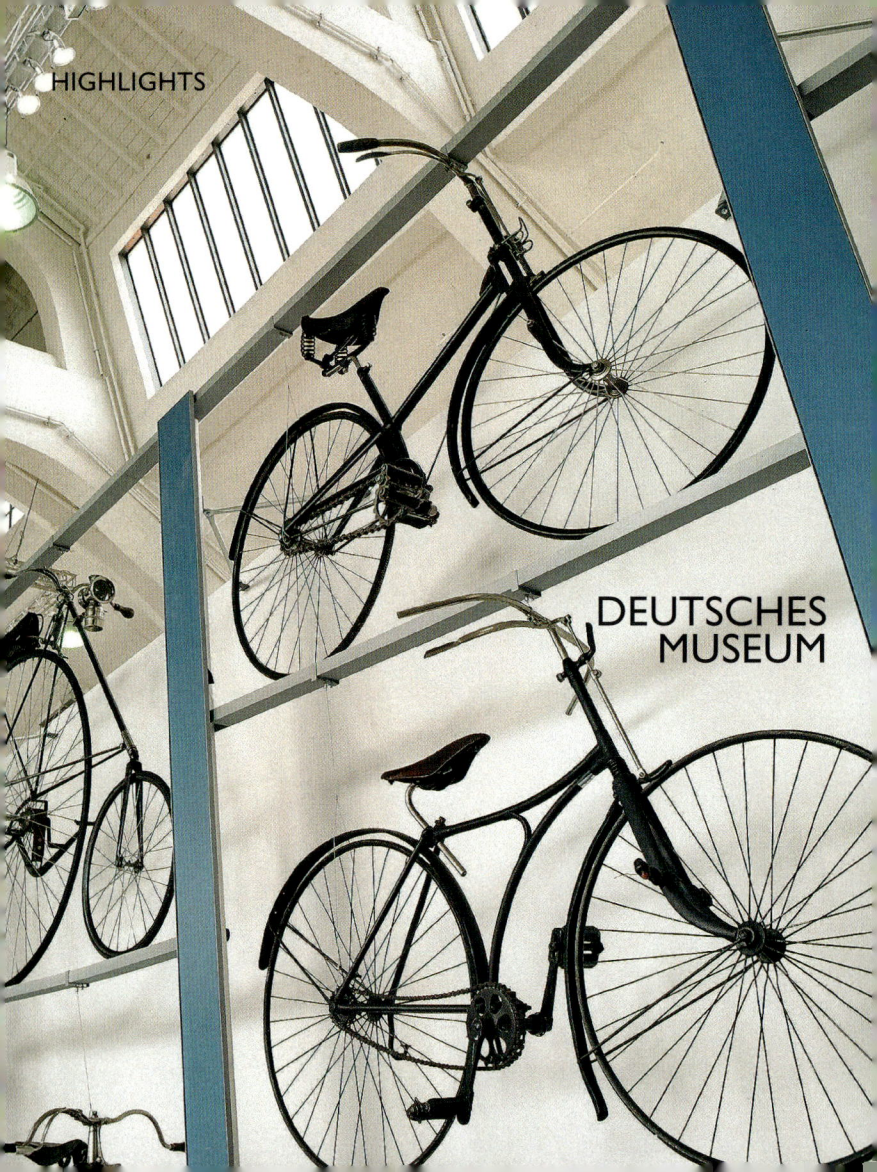

DEUTSCHES
MUSEUM

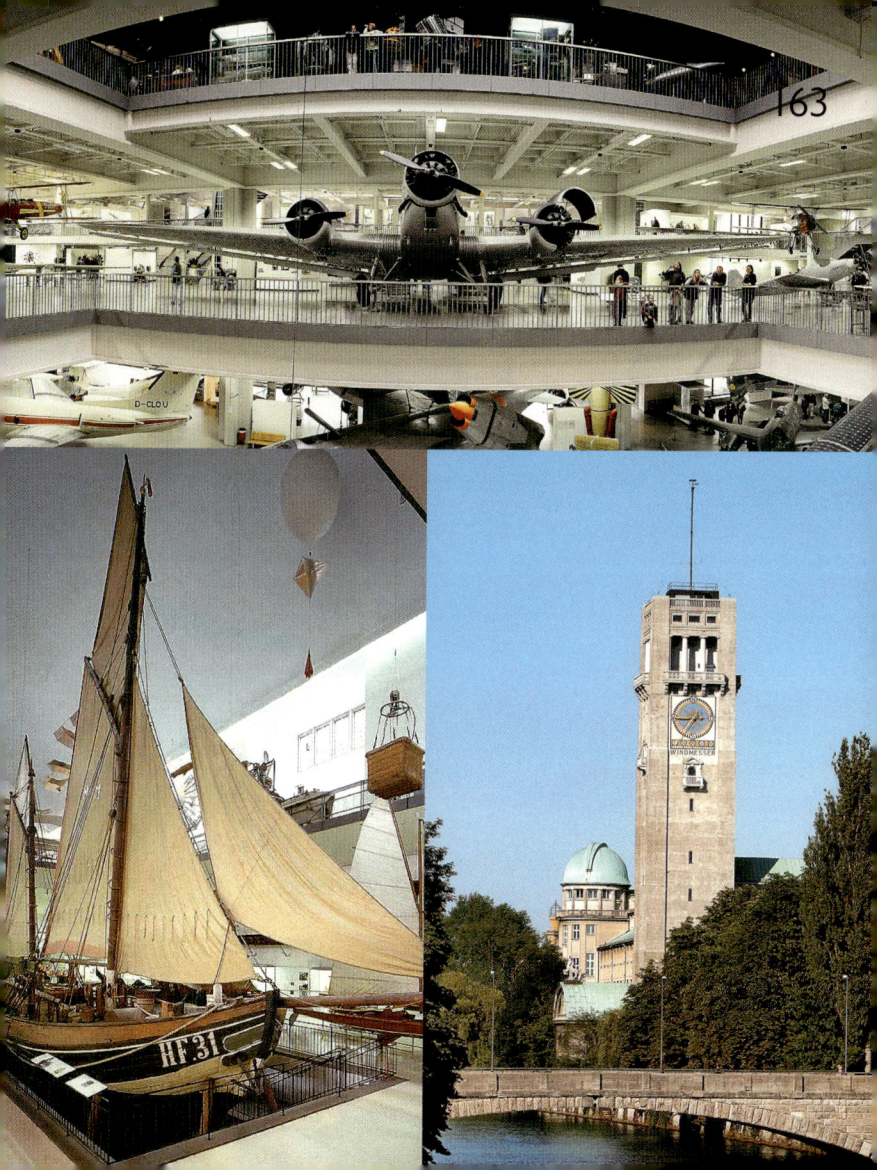

DEUTSCHES MUSEUM

Museumsinsel 1 // Isarvorstadt
Tel.: +49 (0)89 2 17 91
www.deutsches-museum.de

Daily 9 am to 5 pm

Tram 16 Deutsches Museum
S1–8, Tram 18 Isartor

MAP N° 65

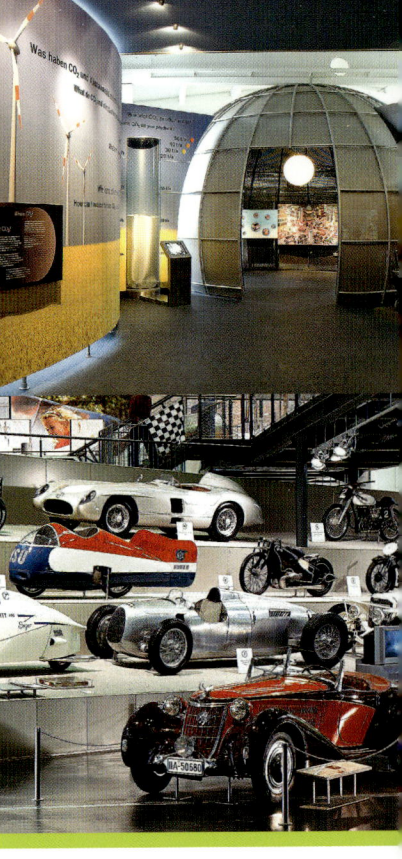

One of the world's most famous science museums stands on what used to be called Coal Island. It was founded by Oskar von Miller in 1903 as the "German Association Museum of Masterpieces of Science and Technology." About one fourth of the collection of some 100,000 objects is displayed in the exhibits. Special highlights include the Wright Brothers' first motor-ized flying machine and the first programmable computer.

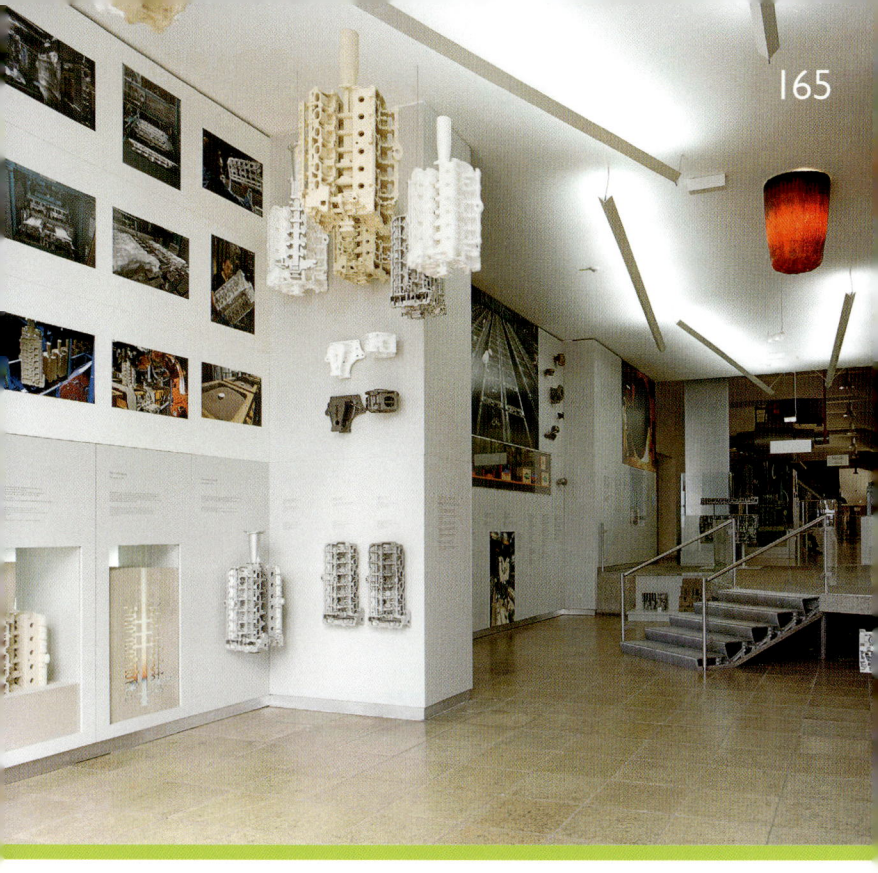

Auf einer ehemaligen Kohleninsel in der Isar steht eines der berühm-testen naturwissenschaftlichen Museen der Welt. 1903 wurde es als „Deutscher Verein Museum von Meisterwerken der Naturwissenschaft und Technik" von Oskar von Miller gegründet. Von den etwa 100 000 Sammlungsobjekten ist rund ein Viertel in den Ausstellungen zu sehen. Zu den besonderen Highlights gehören das erste Motorflugzeug der Gebrüder Wright und der erste programmgesteuerte Computer.

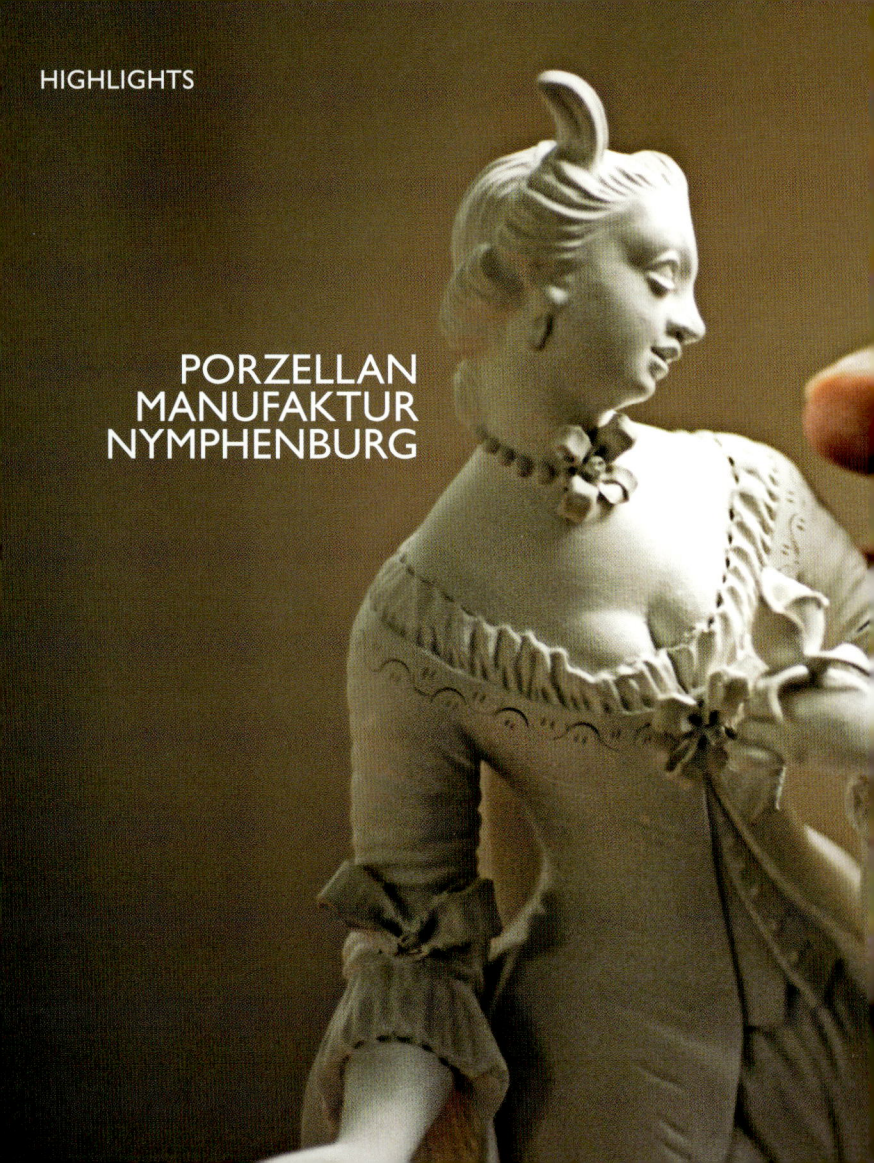

PORZELLAN
MANUFAKTUR
NYMPHENBURG

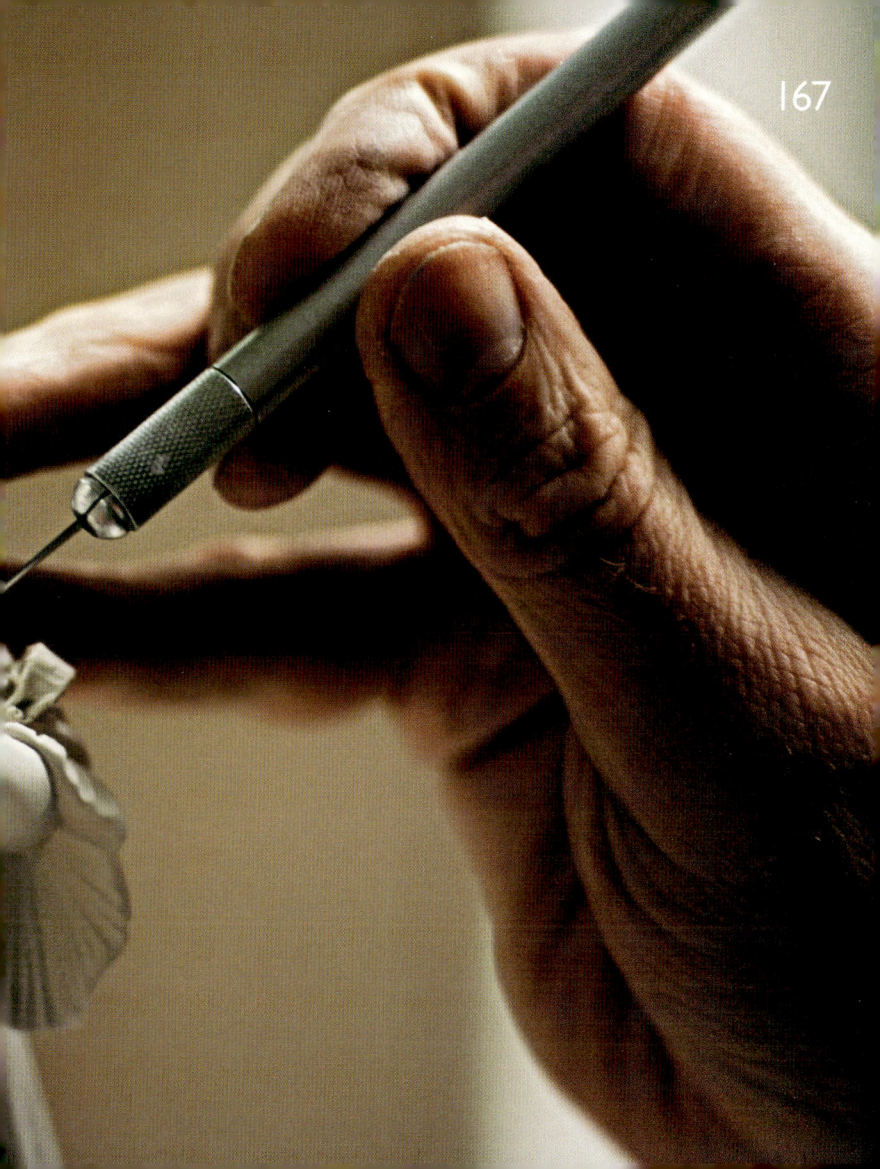

PORZELLAN MANUFAKTUR NYMPHENBURG

Nördliches Schloßrondell 8
Neuhausen-Nymphenburg
Tel.: +49 (0)89 1 79 19 70
www.nymphenburg.com

Mon–Fri 10 am to 5 pm

Tram 17 Dall'Armistraße

Prices: $$$$

MAP N° 66

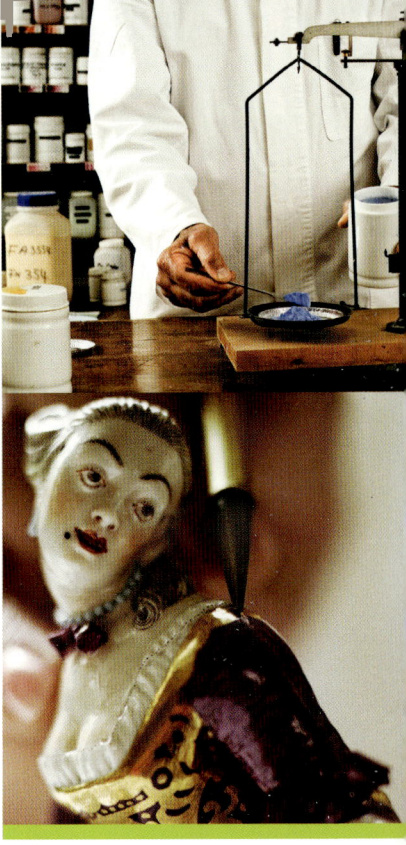

Although the china from the Nymphenburg Porcelain Manufactory is innovative both in terms of shape and style, it is still made using artisan methods that have remained unchanged since the 18th century. The time-consuming proprietary methods once used to produce porcelain for the Wittelsbach dynasty continue to be used today to handcraft dinnerware, figurines, and objets d'art. A tour behind the scenes is available for those who want to get a glimpse of the manufacturing process.

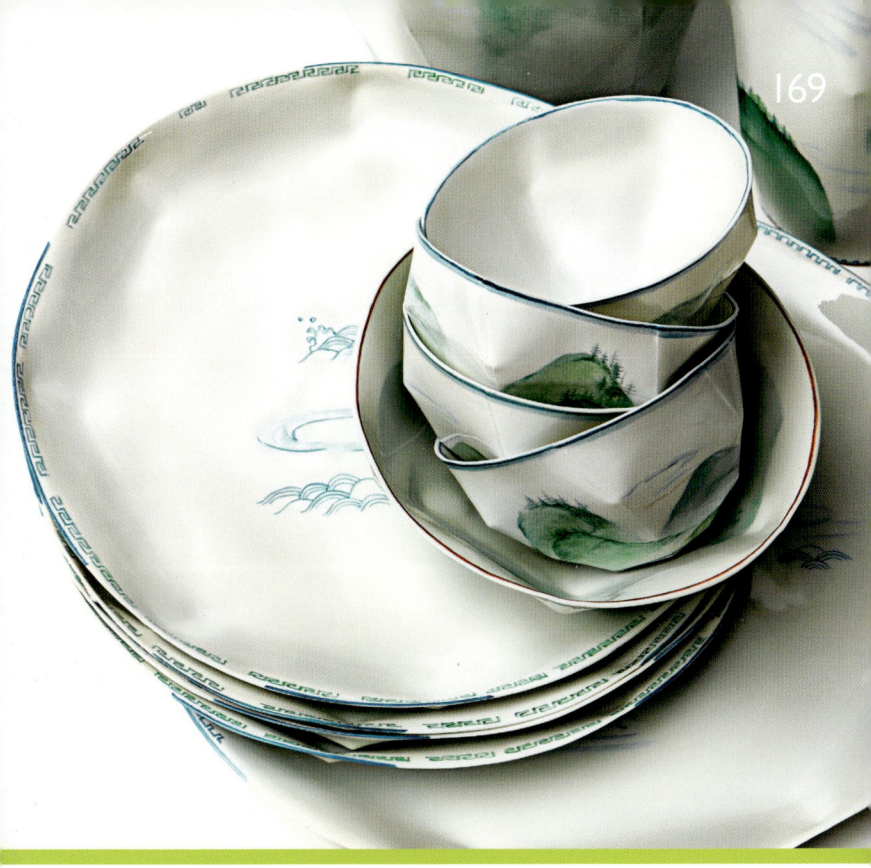

Das Porzellan aus der Manufaktur Nymphenburg ist zwar innovativ in Form und Stil, wird aber mit handwerklichen Methoden hergestellt, die seit dem 18. Jahrhundert unverändert sind. Wie damals das hauseigene Porzellan für die Wittelsbacher produziert wurde, entstehen auch heute noch Service, Figuren und Objekte in aufwendiger Handarbeit. Wer gern hinter die Kulissen der Manufaktur schauen möchte, kann den Herstellungsprozess auch bei einer Führung erkunden.

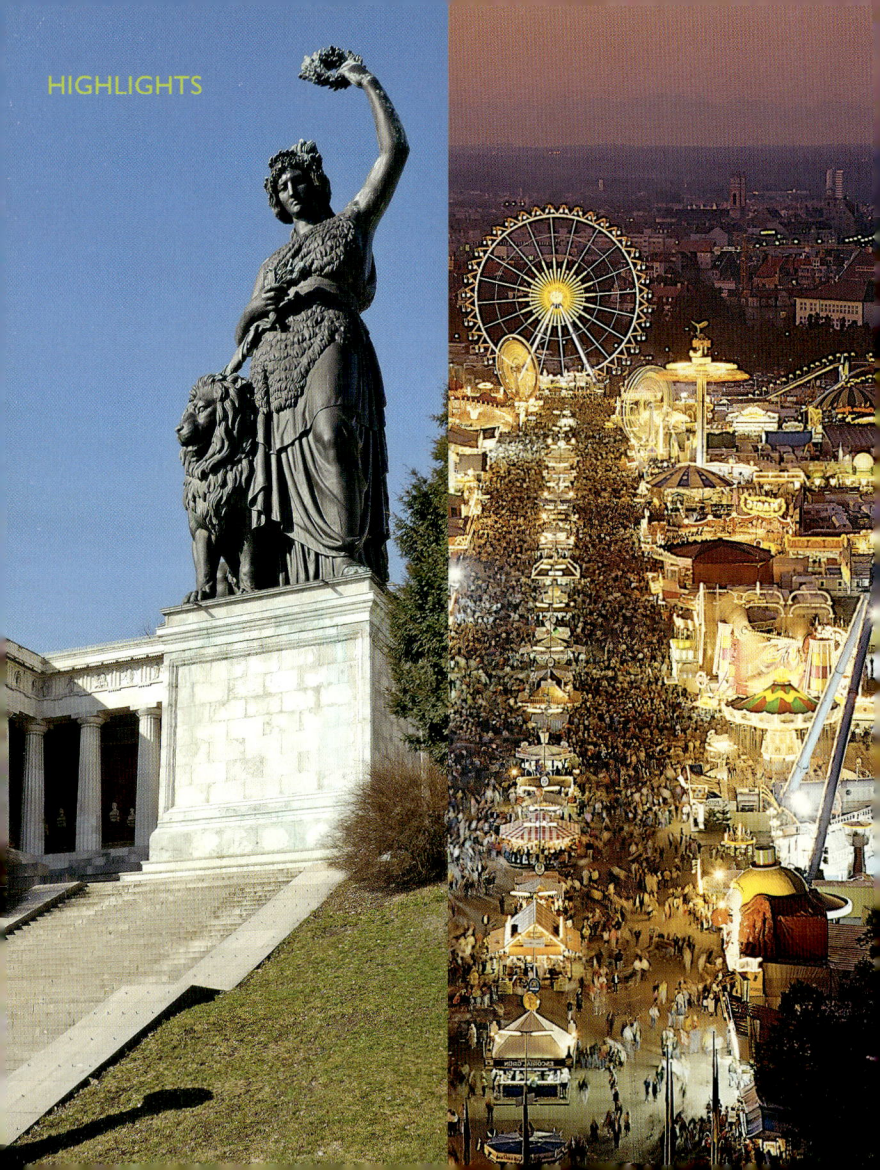

Bavariaring // Ludwigsvorstadt

Bavaria: Apr–Oct daily 9 am to 6 pm
during Oktoberfest until 8 pm

U4, U5 Theresienwiese or
Schwanthalerhöhe

KAREN WEBB'S SPECIAL TIP

Once a year this is simply the place to be! When Miss Bavaria looks down at visitors from all around the world it's the time of the Oktoberfest!

It all began in 1810 with the marriage of Crown Prince Ludwig to Princess Therese of Saxe-Hildburghausen. The public festivities with parades, dancing, and horse racing found great favor among the population—this was the birth of the largest fair in the world: Oktoberfest. Enthroned above it all stands the Bavaria, a monumental statue whose hollow interior you can climb by spiral staircase, backed by the Ruhmeshalle ("Hall of Glory"). Every visitor to Munich should pay a visit to "Miss Bavaria."

Alles begann 1810 mit der Vermählung Kronprinz Ludwigs mit Prinzessin Therese von Sachsen-Hildburghausen. Die öffentlichen Feierlichkeiten mit Paraden, Tanz und Pferderennen fanden großen Anklang in der Bevölkerung – das war die Geburtsstunde des größten Volksfests der Welt: des Oktoberfests. Darüber thront die monumentale, innen begehbare Bavaria, mit der Ruhmeshalle im Rücken. Jeder Münchenbesucher sollte der bronzenen „Miss Bayern" einen Besuch abstatten.

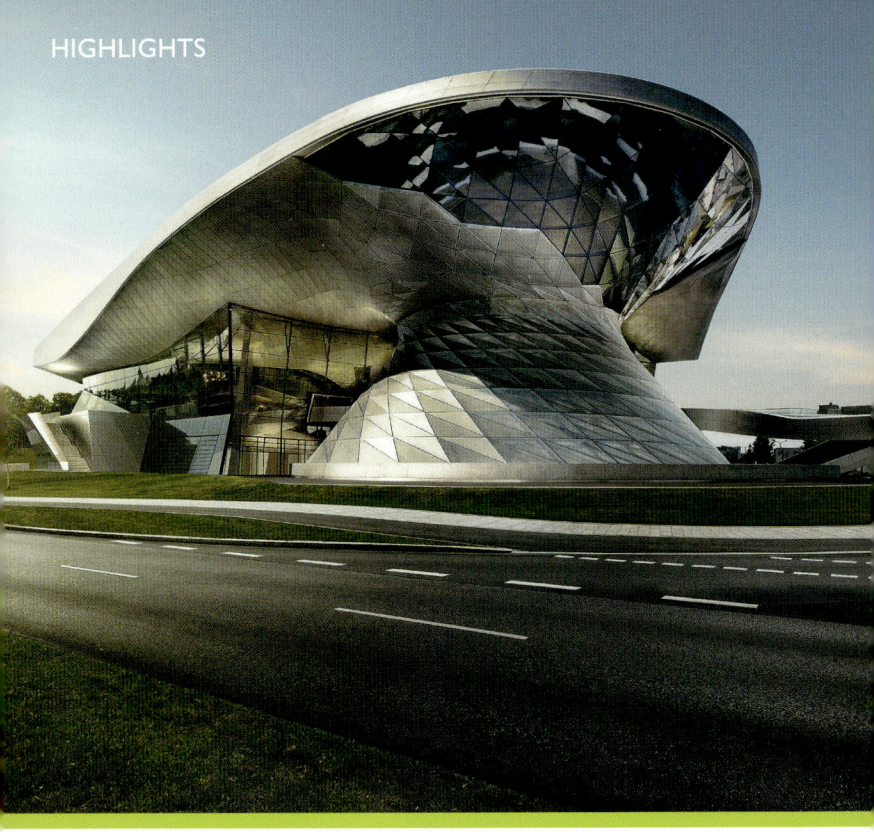

Designed by Coop Himmelb(l)au, BMW Welt is the city's most architecturally spectacular building. Since 2007 the futuristic construct is at once showroom, event headquarters, and signboard of the Bavarian automobile manufacturer. Delivery of the vehicle to its new owner is staged here as a spectacular public happening. The calendar features concerts, parties, and other events in addition to permanent exhibits about the BMW brand.

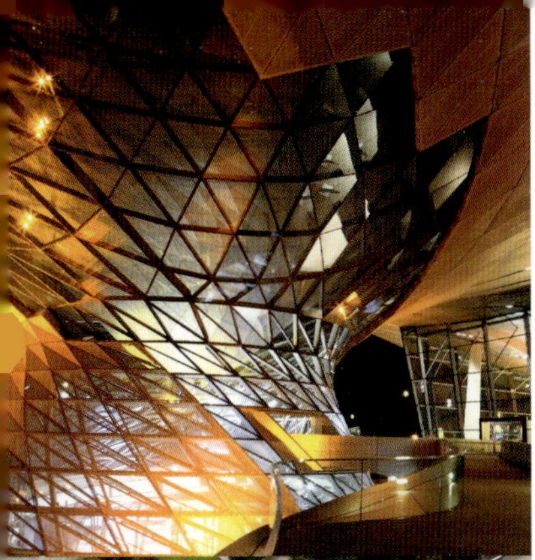

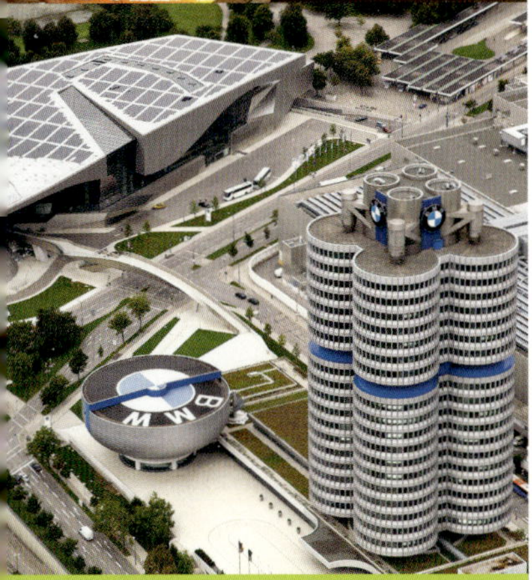

BMW WELT

Am Olympiapark 1 // Milbertshofen
Tel.: +49 (0)1802 11 88 22
www.bmw-welt.com

Daily 9 am to 6 pm

U3 Olympiazentrum

Die von Coop Himmelb(l)au entworfene BMW Welt ist das architektonisch spektakulärste Gebäude der Stadt. Seit 2007 ist das futuristische Konstrukt Showroom, Event-Zentrale und Aushängeschild des bayerischen Automobilherstellers. Hier wird die Übergabe des Autos an seinen neuen Besitzer als spektakuläres Happening öffentlich inszeniert. Neben Dauerausstellungen zur Marke beinhaltet das Programm Konzerte, Partys und andere Veranstaltungen.

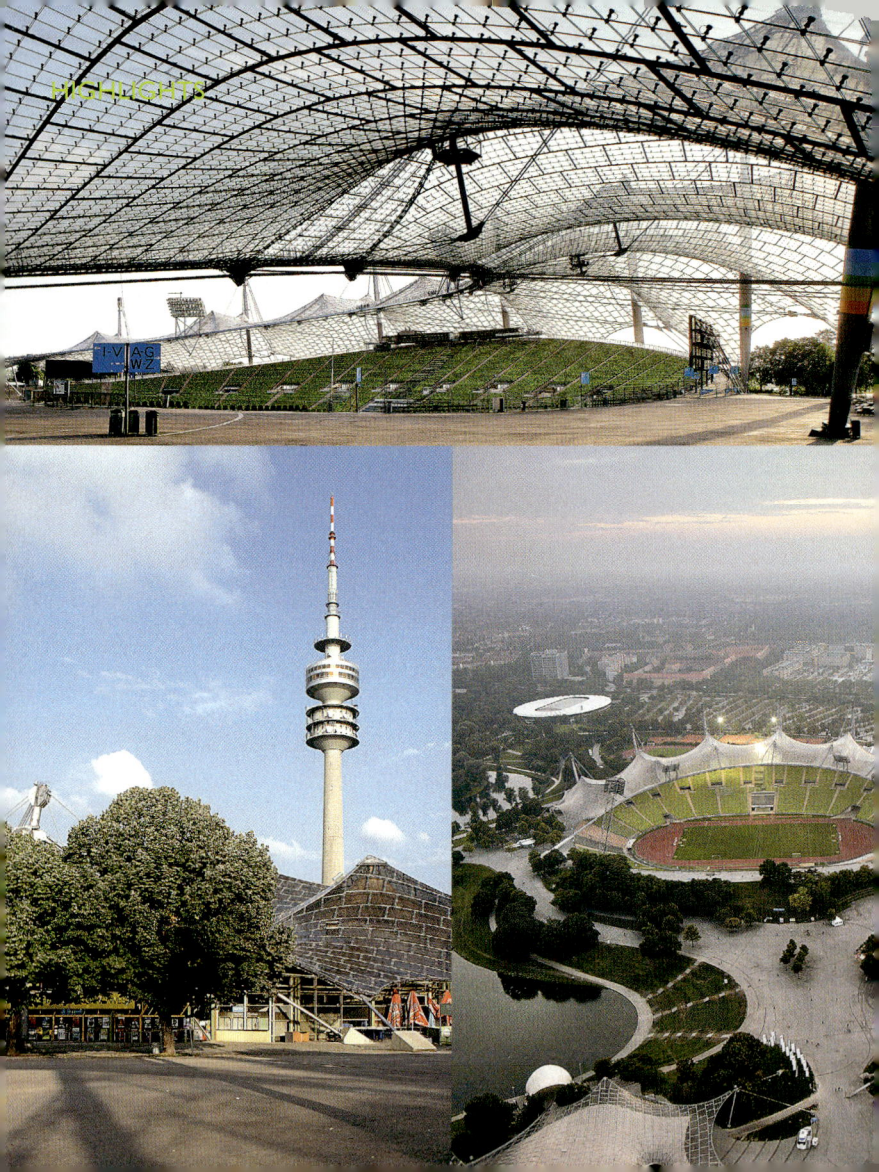

OLYMPIAPARK

Spiridon-Louis-Ring 21 // Neuhausen
Tel.: +49 (0)89 3 06 70
www.olympiapark.de

U3 Olympiazentrum

Built on top of wartime debris, this park is often undervalued even by the locals. At a height of 1,850 ft. atop the Olympiaberg you have a magnificent view of the grounds and the city. There are special tours to acquaint you with the famous architecture or the events of the 1972 Olympic Games. Have a well-grounded meal at the trendy beer garden München 72, or treat yourself to an uplifting dining experience at the revolving restaurant 181. You'll find an odd place of contemplation in the chapel of the Russian hermit Timofei.

Der auf Kriegsschutt errichtete Park wird selbst von Einheimischen gerne unterschätzt. Vom 564 m hohen Olympiaberg genießt man einen spektakulären Blick über das Gelände und die Stadt. Spezielle Touren vermitteln die berühmte Architektur oder die Ereignisse rund um Olympia 1972. Im schicken Biergarten München 72 stärkt man sich bodenständig, im Drehrestaurant 181 „abgehoben". Ein kurioser Ort der Einkehr ist die Kappelle des russischen Eremiten Timofej.

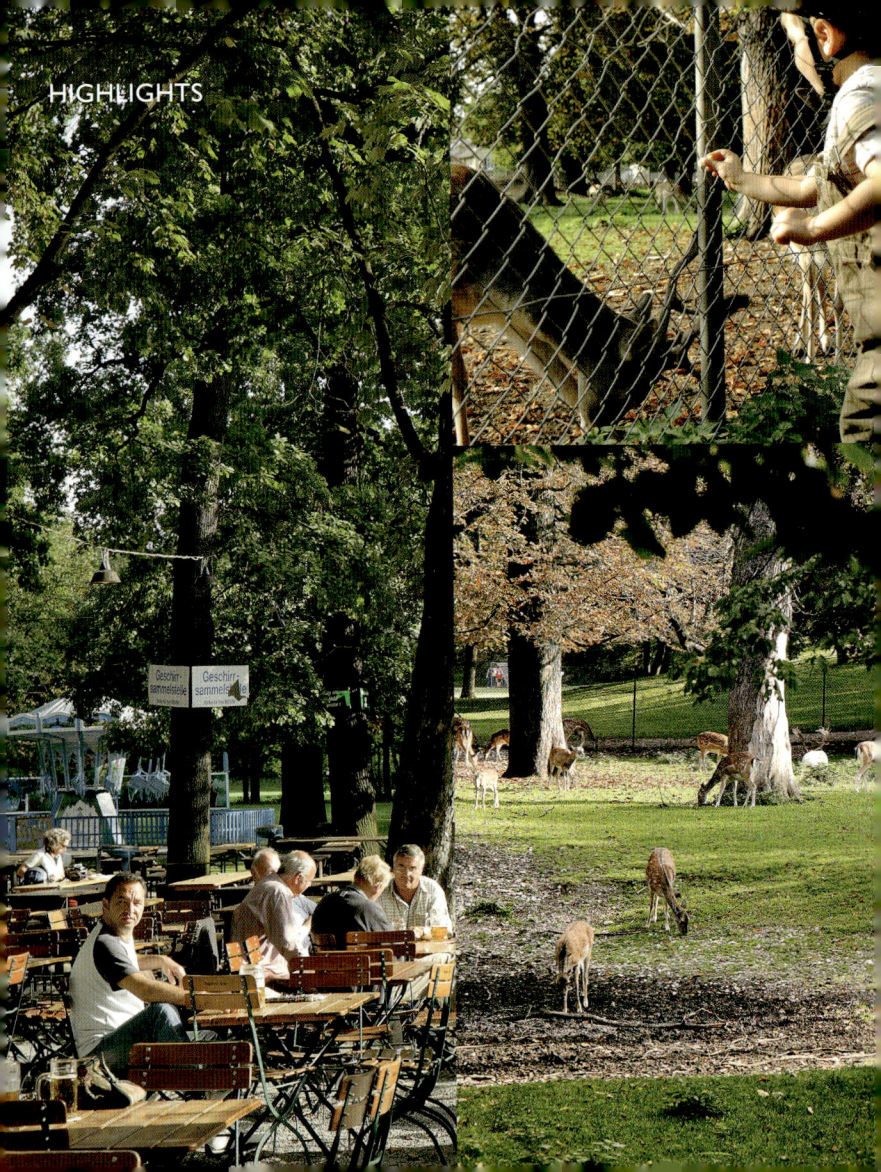

Hirschgarten 1 // Nymphenburg
Tel.: +49 (0)89 17 99 91 19
www.hirschgarten.de

Mon–Sun 9 am to midnight
S1–6, S8 Hirschgarten
Tram 16, 17 Kriemhildenstraße

As soon as it's warm enough Bavarians are drawn to the beer garden. Even knowing this, the sight of almost 8,000 people gathering to enjoy a mug of beer under the open sky can range from unusual to overwhelming. Over the fence a deer bellows and people at the next table are unpacking their picnic lunch—by Bavarian tradition you can bring your own food to a beer garden. Welcome to the royal deer park! That's what Hirschgarten means, after all.

Sobald es warm genug ist, zieht es die Bayern in den Biergarten. Selbst wenn man das weiß, ist der Anblick von knapp 8 000 Menschen, die sich zum gemütlichen Biertrinken unter freiem Himmel einfinden, ungewöhnlich bis überwältigend. Nebenan röhren die Hirsche, jemand packt einen Tisch weiter gerade seine mitgebrachte Brotzeit aus – dass man sich sein Essen selbst mitbringen darf, gehört zur bayerischen Tradition. Willkommen im Königlichen Hirschgarten!

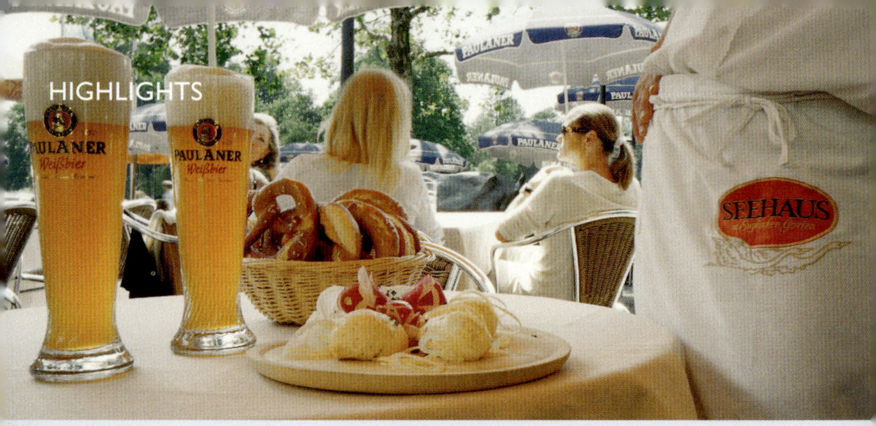

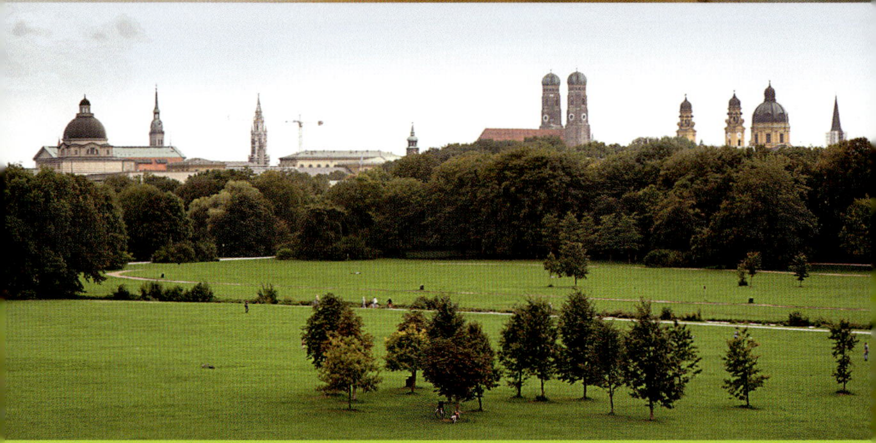

Munich's green lungs stretch over an area larger than New York's Central Park. Just behind the Haus der Kunst, river surfers ride the famous standing wave. Popular attractions include the beer garden at the Chinesischer Turm, the Seehaus, and the view from the Monopteros. Less well-known are the mini-Hofbräuhaus with the so-called ''doggie beer garden,'' the Japanese Teahouse and its tea ceremonies, or the opportunity to sponsor a park bench.

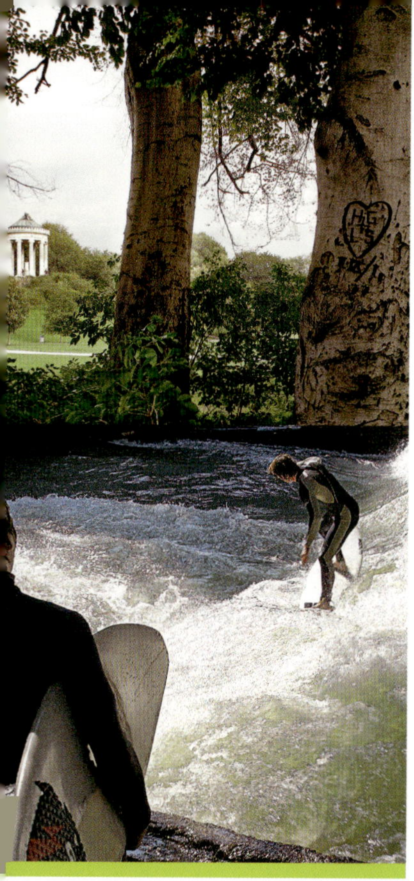

ENGLISCHER GARTEN

Schwabing

U3, U6 Universität, Giselastraße, or Münchner Freiheit

The trick is to keep breathing! There is no better place to relax and enjoy!

Münchens grüne Lunge erstreckt sich auf einer Fläche größer als der Central Park in New York. Gleich hinter dem Haus der Kunst reiten die Stadtsurfer die berühmte stehende Welle. Der Biergarten am Chinesischen Turm, das Seehaus und der Blick vom Monopteros sind ebenfalls bekannte Attraktionen. Weniger bekannt sind das auch als „Hundebiergarten" bezeichnete Minihofbräuhaus, das Japanische Teehaus mit seinen Teezeremonien oder die Möglichkeit, eine „Bank-Patenschaft" zu übernehmen.

BOGENHAUSEN
Today, this district is famous for being a very exclusive residential area with many beautiful Art Nouveau mansions. Also, it is home to the golden Friedensengel and the neoclassical Prinzregententheater.

HAIDHAUSEN
A beautiful historical district, with the so called Au ("meadow") by the river and a lot of green. Haidhausen used to be the craftsmen district—many of their former little houses are still intact, but now renovated and mostly unaffordable for "normal" people.

ISARVORSTADT
The most popular district for living, going out, and for seeing and being seen. It is made up of three quarters: the posh yet laid back and gay-friendly Glockenbachviertel and Gärtnerplatzviertel, and the cool Schlachthofviertel with the graffiti hall of fame.

LEHEL
A very sophisticated district with many impressive old (thoroughly renovated) buildings, the Prinzregenten-straße, and the city's "museum mile." The southern part of the Englischer Garten is part of Lehel.

LUDWIGSVORSTADT
Arguably the liveliest district in Munich—also because of the intriguing mix of red light vibe and multi cultural character in the Bahnhofsviertel, the quarter by the train station. The Theresienwiese, the site of the "Oktoberfest," makes it a major destination.

MAXVORSTADT
An amazing district, with a whole different, almost mediterranean vibe. The universities are located here, as well as several of the best galleries and, of course, museums. Great for sight-seeing, shopping, and chilling out.

ALTSTADT
This is the political, cultural, and commercial center of the city. Countless landmarks and important sights are to be found here, like the Frauenkirche, the Viktualienmarkt, and the infamous Hofbräuhaus.

SCHWABING
Schwabing is famous for the Englischer Garten, the numerous Art Nouveau buildings, and for its wild past. At the end of the 19th century it was the place to be for the painters of "Der Blaue Reiter," writers like Thomas Mann, and a host of artists, actors, and satirists.

SCHWABING-WEST
Schwabing's sister is just as beautiful, yet maybe more relaxed. Many artists used to live here, the poet Rainer Maria Rilke for example. The market at Elisabethplatz is a cosy and authentic alternative to the Viktualienmarkt in the city center.

SCHWANTHALERHÖHE
Also dubbed Westend, this district has seen a steady increase of popularity in the past years. The conversion of former industrial areas into residential space has brought change to the quarter.

COOL
MAP

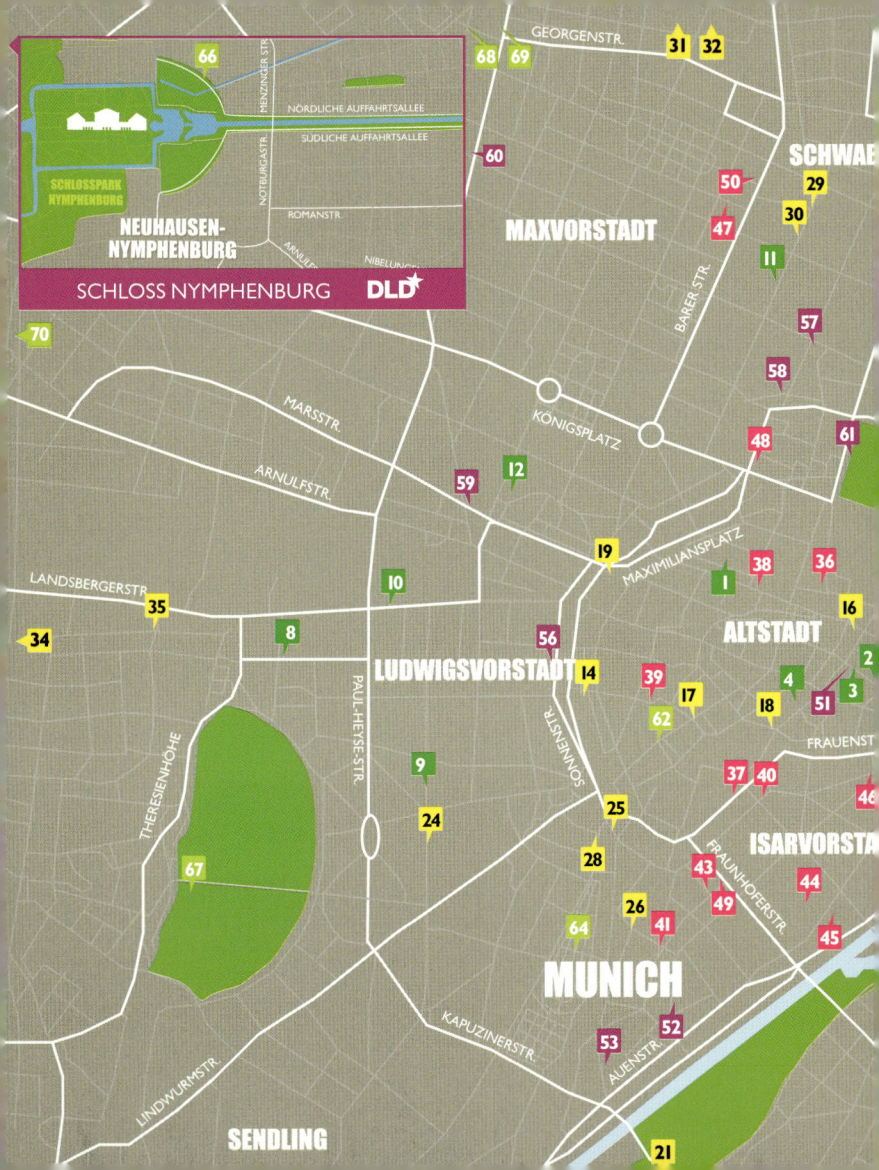

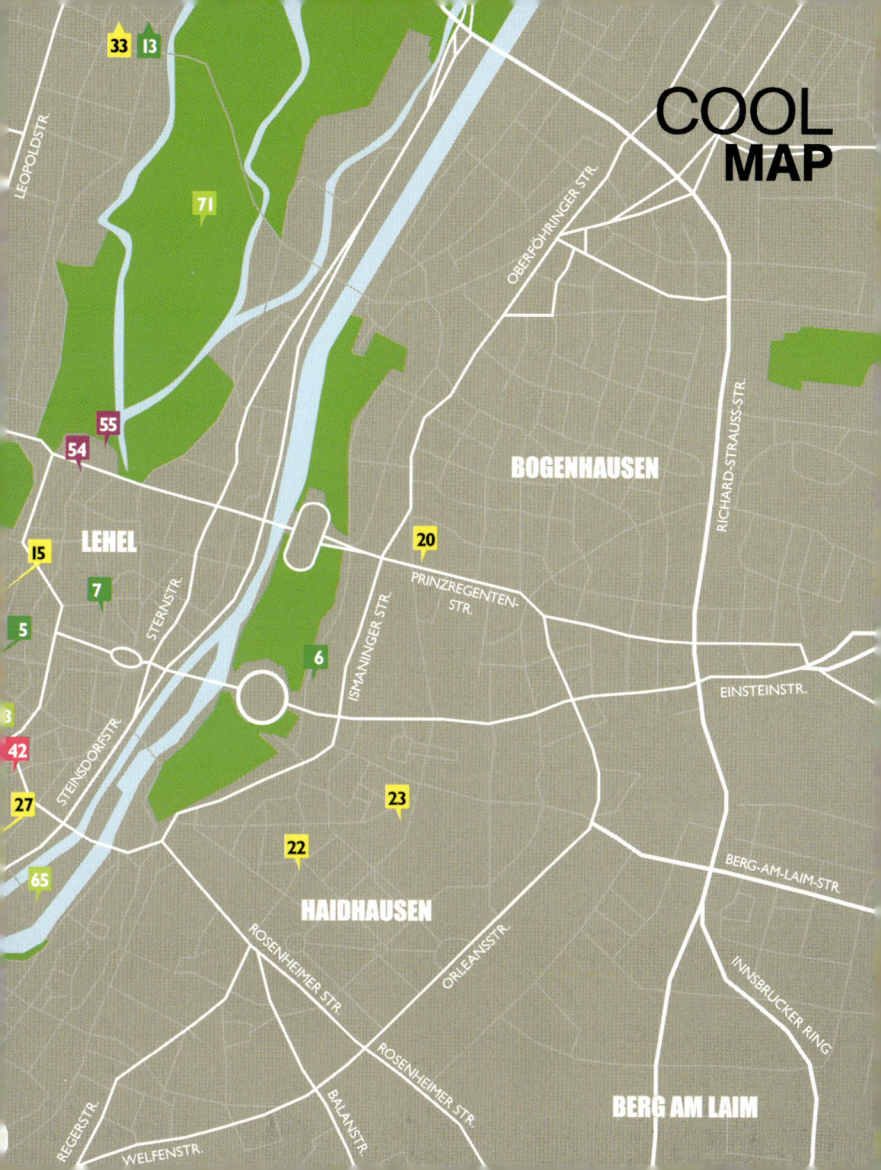

COOL
MAP

EMERGENCY

Ambulance/Fire   Tel.: 112
Police   Tel.: 110

ARRIVAL

BY PLANE

FLUGHAFEN MÜNCHEN
Information on arrivals and departures, security regulations, etc.
www.munich-airport.de
Tel.: +49 (0)89 9 75 00
32 km / 20 miles northeast of the city center. National and international flights. For the city center take the S-Bahn S8 (eastbound) or S1 (westbound), a ride of about 45 minutes, or the airport bus to North Schwabing and Main Station, leaving the airport every 20 minutes from 6.20 am to 9.40 pm. Return buses leave at the main station every 20 minutes from 5.10 am to 7.50 pm. The bus ride takes approximately 40 minutes.
www.s-bahn-muenchen.de
www.airportbus-muenchen.de

BY TRAIN

HAUPTBAHNHOF MÜNCHEN
www.hauptbahnhof-muenchen.de
Munich's main station is located conveniently close to the Marienplatz and is well connected with all the main S-Bahn trains (S1–8),

U-Bahn lines U1, U2, U4, and U5, Trams 17–21, and Bus 58 and 100.
www.bahn.de – official website of the Deutsche Bahn, for detailed information on train schedules, fares, etc.

TOURIST INFORMATION

Tourismusamt München, Sendlinger Str. 1
Offers assistance in planning and organising your trip and any kind of advice.
www.muenchen.de/tam
tourismus@muenchen.de
Tel.: +49 (0)89 23 39 65 55
Tourist Information Hauptbahnhof (Main Station)
Bahnhofsplatz 2, open Mon–Sat 9 am to 8 pm, Sun 10 am to 6 pm.
Tourist Information Marienplatz
Inside the Neues Rathaus, open Mon–Fri 10 am to 8 pm, Sat 10 am to 5 pm, Sun 10 am to 4 pm, closed on holidays.

ACCOMMODATION

www.muenchen.de - Download an extensive list with accommodation options or send an email to hotelservice@muenchen.de.

TICKETS

Book online on **www.muenchen.de** or at a München Ticket booth:
München Ticket at Main Station,

COOL
CITY INFO

Mon–Sat 10 am to 8 pm.
München Ticket at Rathaus,
Mon–Fri 10 am to 8 pm, Sat 10 am to 4 pm.
München Ticket at Glashalle im Gasteig,
Mon–Fri 10 am to 8 pm, Sat 10 am to 4 pm.
Info-Pavillon at Olympia-Eissportzentrum,
Mon–Fri 1 pm to 6 pm, Sat 10 am to 4 pm.

CityTourCard – 1 day or 3 day ticket for free use of all public transportation in the MVV inner district or entire network, as well as discounts at over 30 tourist destinations. Available as single or partner ticket from ticket vending machines and ticket booths. Prices from €9.90 EUR to €51.50. More information on **www.citytourcard.com.**

GETTING AROUND

PUBLIC TRANSPORTATION
www.mvv-muenchen.de
Münchener Verkehrs- und Tarifverbund (MVV), Service Line for information on time tables and fares, Tel.: +49 (0)89 41 42 43 44.

TAXI
Tel.: +49 (0)89 45 05 40
Tel.: +49 (0)89 2 16 10
Tel.: +49 (0)89 1 94 10

BICYCLE RENTAL
www.radiustours.com
Tel.: +49 (0)89 55 02 93 74, from €14.40 per day. Office hours Apr 1st–Oct 15th: Mon–Fri 9 am to 6 pm, Sat–Sun 9 am to 8 pm. Oct 16th– March 31st dependent on weather. The Bike Rental is located in the vicinity of platform 32–34 at the Main Station.

www.callabike-interaktiv.de
Call a bike, Tel.: +49 (0)7000 5 22 55 22 (Mon–Fri 9 am to 6 pm 13 ct/min., at off-peak times 6 ct/min. from German land line). Registration online for €7.50 or by phone for €15. Rent is 8 ct/min. and €15/day.

CAR RENTAL
Besides the international companies there are some Munich-based ones like:
www.buchbinder.de
www.autoverleih-sander.de
www.autovermietung.de
www.avm-autovermietung.de

CITY TOURS

BUSES AND TRAMS
Bus No. 100, the "Museum Line," goes from the Main Station to Ostbahnhof, stopping at Königsplatz, Pinakotheken, Odeonsplatz, Haus der Kunst, Friedensengel, and passing by 22 museums on its route. Tram lines 17, 18, 19, and 27 are great ways to discover the city and its most beautiful sights.
www.spurwechsel-muenchen.de
City Tour by tram in a real "oldtimer" built in 1958. The tour takes about 50 min. and takes you to all the sights in the center of Munich. Jun–Oct. English tour available once a week.

SIGHTSEEING BUSES
www.sightseeing-munich.com
Tel.: +49 (0)89 54 90 75 60
www.citysightseeing-muenchen.de
Tel. +49 (0)176 86 47 41 24

COOL
CITY INFO

BOAT TOUR
www.flossfahrt.de – Float down the Isar
from Wolfratshausen to Thalkirchen on a raft.
Tel.: +49 (0)8171 7 85 18

GUIDED TOURS
www.weisser-stadtvogel.de
Tel.: +49 (0)89 2 03 24 53 60
www.stattreisen-muenchen.de
Tel.: +49 (0)89 54 40 42 30
www.spurwechsel-muenchen.de
Tel.: +49 (0)89 6 92 46 99
www.radiustours.com
Tel.: +49 (0)89 55 02 93 74

VIEWING THE CITY FROM ABOVE

www.olympiapark.de – Olympiaturm
www.muenchner-dom.de – Frauenkirche
www.schloesser.bayern.de – Bavaria
Monopteros in the Englischer Garten

ART & CULTURE
www.museen-in-muenchen.de
Portal of Munich's museums
www.muenchner-galerien.de
Galleries in Munich
www.muenchen.de
Events Calendar and Cinema Program
www.kultmuenchen.de
Cultural events in Munich

GOING OUT
www.derkongress.com – music and culture
www.in-muenchen.de – free magazine
www.munichx.de

EVENTS

JANUARY TO MARCH
www.lange-nacht-der-architektur.de
Long night of architecture (Jan, biyearly)
www.nockherberg.com
Starkbier ("strong beer") festival (Mar)

APRIL TO JUNE
www.stroke-artfair.com – (May)
www.auerdult.de
Traditional fun fair around May 1st with beer
and food tents and stands with local artisanry.
Also takes place in July and October.
www.dokfest-muenchen.de
International Documentary Filmfestival (May)
www.muenchner.de/musiknacht
Long night of music (May)
www.bayerische.staatsoper.de
Munich Opera Festival (Jun/Jul)
www.tollwood.de
Cultural summer festival (Jun/Jul)
www.filmfest-muenchen.de
International Filmfestival Munich (Jun/Jul)

JULY TO SEPTEMBER
www.klassik-am-odeonsplatz.de
Classical music open-air festival (Jul)
www.oktoberfest.de – (Sep/Oct)

OCTOBER TO DECEMBER
www.muenchner.de/museumsnacht
Long night of the museums (Oct)
www.tollwood.de
Cultural winter festival (Nov/Dec)

COOL
CREDITS

Cover photo (Schloss Nymphenburg) by Roland Bauer
Back cover photos by Roland Bauer,
courtesy of Hotel Bayerischer Hof, Haydar Koyupinar
Illustrations by Christin Steirat

Greeting photo courtesy of flohagena.com/DLD;
p 2–3 (Intro) (Schloss Nymphenburg) by Roland Bauer;
p 6–7 (Intro) by Sergey Borisov/istockphoto

HOTELS

p 10–11 (Bayerischer Hof) p 11 left by Roland Bauer (further credited as rb), all others courtesy of Bayerischer Hof; p 12–13 (Cortiina) all photos by rb; p 14–15 (Hotel Lux) all photos courtesy of Hotel Lux; p 16–19 (Louis Hotel) p 16-17 by Martin Nicholas Kunz, p 18 photos at the top by Stefan Braun/courtesy of Louis Hotel, p 18 photos down at the bottom courtesy of Louis Hotel; p 20–21 (Mandarin Oriental Munich) all photos by rb; p 22–23 (Hotel Ritzi) all photos courtesy of Hotel Ritzi; p 24–25 (Hotel Opéra) all photos by rb; p 26–27 (Hotel Achterbahn) all photos by rb; p 28–29 (Hotel Mariandl) all photos courtesy of Hotel Mariandl; p 30–31 (Sofitel Munich Bayerpost) all photos by Stephen Huljak; p 32–33 (das HOTEL in München) all photos courtesy of das HOTEL in München; p 34–35 (The Charles Hotel) all photos courtesy of The Charles Hotel/Rocco Forte Collection; p 36–37 (Hotel La Maison) all photos by rb

RESTAURANTS + CAFÉS

p 40–41 (Bon Valeur) p 40 at the top courtesy of Bon Valeur, all others by rb; p 42–43 (Brenner) all photos courtesy of Brenner Grill; p 44–45 (Schuhbecks in den Südtiroler Stuben) all photos by Südtiroler Stuben; p 46–47 (Prinz Myshkin) all photos courtesy of Prinz Myshkin; p 48–49 (Schiffmacher Eis Café Bar) all photos by rb; p 50–53 (The Grill) all photos by Markus Kehl; p 54–55 (Käfer-Schänke) p 52 at the bottom courtesy of Feinkost Käfer, all others by rb; p 56–57 (Charlie) all photos courtesy of Charlie; p 58–59 (Saint Laurent) all photos by rb; p 60–61 (Zum Kloster) all photos by rb; p 62–63 (Banyan) all photos courtesy of Banyan; p 64–65 (Bar Corso) all photos courtesy of Bar Corso; p 66–67 (Hey Luigi) all photos by rb; p 68–69 (München 72) all photos by rb; p 70–71 (Schnelle Liebe) all photos by rb; p 72–73 (Gartensalon) all photos courtesy of Gartensalon; p 74–75 (Pavesi Picnic) all photos courtesy of Pavesi Picnic; p 76–79 (Die Blaue Donau) all photos by Georg Zellentin, www.georgzellentin.de/courtesy of Die Blaue Donau; p 80–81 (Schöntag) all photos by rb; p 82–83 (Tantris) all photos by Roman Job/Tantris; p 84–85 (Marais) all photos courtesy of Café Marais; p 86–87 (Josefa) all photos by Gyula Tomcsányi/courtesy of Josefa

SHOPS

p 90–91 (Bogner) all photos courtesy of Bogner; p 92–93 (Kräuter- und Wurzelsepp) all photos by rb; p 94–95 (Lodenfrey) all photos by courtesy of Lodenfrey; p 96–97 (servus.heimat) all photos courtesy of servus.heimat; p 98–99 (Amen Store) all photos courtesy of Amen; p 100–103 (Götterspeise) p 101 at the top left and p 102 left courtesy of Götterspeise, all others by rb; p 104–105 (Literatur Moths) all photos by Markus Bachmann; p 106–107 (Optimal) all photos courtesy of Echt Optimal Schallplatten; p 108–109 (Ruby Store) all photos by Jann Averwerser/www.jannaverwerser.com; p 110–111 (rocket.) all photos courtesy of rocket./Kirsten Almanstötter; p 112–113 (Wash & Coffee) all photos by rb; p 114–117 (Harvest) all photos by rb; p 118–119 (teNeues Store @ Freso Home) all photos by rb; p 120–121 (iki M.) all photos courtesy of iki M.; p 122–125 (Nia. Chaussures) all photos by rb

CLUBS, LOUNGES + BARS

p 128–129 (Bar Lux) all photos by rb; p 130–131 (Josef Bar) all photos by Lukas Schramm; p 132–133 (Rennsalon) all photos by rb; p 134–135 (Ed Moses) all photos courtesy of Ed Moses; p 136–137 (Goldene Bar) all photos by Fabian Beger/www.begerfabian.com; p 138–139 (Harry Klein) all photos by rb; p 140–143 (Bar Sehnsucht) all photos by Florian Deventer/www.deventer-photography.com; p 144–145 (Bob Beaman) all photos by Benjamin Monn, light installation by Fantomas (München); p 146–147 (Café Kosmos) all photos by Manfred Lehner/www.bluecatdesign.de; p 148–149 (Eat the Rich) p 148 all photos by Alex Schelbert/www.wildcard.de, p 149 photo courtesy of Eat the Rich; p 150–151 (Schumann's Bar am Hofgarten) all photos by Klaus Brenninger

HIGHLIGHTS

p 154–155 (Asamkirche) p 154 right by rb, left at the top and bottom by Sean Nel/Shutterstock (2); p 156–157 (Valentin-Karlstadt-Musäum) all photos courtesy of Valentin-Karlstadt-Musäum, München; p 158–161 (Alter südlicher Friedhof) all photos by rb; p 162–165 (Deutsches Museum) all photos courtesy of Deutsches Museum; p 166–169 (Porzellan Manufaktur Nymphenburg) all photos courtesy of Porzellan Manufaktur Nymphenburg; p 170–171 (Bavaria/Theresienwiese) p 170 left by xyno/istockphoto, right by Alfred Müller/Fremdenverkehrsamt München; p 172–173 (BMW Welt) all photos by eb.andriuolo/BMW AG; p 174–175 (Olympiapark) all photos by rb; p 176–177 (Hirschgarten) all photos by rb; p 178–179 (Englischer Garten) p 178 at the bottom by rb, p 178 at the top by Nicolas Bruant, p 179 at the bottom by Georg Winkens/istockphoto, p 179 at the top by rb

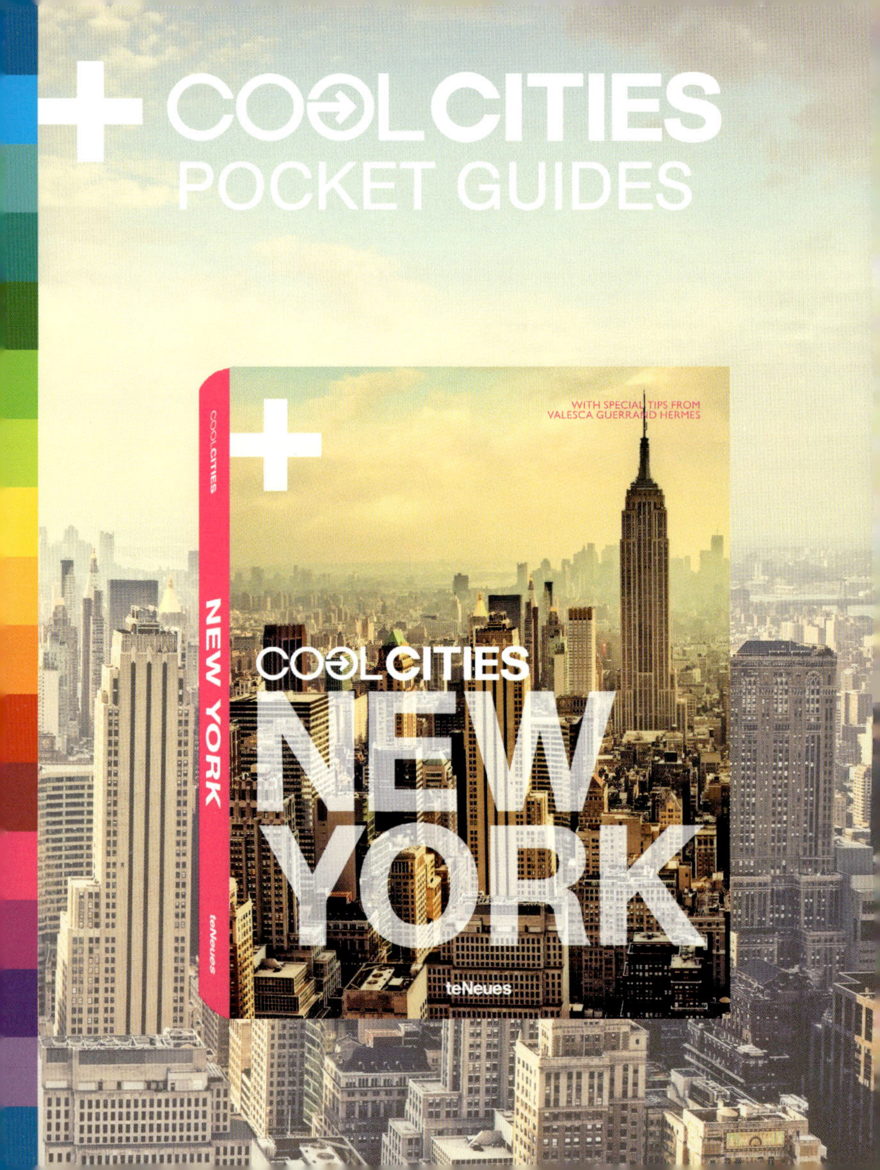

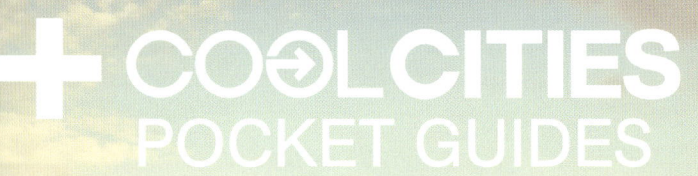

COOLCITIES
POCKET GUIDES

WITH SPECIAL TIPS FROM
VALESCA GUERRAND HERMES

COOLCITIES
NEW YORK

NEW YORK

COOL CITIES

teNeues

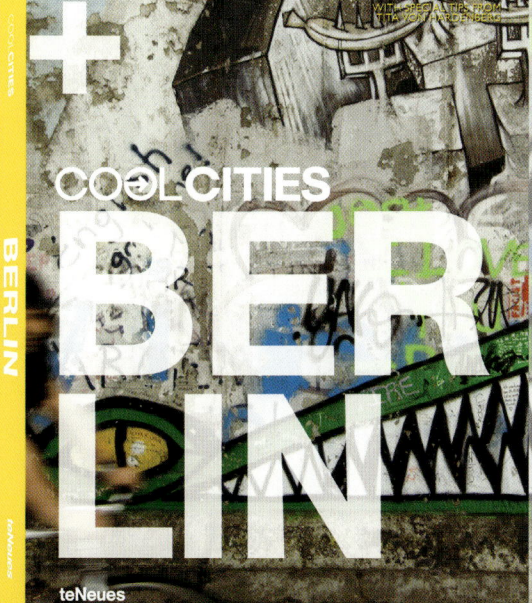

COOL→CITIES
APPS for iPhone/iPad/iPod Touch

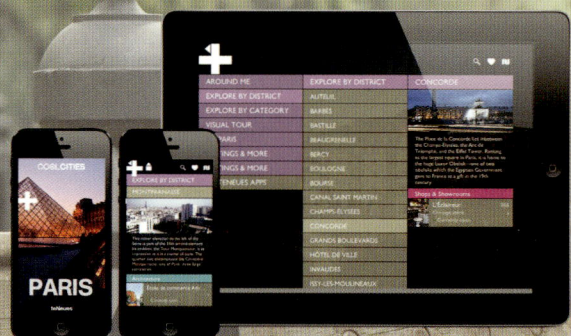

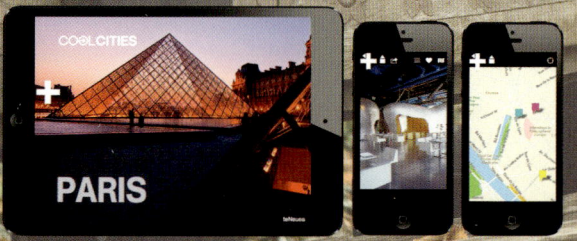

APP FEATURES
**Search by categories, districts, or geolocator;
get directions or create your own tour.**

VISUAL
Discover the city with tons of brilliant photos and videos.

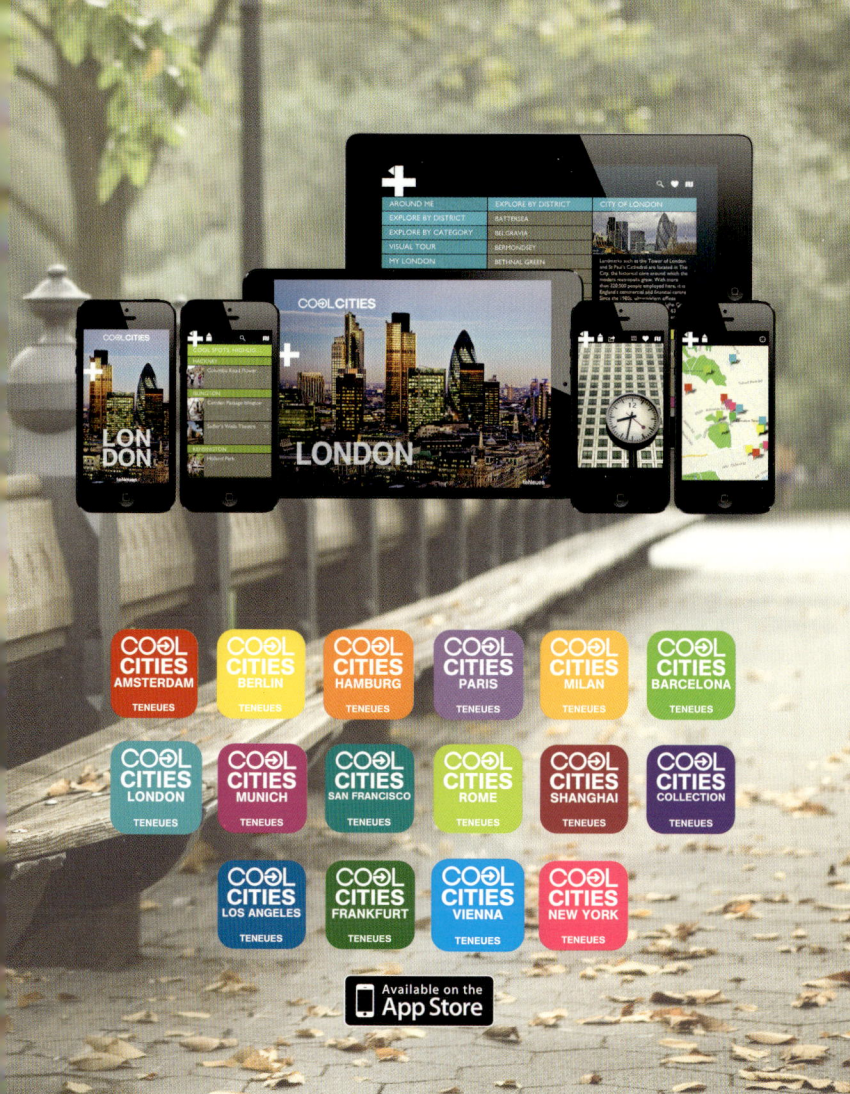

© 2011 Idea & concept by Martin Nicholas Kunz, Lizzy Courage Berlin
Selected and edited by Aishah El Muntasser
Introduction and location texts by Aishah El Muntasser
Executive Photo Editor: David Burghardt
Copy Editor: Dr. Simone Bischoff, Maria Regina Madarang
Layout: Christin Steirat, Peter Krämer, Sonja Oehmke
Imaging and pre-press production: Norbert Dietsche - Imageproduction, David Burghardt
Translations: Übersetzungsbüro Romina Russo, RR Communications
Robert Rosenbaum, Romina Russo

© 2011 teNeues Verlag GmbH + Co. KG, Kempen

teNeues Verlag GmbH + Co. KG
Am Selder 37, 47906 Kempen // Germany
Tel.: +49 (0)2152 916-0, Fax: +49 (0)2152 916-111
e-mail: books@teneues.de

Press department: Andrea Rehn
Tel.: +49 (0)2152 916-202 // e-mail: arehn@teneues.de

teNeues Digital Media GmbH
Kohlfurter Straße 41–43, 10999 Berlin // Germany
Tel.: +49 (0)30 7 00 77 65-0

teNeues Publishing Company
7 West 18th Street, New York, NY 10011 // USA
Tel.: +1 212 627 9090, Fax: +1 212 627 9511

teNeues Publishing UK Ltd.
21 Marlowe Court, Lymer Avenue, London SE19 1LP // UK
Tel.: +44 (0)20 8670 7522, Fax: +44 (0)20 8670 7523

teNeues France S.A.R.L.
39, rue des Billets, 18250 Henrichemont // France
Tel.: +33 (0)2 4826 9348, Fax: +33 (0)1 7072 3482

www.teneues.com

Bibliographic information published by the Deutsche Nationalbibliothek.
The Deutsche Nationalbibliothek lists this publication in the
Deutsche Nationalbibliografie; detailed bibliographic data are
available in the Internet at http://dnb.d-nb.de.

v 1.3 // 2013
Printed in the Czech Republic
ISBN: 978-3-8327-9496-5

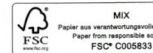

MIX
Papier aus verantwortungsvollen (
Paper from responsible sourc
FSC   FSC® C005833